The New
Oxford Book of
CHILDREN'S
VERSE

# The New
# Oxford Book of
# CHILDREN'S
# VERSE

EDITED BY

*Neil Philip*

Oxford   New York

OXFORD UNIVERSITY PRESS

1996

Oxford University Press, Walton Street, Oxford OX2 6DP

Oxford New York
Athens Auckland Bangkok Bogota Bombay
Buenos Aires Calcutta Cape Town Dar es Salaam
Delhi Florence Hong Kong Istanbul Karachi
Kuala Lumpur Madras Madrid Melbourne
Mexico City Nairobi Paris Singapore
Taipei Tokyo Toronto
and associated companies in
Berlin Ibadan

Oxford is a trade mark of Oxford University Press

British Library Cataloguing in Publication Data
Data available

Library of Congress Cataloging in Publication Data
The new Oxford book of children's verse / edited by Neil Philip.
p. cm.
Includes bibliographical references and indexes.
1. Children's poetry, English. 2. Children's poetry, Commonwealth
(English) 3. Children's poetry, American. I. Philip, Neil.
RR1175.3.N46 1996. 821.008'09282—dc20 96–2398
ISBN 0-19-214247-X

1 3 5 7 9 10 8 6 4 2

Typeset by Rowland Phototypesetting Limited
Printed in Great Britain by
Bookcraft (Bath) Limited, Midsomer Norton, Avon

For Heather Neill

# ACKNOWLEDGEMENTS

I would like to thank the following people for their encouragement and friendship in the study of children's literature over the last two decades: Brian and Valerie Alderson; Professor J. S. Bratton; Nancy Chambers; Mary Cruickshank; Gillian Dickinson, Rosemary Hood, and Fiona Lafferty; Heather Neill, Arts Editor of *The Times Educational Supplement*, who gave me my first opportunity to write on the subject in a public forum; and John Rowe Townsend and Jill Paton Walsh. I am particularly grateful to Nancy Chambers, editor of the magazine *Signal: Approaches to Children's Books*, for asking me to be for the years 1982–4 a judge of the Signal Poetry Award, and to my fellow judges Margaret Meek and Anthea Bell for their stimulating perspectives on the books we discussed. Iona Opie was generous and gracious in her support of this book, which is meant to stand alongside Iona and Peter Opie's magisterial *Oxford Book of Children's Verse*, not supplant it. In America, I have greatly valued the advice of Julie Cummins, Coordinator of Children's Services at the New York Public Library. Judith Luna and her colleagues at Oxford University Press have made my path as easy as possible, and I also appreciate the assistance of Connie Hallam in clearing permissions and Dr Robyn Marsack in preparing the indexes. Last but not least, I must thank my friend Elizabeth Wilkes, and my wife Emma Bradford, for their cheerful help over the course of this project from contract to finished book.

# CONTENTS

## Contents

# INTRODUCTION

This anthology is, as its title proclaims, a collection of 'children's verse.' This is a term that covers a multitude of sins. In practical terms, I have taken it to mean verse written for children, or with them prominently in mind, or published for them with the explicit or implicit endorsement of the author. Even then there remains a handful of poems that are, I think, legitimately chosen—such as Poe's 'Eldorado'—which fall into none of these categories, but nevertheless seem anchored to the children's verse tradition by a kind of gravitational pull.

The problem is essentially one of definition. What is children's poetry, and how does it differ from poetry in general? This anthology is itself a full answer to this difficult question, but it is not an answer that is easy to summarize.

Some would argue that the very notion of poetry for children is a nonsense. The poetry that has been written and published for children is by no means the only poetry to which they respond; indeed some of the best anthologies for the young scarcely contain any poems expressly written for them. There is only poetry, good or bad.

Yet there is a recognizable tradition of children's verse, which this book traces. It is a tradition that is at once separate from and intermingled with the larger poetic tradition, but it has its own landmarks and its own rhetoric.

It is, most crucially, a tradition of immediate apprehension. There is in the best children's poetry a sense of the world being seen as for the first time, and of language being plucked from the air to describe it. Everything is freshly created, and the poet's senses are quiveringly alert to each new sound, scent and sight of what William Brighty Rands calls this 'great, wide, beautiful, wonderful world.'

Of course this description also fits much adult poetry, but it is important to note that the immediate sense perceptions have an overriding importance in children's poetry, quite beyond the workings of memory and reflection, or the filters of spiritual, philosophical, or political ideas. This does not necessarily mean that children's poems are 'simple' in any reductive sense. I would argue that no poem can be called a poem that does not have at its heart some unknowable mystery; as Emily Dickinson scrawled on the back of one of her poems, 'Bliss is the Plaything of the Child': 'Dont think you could understand if you tried—.' But a children's poem will in general take the direct route from one thought to another.

A true children's poem is distinguished by a clarity of thought, language and rhythm that stems from this directness. The guiding principle is that expressed by Bertolt Brecht in his poem 'And I always thought', translated here by Michael Hamburger:

> And I always thought: the very simplest words
> Must be enough.

The case of Emily Dickinson (mirrored to some extent by that of Stevie Smith) tests any makeshift boundary lines between poetry for children and poetry for adults to their limits. Shortly after her death, her poems began to appear in children's journals such as *St Nicholas* and *Youth's Companion*. Some of her poems such as 'A Narrow Fellow in the Grass' or 'Dear March—Come in—', speak strongly and directly to children. But can they, in the absence of any guidance from the author, be regarded as children's poems? A very strong case could be made for such a decision, but it would have to ignore the congruence of these poems with the remainder of her work, in which the ideas and feelings are quite definitely outside a child's grasp. So I have reluctantly confined myself in this book to three poems that Emily Dickinson herself sent to children.

If Emily Dickinson is not essentially a children's poet, it has something to do with the sense that she is not so much a participant in life as a witness to it, sworn on oath in some metaphysical court. Yet the overriding qualities of her work are also those of children's poetry: clarity, directness, mystery. She writes, for instance:

> When I have seen the Sun emerge
> From His amazing House—
> And leave a Day at every Door
> A Deed, in every place—

This is, in its clear-eyed economy, perfect children's verse.

The secret as to why a poet whose themes are profoundly unchildish should nevertheless skirt so close to being a children's poet lies in the sense of wonder. Everyone has seen the sun rise; only someone doing so as if for the first time has seen it 'leave a Day at every Door.' Emily Dickinson also wrote,

> I dwell in Possibility—
> A fairer House than Prose

and this is perhaps as good a definition as any of poetry for children. It is the poetry of Possibility. Or, as John Clare put it, 'There is nothing but poetry about the existance of childhood real simple soul moving poetry the laughter and joy of poetry and not its philosophy.'

Today, people tend to two different views about poetry for children. The first is that it is something that was defined and perfected in a lost golden age, spanning from Robert Louis Stevenson and Eugene Field to A. A. Milne and Eleanor Farjeon. Here, a succession of poets, attuned to the child's viewpoint, captured in traditional forms the essence of childhood.

The opposing view is that these are poets for the nursery, irrelevant to the modern world: comforting, sentimental, and drenched in nostalgia. Children today, it is argued, require something shorter and snappier: what Spike Milligan has proudly termed, 'silly verse for kids'.

Both views are too simplistic, and it is one of the aims of this anthology to reconcile them. Silliness has been essential to children's poetry from the beginning, and was brought to its apogee by Edward Lear; even Isaac Watts, whom I regard as the first true children's poet, urged that verse for children should be 'flowing with cheerfulness'. Word-play, parody, nonsense, and all kinds of mickey-taking and topsy-turviness are part of the central tradition of children's verse.

So, too, is the serious treatment of serious themes. A lot of early children's verse is about death; as Kenneth Grahame noted in the preface to his *Cambridge Book of Poetry for Children* in 1916, 'a compiler of Obituary Verse for the delight of children could make a fine fat volume with little difficulty'. It is in this context that the fresh unforced celebration of the child's world that we find in writers such as Stevenson and Milne should be viewed. They are such poets as Blake aspired to be, writing

> happy songs
> Every child may joy to hear.

But Blake paired his merry *Songs of Innocence* with darker *Songs of Experience*, even, as with 'Holy Thursday', writing parallel poems with the same title. Children's lives are full of wonder and delight, but they are also fraught with worries, disappointments, and sadnesses; the best children's poets come to terms with grief as well as joy.

Edward Lear, for instance, may offer a prototype for today's 'silly verse', but his nonsense is shadowed by a sense of loss and loneliness:

> Calico Pie,
> The little Birds fly
> Down to the calico tree,
> Their wings were blue,
> And they sang 'Tilly-loo!'
> Till away they flew,—
> And they never came back to me!
> They never came back!
> They never came back!
> They never came back to me!

This plangent quality in Lear, an inextricable tangle of happy and sad feelings, has resurfaced strongly in the work of one of today's finest children's poets, Charles Causley, but it can be felt in that of many others, from Walter de la Mare and Eleanor Farjeon to Roger McGough and John Mole.

Spike Milligan has it too, but the 'silly verse' of some others can seem not so much silly as empty, offering instant gratification but no sustenance. The absence of Lear's discords and minor keys turns tunes into jingles. It is easy for children's poets to fall into this trap. The resultant verse may be fun, but it offers nothing to digest, and will soon be forgotten. The basis of much of it is the pun, which is no bad thing, for at least it gives children the idea that poetry is what happens when words collide.

The problem is one of form as much as of content. Today's children's poets have deconstructed the rhetoric of children's poetry in much the same way as postmodernist writers in other modes. This has left them with a formal freedom that the skilful—Valerie Worth, or Michael Rosen, say—can exploit to powerful effect. Poets such as Sonia Sanchez and e. e. cummings make no stylistic allowances for the child reader, and as a consequence offer their readers an exhilarating experience.

But not all children's poets have the technical confidence to negotiate free verse, and the result is that some offer prose limply arranged in lines and hope for the best, while others revert to doggerel metrics. The glee with which children's poets adopted the haiku shows how far adrift many have come from the adroit mastery of traditional verse technique that we find in A. A. Milne or David McCord—you can almost hear the collective sigh of relief, 'All you've got to do is count to seventeen!'

That quintessentially English poet James Reeves published in 1971 a book entitled *How to Write Poems for Children*. It was really a study of his own practice, rather than a prescriptive 'fit one—fit all' pattern for aspiring children's poets, and it is full of insights gained from his experience. Reeves claims that 'Three things are necessary for a writer of children's poems: imagination, technique and taste.' Although Reeves himself was by nature a conservative, he does not rule out free verse, 'provided it makes its own music and fulfils its own pattern'. This, it seems to me, is the key: poetry must make its own music.

Sometimes that music can be made by the look of the poem on the page. Lewis Carroll's 'The Mouse's Tale' from *Alice in Wonderland* can probably claim to be the first concrete poem for children, the forerunner of such modern delights as Wes Magee's 'Giant Rocket' or 'Coyotes' by the Canadian, Jon Whyte. These are poems that only work on the page: you couldn't read them aloud.

Conversely, there is now a thriving tradition of performance poetry for children. Again, this has deep historical roots; for instance I would class Browning's 'The Pied Piper of Hamelin' as a performance poem. But, as with song lyrics, the virtues of performance poetry are hard to capture in print. The poets in this collection who might loosely be termed performance poets, such as Roger McGough, Michael Rosen, Adrian Mitchell, Michael Smith, and Benjamin Zephaniah, are the very best of their kind. The printed words are not so much a blueprint for performance as the performance is an expression of the text. The critic Margaret Meek writes of Michael Rosen, 'I would argue that when Michael recites his own poetry, as he often does in schools, he has to do it so that the graphematic features of its shape, what it would look like on the page, become audible rather than visible, and *not the other way round.*' In Zephaniah's case, the whole point of the poem I have chosen, 'According to My Mood', is the impossibility of confining the free voice in the strait-jacket of type.

Children's poetry is by its nature especially apt to be read aloud, and the performance qualities of many modern writers extend rather than disrupt the tradition. A lot of the poems in this book, from Blake to Prelutsky, positively beg to be read aloud. In the case of David McCord's 'Five Chants', for instance, the poem almost says the words for you:

> The goose has a hiss
> And it goes like this

'Fireflies' by Paul Fleischman (son of the children's writer Sid Fleischman) is a virtuoso performance in two ways. Fleischman's poems are intended to be read aloud by two voices. In this particular poem, the flickering effect of the double column grid on the printed page gives a thrilling typographical equivalent of such a performance. Whether reading or listening, the form captures the pulsing quality of the subject.

Children first encounter poetry through listening to nursery rhymes. The old rhymes just go on and on, satisfying precisely because they have been shaped by so many mouths, and battered by so many accidents of life. It is one of the highest accolades of a children's poet for a verse to be silently appropriated by the world and reshaped by Anon., as happened for instance to Hughes Mearns with 'A Little Man'. Samuel Griswold Goodrich wrote his contribution to the nursery classics, 'Higglety, Pigglety, Pop!', precisely to show what facile nonsense such rhymes are, yet it has outlived all his other achievements. We can fairly assume that the best nursery rhymes of Eleanor Farjeon, Rose Fyleman, and Clyde Watson will in time join the canon, together with Christopher Isherwood's 'The Common Cormorant'—though Isherwood stole a march on the others by crediting the poem to Anon. on its first appearance, in Auden and Garrett's *The Poet's Tongue*.

Poetry for children ranges from the brevity of the new-fashioned nursery rhyme to the formidable length of a narrative poem such as 'The Pied Piper of Hamelin', or Mick Gowar's modern rewrite, 'Rat Trap'. It can accommodate every mood from lullaby to elegy, and speak both to the child and to the adult the child will become. No one person's choice from such a wide-ranging body of work could satisfy all readers on all points. But I hope that this new selection, in charting the journey from Isaac Watts to Janet S. Wong, will show the development of poetry for children as a living, separate tradition. From early days, children's poets have attended to their predecessors and anticipated their successors. Lewis Carroll, for instance, paid homage to Isaac Watts and Jane Taylor in his parodies, and in poems such as 'Brother and Sister' (*'Moral*: Never stew your sister') laid the ground rules for the *Cautionary Verses* of Hilaire Belloc, the *Ruthless Rhymes* of Harry Graham, and their contemporary equivalents.

In preparing *The New Oxford Book of Children's Verse* I have had the advantage of following in the footsteps of Iona and Peter Opie's *Oxford Book of Children's Verse* and Donald Hall's *Oxford Book of Children's Verse in America*. While the amount of actual overlap between the three volumes is minimal, Opie and Hall have been constantly at my side. My admiration for both books has, if possible, grown in the process, and I have also been grateful that the assiduous scholarship of their editors has freed me from the need to include work simply for its historical importance.

If you look in this book for some half-remembered poem from your childhood and do not find it, it is probably in Opie or Hall; I want the poems in this book to speak to today's children, as well as yesterday's. This has tipped the scales towards modern work, and towards a lively mix of authors and cultures which I hope will both surprise and please readers whose idea of English-language children's verse has been defined by my predecessors.

Within the arguable range of 'children's verse', my search was for poetry that is, in Hugh MacDiarmid's words, 'alive as a bout of all-in wrestling'—for words that sing.

In his 1967 essay 'Poetry for Children', David McCord quotes Emerson: 'Every word was once a poem.' This is the rock bottom truth about poetry, and I have looked for a sense of that truth in each poem I considered for this book. Not every poem can be a masterpiece, but they can all aspire, in Browning's words about Christopher Smart, to adjust 'Real vision to right language.'

An example might be McCord's 'Father and I in the Woods'. This might seem on first encounter a slight poem, but in my opinion it is the best thing McCord ever wrote, over a long career that produced an œuvre to rival that of James Reeves. The reason is the perfect harmony of form, style, and subject. The elegant restraint of the language, and the delicate stepping quality of the rhythm, are inseparable from the meaning of the words.

Another test is that 'Father and I in the Woods' could not have been written by anyone else. It is original in the true sense. By originality I do not mean a straining after novelty, but a refusal to deal in second-hand words and images. Ebenezer Elliott, 'the Corn-Law Rhymer', writes in his autobiography (written 1841, published in *The Athenaeum*, 1850), 'There is not in my writings one good idea that has not been suggested to me by some real occurrence, or by some object actually before my eyes, or by some remembered object or occurrence, or by the thoughts of other men, heard or read.' Yet Elliott, though a pedestrian and unskilful writer, was 'original' in the sense I mean. What he wrote could not have been produced by any other man, and he wrote it from the centre of himself.

The book is arranged in historical sequence by the year of the poet's birth. This has obvious advantages in tracing the historical development of poetry for children (allowing for the odd trap set by publication dates of particular poems). The disadvantage is that the earlier work, by writers who, because of the passage of time, require more effort from today's child reader, comes first.

This would be a problem if I felt that the earlier work was dead and done with; but I do not. Anyone, adult or child, who opens this book at Blake's 'The Tyger', Charles and Mary Lamb's 'Anger', or Southey's 'The

Devil', may like or dislike the poem, but it will not be on the grounds of being old-fashioned. Southey's poem, incidentally, is usually printed as the first three stanzas of Samuel Taylor Coleridge's 'The Devil's Thoughts'.

Within the historical selections, I hope that my choices will inspire a reassessment of some poets. Ann Taylor, for instance, is usually represented by the sentiment of 'My Mother', or the moralizing of 'Meddlesome Matty' (both in Opie). Her poems 'Fire', 'Air', 'Earth', and 'Water' will come as a surprise to those who thought her range was limited to such work. These are poems of great power and movement. At the end of 'Fire', the poet, quite contrary to her sentimental and timid reputation, positively exults in the coming destruction:

> And when the great morning of judgment shall rise,
> How wide will its blazes be curled!
> With heat, fervent heat, it shall melt down the skies,
> And burn up this beautiful world.

Another woman poet whose work is much more interesting than commonly supposed is Rose Fyleman, author of 'Fairies' ('There are fairies at the bottom of our garden!'). The Opies print several of her now outmoded fairy poems; I have chosen two of her lively and witty nursery rhymes, as well as a lovely little poem, 'Solo with Chorus', that might have been written for an Oxford Book. Rose Fyleman's is a case of a poet's true talent being overshadowed by popular success; we should remember that it was she who encouraged A. A. Milne to write children's poetry, thus acting as midwife to one of the untarnished classics of the genre, *When We Were Very Young*.

Such is the nostalgic fondness that adults brought up on Milne and Stevenson, or their American equivalent, Eugene Field, feel for the classic children's poems, it is sometimes hard for them to register the vitality and quality of more recent work. The middle years of this century saw some excellent children's poets emerge—for instance James Reeves in Britain, David McCord and Elizabeth Madox Roberts in the USA—but the last quarter of a century has seen a positive explosion of children's poetry on both sides of the Atlantic.

In Britain, there has been a seismic shift in children's poetry. The line running from Stevenson and Rossetti, through de la Mare, Farjeon, and Reeves, to Charles Causley has been disrupted by a more boisterous, less reflective street-smart poetry, characterized by the critic John Rowe Townsend as 'urchin verse'. The focus is on shared not unique experience, on the rhythms of speech not the patterns of prosody, on school not home.

Some of this new poetry is facile and superficial, but the best of it is doing something new and exciting. Each of the three leading poets in this mode—Allan Ahlberg, Roger McGough, and Michael Rosen—speaks very much in his own voice; it is not their fault if their imitators can manage the mannerisms but not the manner. Michael Rosen published a striking defence of such work in *The Times Educational Supplement* in 1984, 'Memorable Speech?', in which he argues for the availability of a variety of poetic registers in which to speak to children, one of which is 'to use a child's speech mode'. In his frequent visits to schools he sees 'children fastening on to their own speech patterns as an ideal mode for expressing themselves. I see them using my writing like a catalyst, tuning in to its small hurts, jokes and fantasies of everyday life as a means to explore their own.'

Rosen's success in the classroom is supported by Brian Morse, a teacher who is also himself a notable poet ('A Day on the Planet'), writing in the journal *Signal: Approaches to Children's Books* in 1986. 'Perhaps it's dangerous to quote children's reactions, but my class of six- and seven-year-olds are still demanding rereadings of "Eddie and the Birthday", "Eddie and the Nappy" (in fact all the baby-Eddie poems) and "Chocolate Cake" six months after they first heard them, and greeting me "Nappy nappy nappy" in the morning.' Rosen's skill, writes Morse, is 'to put children in touch with themselves'.

These poems for the classroom and the playground, rather than the solitary reading child, have injected a new energy into poetry for children, that can be felt in the work of poets such as John Mole and Jackie Kay, who combine the subtler layered quality of the older tradition with the fresh demotic appeal of the newer. The Caribbean inflections of poets such as James Berry and John Agard have also added a new note to children's poetry in Britain.

Nevertheless the two most impressive British children's poets of this period have worked utterly outside this movement. Charles Causley and Ted Hughes are two highly regarded poets for adults who have also devoted considerable energies to children's poetry. Causley's 1970 collection *Figgie Hobbin* remains his best work, but it has been followed by a series of books nearly as good. His *Collected Poems for Children* will stand as one of the peak achievements of children's poetry, alongside Blake, Lear, and Stevenson.

'All poetry is magic,' writes Causley in the introduction to his *Puffin*

*Book of Magic Verse*. A poem is a spell. And what is the essential of a spell? Constantine the poet, in Rebecca West's masterpiece *Black Lamb and Grey Falcon*, tells us: '*That if one word is left out it is no longer a spell.*'

Causley is essentially a poet of loss, striving to see the world anew; to see it, in a key Causley phrase, 'Eden-fresh'. Part of this task is to recapture a child's sense of wonder. He achieves this by means of subtle verbal dislocations, effecting the sort of shift of sensibility that makes one believe, sitting in a moving train, that it is the world that is moving and the train alone that is still. Thus in the ballad 'Young Edgcumbe' from his children's collection *Figure of 8*, he writes:

> Down by the Tamar river
>   As young Edgcumbe walked by
> He heard from sleep the woodcock leap
>   Into the sudden sky.

The sudden sky. There is a magic phrase. Replace it with description rather than action—'into the cloudy sky', 'into the bright blue sky'—and the whole stanza crumbles into nothing. Rephrase it—'Suddenly to the sky'—and the feeling is completely lost. It is the sky moving not the birds.

If one word is left out, it is no longer a spell.

If Causley is a poet of loss, then Ted Hughes is a poet of repossession. The intense vitality of his vision offers his readers the whole world as a gift. Like the bear in 'I See a Bear' from *Moon-Bells*,

> You have got it everything for nothing

Hughes has published several landmark collections for the young, winning the prestigious Signal Poetry Award for both *Moon-Bells*, and *What is the Truth?* Each shows a major poet working at his full power.

*What is the Truth?*—from which I have chosen three poems, 'Yesterday he was nowhere to be found,' 'Rooks love excitement', and 'An October robin'—is packed with genuine poetry: harsh, funny, urgent, potent. The whole book, slotted into a loose frame story in which God and his Son question a number of villagers about the natural world, has a marvellous quality of improvised speech, jingle, and song, of issuing out on the breath rather than through the pen. Yet there is also a sense of craft and control: most of all in the free verse, in which each phrase, each image responds to its predecessor and expects it successor.

The lithe muscularity of these poems, their compassion, their delicate balance between stillness and movement, their stunningly compact and vivid visual imagery, are typical of the mature confidence of Hughes's work for children, both in verse and prose.

Children's poetry in the USA has, like American poetry in general, developed on a separate track. Much of the best American children's verse is scarcely known in Britain, and the poets themselves represented only by a few hackneyed anthology pieces. Yet since Eugene Field and James Whitcomb Riley, America has consistently produced children's poets of great energy and invention.

Donald Hall's *Oxford Book of Children's Verse in America* deftly traces the origins of American children's verse in the pages of nineteenth-century children's magazines such as *St Nicholas*. From this rich soil came poets such as Lucy Larcom, Celia Thaxter, Laura E. Richards, and Katharine Pyle (sister of the children's writer Howard Pyle).

By the middle years of this century, America's children's poets such as David McCord, Elizabeth Coatsworth, Elizabeth Madox Roberts, Rachel Field, and Aileen Fisher were producing a body of work that, in its quiet observation, delicately controlled rhythms, and child's-eye view-point, offers a distinctly American counterpoint to the work of English writers such as de la Mare, Farjeon, and Reeves. In the meantime, major adult poets such as Carl Sandburg, Vachel Lindsay, Theodore Roethke, e. e. cummings, and Langston Hughes were turning their attention to children's verse, producing poems, as Sandburg said of his children's stories, 'in the American lingo'.

Langston Hughes is of particular importance, as the first major African American writer to address America's children. Hughes's magnificent 1932 collection *The Dream Keeper* (reissued in 1994) contains his addendum to Whitman's 'I Hear America Singing':

> I, too, sing America.

The memory of childhood racial abuse in Hughes's colleague Countee Cullen's poem 'Incident' strikes a kind of rueful sadder-but-wiser note that also echoes in Hughes's own work. The spark of anger in a poem such as 'Children's Rhymes' was to leap into flame in the 1960s, and the work of poets such as Nikki Giovanni and Sonia Sanchez.

Sanchez's 'definition for blk/children' is about as far from the comforting nursery world of A. A. Milne as it is possible to get:

```
a policeman
            is a pig
and he shd be in
       a zoo
with all the other piggy
                  animals.   and
until he stops
       killing blk/people
cracking open their heads
remember.
            the policeman
       is a pig.
            (oink/
              oink.)
```

A less aggressive but equally uncompromising message could be found in June Jordan's verse picture book of 1969, *Who Look at Me?*, with at its heart the line,

> I am black alive and looking back at you.

This process of 'looking back' at America, coming, in Langston Hughes's words, 'to sit at the table', has brought forth in recent years some marvellous children's poetry not just from African American writers but from every part of America's cultural 'melting pot'.

Today, children's poetry is thriving in America, with a multiplicity of voices and modes of expression. Writers such as Jack Prelutsky and X. J. Kennedy fill the McGough/Rosen role, while more traditional poets such as Myra Cohn Livingston continue to extend the core tradition that extends from Field to McCord to writers such as Eve Merriam, John Ciardi, and Lucille Clifton.

What connects all these poets—and their colleagues in the rest of the English-speaking world—is a commitment to the primacy of the word as the means to shape and understand our interior life. All are engaged in the task defined by Browning in the poem on Smart I quoted earlier: to pierce

> the screen
> 'Twixt thing and word.

It is sometimes assumed that children cannot cope with undiluted poetry; that it is too difficult, too esoteric. But this is a measure of the adult's nervousness, not the child's. Children's own use of language—as shown in anthologies of their writing, such as Timothy Roger's wonderful *Those First Affections* (1979) or Jill Pirrie's inspiring collection of work from Halesworth Middle School, *Apple Fire* (1993)—shares a dimension with poetry. Indeed, the adult struggle to merge thing and word is to some extent an attempt to redeem the child's magical assumption of the identity of thought and action.

Brian Sutton-Smith's essay 'Early Stories as Poetry' in volume ix of the American annual *Children's Literature* (1981) discusses the prosodic elements of young children's narratives. Though this is a book of poems for children, not by them, I shall close with one of these story-poems, from a boy aged five years and one month.

> Once upon a time the once upon a time ate the once upon a time which
> ate the once upon a time
> And then the once upon a time which ate the once upon a time ate the
> princess once upon a time with the king
> And then the once upon a times died
> Then the end ate the end
> The end
> The end
> Then the end died
> Then the end died
> Then the end died
> Then the end died
> And then the end the end the end died
> The end with a the end
> The end
> The end.

This is verbal play raised to the level of magical creation: like being in the mind of God as he made the world. Here, as for Brecht, the very simplest words have been enough.

The New
Oxford Book of
# CHILDREN'S
# VERSE

# ISAAC WATTS
## 1674–1748

### *Our Saviour's Golden Rule*

MATT. VII. 12.

Be thou to others kind and true,
As you'd have others be to you;
And neither do nor say to men,
Whate'er you would not take again.


# CHRISTOPHER SMART
## 1722–1771

### *Hymns for Saturday*

Now's the time for mirth and play,
Saturday's an holiday;
Praise to heaven unceasing yield,
I've found a lark's nest in the field.

A lark's nest, then your playmate begs
You'd spare herself and speckled eggs;
Soon she shall ascend and sing
Your praises to the eternal King.


# WILLIAM BLAKE
## 1757–1827

### *'Piping down the valleys wild'*

Piping down the valleys wild,
Piping songs of pleasant glee,
On a cloud I saw a child,
And he laughing said to me:

'Pipe a song about a Lamb!'
So I piped with merry cheer.
'Piper, pipe that song again';
So I piped: he wept to hear.

'Drop thy pipe, thy happy pipe;
Sing thy songs of happy cheer':
So I sung the same again,
While he wept with joy to hear.

'Piper, sit thee down and write
In a book that all may read.'
So he vanished from my sight,
And I plucked a hollow reed,

And I made a rural pen,
And I stained the water clear,
And I wrote my happy songs
Every child may joy to hear.


## *Spring*

Sound the Flute!
Now it's mute.
Birds delight
Day and Night;
Nightingale
In the dale,
Lark in Sky,
Merrily,
Merrily, Merrily, to welcome in the Year.

Little Boy,
Full of joy;
Little Girl,
Sweet and small;

Cock does crow,
So do you;
Merry voice,
Infant noise,
Merrily, Merrily, to welcome in the Year.

Little Lamb,
Here I am;
Come and lick
My white neck;
Let me pull
Your soft Wool;
Let me kiss
Your soft face:
Merrily, Merrily, we welcome in the Year.


## Holy Thursday (Innocence)

'Twas on a Holy Thursday, their innocent faces clean,
The children walking two and two, in red and blue and green,
Grey-headed beadles walked before, with wands as white as snow,
Till into the high dome of Paul's they like Thames' waters flow.

O what a multitude they seemed, these flowers of London town!
Seated in companies they sit with radiance all their own.
The hum of multitudes was there, but multitudes of lambs,
Thousands of little boys and girls raising their innocent hands.

Now like a mighty wind they raise to heaven the voice of song,
Or like harmonious thunderings the seats of heaven among.
Beneath them sit the aged men, wise guardians of the poor;
Then cherish pity, lest you drive an angel from your door.

## Holy Thursday (Experience)

Is this a holy thing to see
In a rich and fruitful land,
Babes reduced to misery,
Fed with cold and usurous hand?

Is that trembling cry a song?
Can it be a song of joy?
And so many children poor?
It is a land of poverty!

And their sun does never shine,
And their fields are black and bare,
And their ways are filled with thorns:
It is eternal winter there.

For where-e'er the sun does shine,
And where-e'er the rain does fall,
Babe can never hunger there,
Nor poverty the mind appall.

## The Fly

Little Fly,
Thy summer's play
My thoughtless hand
Has brushed away.

Am not I
A fly like thee?
Or art not thou
A man like me?

For I dance,
And drink, and sing,
Till some blind hand
Shall brush my wing.

If thought is life
And strength and breath,
And the want
Of thought is death;

Then am I
A happy fly,
If I live
Or if I die.

## The Tyger

Tyger! Tyger! burning bright
In the forests of the night,
What immortal hand or eye
Could frame thy fearful symmetry?

In what distant deeps or skies
Burnt the fire of thine eyes?
On what wings dare he aspire?
What the hand dare seize the fire?

And what shoulder, and what art,
Could twist the sinews of thy heart?
And when thy heart began to beat,
What dread hand? And what dread feet?

What the hammer? what the chain?
In what furnace was thy brain?
What the anvil? what dread grasp
Dare its deadly terrors clasp?

When the stars threw down their spears,
And water'd heaven with their tears,
Did he smile his work to see?
Did he who made the Lamb make thee?

*William Blake*

Tyger! Tyger! burning bright
In the forests of the night,
What immortal hand or eye
Dare frame thy fearful symmetry?

# JAMES HOGG
## 1770—1835

### *A Boy's Song*

Where the pools are bright and deep,
Where the grey trout lies asleep,
Up the river and o'er the lea,
That's the way for Billy and me.

Where the blackbird sings the latest,
Where the hawthorn blooms the sweetest,
Where the nestlings chirp and flee,
That's the way for Billy and me.

Where the mowers mow the cleanest,
Where the hay lies thick and greenest;
There to trace the homeward bee,
That's the way for Billy and me.

Where the hazel bank is steepest,
Where the shadow falls the deepest,
Where the clustering nuts fall free,
That's the way for Billy and me.

Why the boys should drive away
Little sweet maidens from the play,
Or love to banter and fight so well,
That's the thing I never could tell.

But this I know, I love to play,
Through the meadow, among the hay;
Up the water and o'er the lea,
That's the way for Billy and me.

# CHARLES AND MARY LAMB
## 1775–1834 and 1764–1847

### *Anger*

Anger in its time and place
May assume a kind of grace.
It must have some reason in it,
And not last beyond a minute.
If to further lengths it go,
It does into malice grow.
'Tis the difference we see
'Twixt the serpent and the bee.
If the latter you provoke
It inflicts a hasty stroke,
Puts you to some little pain,
But it *never stings again*.
Close in tuften bush or brake
Lurks the poison-swellèd snake
Nursing up his cherished wrath;
In the purlieux of his path,
In the cold, or in the warm,
Mean him good, or mean him harm,
Whensoever fate may bring you,
The vile snake will *always sting you*.

# DOROTHY WORDSWORTH
## 1771–1885

### *Address to a Child during a Boisterous Winter Evening*

What way does the Wind come? What way does he go?
He rides over the water, and over the snow,
Through wood, and through vale; and o'er rocky height,
Which the goat cannot climb, takes his sounding flight;
He tosses about in every bare tree,
As, if you look up, you plainly may see;
But how he will come, and whither he goes,
There's never a scholar in England knows.

He will suddenly stop in a cunning nook,
And rings a sharp 'larum; but, if you should look,
There's nothing to see but a cushion of snow
Round as a pillow, and whiter than milk,
And softer than if it were covered with silk.
Sometimes he'll hide in the cave of a rock,
Then whistle as shrill as the buzzard cock.
Yet seek him—and what shall you find in his place?
Nothing but silence and empty space;
Save, in a corner, a heap of dry leaves,
That he's left, for a bed, to beggars or thieves!

As soon as 'tis daylight, tomorrow with me
You shall go to the orchard, and then you will see
That he has been there, and made a great rout,
And cracked the branches, and strewn them about:
Heaven grant that he spare but that one upright twig
That looked up at the sky so proud and big
All last summer, as well you know,
Studded with apples, a beautiful show!

Hark! over the roof he makes a pause,
And growls as if he would fix his claws
Right in the slates, and with a huge rattle
Drive them down, like men in a battle.

But let him range round; he does us no harm,
We build up the fire, we're snug and warm;
Untouched by his breath, see the candle shines bright,
And burns with a clear and steady light.
Books have we to read—but that half-stifled knell,
Alas! 'tis the sound of the eight o'clock bell.

Come, now we'll to bed! and when we are there
He may work his own will, and what shall we care?
He may knock at the door—we'll not let him in;
May drive at the windows—we'll laugh at his din.
Let him seek his own home, wherever it be:
Here's a cosy warm house for Edward and me.

# SAMUEL TAYLOR COLERIDGE
## 1772–1834

### The Raven

A CHRISTMAS TALE, TOLD BY A SCHOOL-BOY TO
HIS LITTLE BROTHERS AND SISTERS

Underneath an old oak tree
There was of swine a huge company,
That grunted as they crunched the mast:
For that was ripe, and fell full fast.
Then they trotted away, for the wind grew high:
One acorn they left, and no more might you spy.
Next came a Raven, that liked not such folly:
He belonged, they did say, to the witch Melancholy!
Blacker was he than blackest jet,
Flew low in the rain, and his feathers not wet.
He picked up the acorn and buried it straight
By the side of a river both deep and great.
Where then did the Raven go?
He went high and low,
Over hill, over dale, did the black Raven go.

Many Autumns, many Springs
Travelled he with wandering wings:
Many Summers, many Winters—
I can't tell half his adventures.

At length he came back, and with him a She,
And the acorn was grown to a tall oak tree.
They built them a nest in the topmost bough,
And young ones they had, and were happy enow.
But soon came a Woodman in leathern guise,
His brow, like a pent-house, hung over his eyes.
He'd an axe in his hand, not a word he spoke,
But with many a hem! and a sturdy stroke,
At length he brought down the poor Raven's own oak.
His young ones were killed; for they could not depart,
And their mother did die of a broken heart.

The boughs from the trunk the Woodman did sever;
And they floated it down on the course of the river.
They sawed it in planks, and its bark they did strip,
And with this tree and others they made a good ship.
The ship, it was launched; but in sight of the land
Such a storm there did rise as no ship could withstand.
It bulged on a rock, and the waves rush'd in fast:
Round and round flew the raven, and cawed to the blast.
He heard the last shriek of the perishing souls—
See! see! o'er the topmast the mad water rolls!
    Right glad was the Raven, and off he went fleet.
And Death riding home on a cloud he did meet,
And he thank'd him again and again for this treat:
    They had taken his all, and REVENGE IT WAS SWEET!

## Answer to a Child's Question

Do you ask what the birds say? The sparrow, the dove,
The linnet and thrush say, 'I love and I love!'
In the winter they're silent—the wind is so strong;
What it says, I don't know, but it sings a loud song.

But green leaves, and blossoms, and sunny warm weather,
And singing, and loving—all come back together.
But the lark is so brimful of gladness and love,
The green fields below him, the blue sky above,
That he sings, and he sings; and for ever sings he—
'I love my Love, and my Love loves me!'

# ROBERT SOUTHEY
## 1774–1843

### *The Devil*

From his brimstone bed at the break of day
  A walking the Devil is gone
To visit his snug little farm, the earth
  And see how his stock goes on.

Over the hill and over the dale,
  And he went over the plain,
And backward and forward he switched his long tail
  As a gentleman switches his cane.

And how then was the Devil dressed?
  Oh! he was in his Sunday's best:
His jacket was red and his breeches were blue
  And there was a hole where the tail came through.

### *The Cataract of Lodore*

'How does the Water
Come down at Lodore?'
My little boy asked me
Thus, once on a time;
And moreover he tasked me
To tell him in rhyme.

Anon at the word,
There first came one daughter
And then came another,
To second and third
The request of their brother,
And to hear how the water
Comes down at Lodore,
With its rush and its roar,
As many a time
They had seen it before.
So I told them in rhyme,
For of rhymes I had store:
And 'twas in my vocation
For their recreation
That so I should sing;
Because I was Laureate
To them and the King.

From its sources which well
In the Tarn on the fell;
From its fountains
In the mountains,
Its rills and its gills;
Through moss and through brake,
It runs and it creeps
For awhile, till it sleeps
In its own little lake.
And thence at departing,
Awakening and starting,
It runs through the reeds
And away it proceeds,
Through meadow and glade,
In sun and in shade,
And through the wood-shelter,
Among crags in its flurry,
Helter-skelter,
Hurry-scurry.
Here it comes sparkling,
And there it lies darkling;

Now smoking and frothing
Its tumult and wrath in,
Till in this rapid race
On which it is bent,
It reaches the place
Of its steep descent.

The Cataract strong
Then plunges along,
Striking and raging
As if a war waging
Its caverns and rocks among:
Rising and leaping,
Sinking and creeping,
Swelling and sweeping,
Showering and springing,
Flying and flinging,
Writhing and ringing,
Eddying and whisking,
Spouting and frisking,
Turning and twisting,
Around and around
With endless rebound!
Smiting and fighting,
A sight to delight in;
Confounding, astounding,
Dizzying and deafening the ear with its sound.

Collecting, projecting,
Receding and speeding,
And shocking and rocking,
And darting and parting,
And threading and spreading,
And whizzing and hissing,
And dripping and skipping,
And hitting and splitting,
And shining and twining,
And rattling and battling,
And shaking and quaking,
And pouring and roaring,
And waving and raving,

And tossing and crossing,
And flowing and going,
And running and stunning,
And foaming and roaming,
And dinning and spinning,
And dropping and hopping,
And working and jerking,
And guggling and struggling,
And heaving and cleaving,
And moaning and groaning;

And glittering and frittering,
And gathering and feathering,
And whitening and brightening,
And quivering and shivering,
And hurrying and scurrying,
And thundering and floundering;

Dividing and gliding and sliding,
And falling and brawling and sprawling,
And driving and riving and striving,
And sprinkling and twinkling and wrinkling,
And sounding and bounding and rounding,
And bubbling and troubling and doubling,
And grumbling and rumbling and tumbling,
And clattering and battering and shattering;

Retreating and beating and meeting and sheeting,
Delaying and straying and playing and spraying,
Advancing and prancing and glancing and dancing,
Recoiling, turmoiling and toiling and boiling,
And gleaming and streaming and steaming and beaming,
And rushing and flushing and brushing and gushing,
And flapping and rapping and clapping and slapping,
And curling and whirling and purling and twirling,
And thumping and plumping and bumping and jumping,
And dashing and flashing and splashing and clashing;
And so never ending, but always descending,
Sounds and motions for ever and ever are blending,
All at once and all o'er, with a mighty uproar,
And this way the Water comes down at Lodore.

# ADELAIDE O'KEEFFE
## 1776–1855

### *The Kite*

My kite is three feet broad, and six feet long;
 The standard straight, the bender tough and strong,
And to its milk-white breast five painted stars belong.

Grand and majestic soars my paper kite,
 Through trackless skies it takes its lofty flight:
Nor lark nor eagle flies to such a noble height.

As in the field I stand and hold the twine,
 Swift I unwind, to give it length of line,
Yet swifter it ascends, nor will to earth incline.

Like a small speck, so high I see it sail,
 I hear its pinions flutter in the gale,
And, like a flock of wild geese, sweeps its flowing tail.

# ANN TAYLOR
## 1782–1866

### *Fire*

What is it that shoots from the mountains so high,
 In many a beautiful spire?
What is it that blazes and curls to the sky?
 This beautiful something is fire.

Loud noises are heard in the caverns to groan,
 Hot cinders fall thicker than snow;
Huge stones to a wonderful distance are thrown,
 For burning fire rages below.

*Ann Taylor*

When winter blows bleak, and loud bellows the storm,
  And frostily twinkle the stars;
Then bright burns the fire in the chimney so warm,
  And the kettle sings shrill on the bars.

Then call the poor trav'ller in, cover'd with snow,
  And warm him with charity kind;
Fire is not so warm as the feelings that glow
  In the friendly, benevolent mind.

By fire rugged metals are fitted for use:
  Iron, copper, gold, silver, and tin;
Without its assistance we could not produce
  So much as a minikin pin.

Fire rages with fury, wherever it comes;
  If only one spark should be dropt,
Whole houses, or cities, sometimes it consumes,
  Where its violence cannot be stopt.

And when the great morning of judgment shall rise,
  How wide will its blazes be curl'd!
With heat, fervent heat, it shall melt down the skies,
  And burn up this beautiful world.


## Air

What is it that winds about over the world,
  Spread thin like a covering fair?
Into each little corner and crevice 'tis curl'd;
  This wonderful fluid is—air.

In summer's still ev'ning how peaceful it floats,
  When not a leaf moves on the spray;
And no sound is heard but the nightingale's notes,
  And merry gnats dancing away.

The village bells glide on its bosom serene,
    And steal in sweet cadence along;
The shepherd's soft pipe warbles over the green,
    And the cottage girls join in the song.

But oft in the winter it bellows aloud,
    And roars in the northerly blast;
With fury drives onward the snowy blue cloud,
    And cracks the tall, tapering mast.

The sea rages wildly, and mounts to the skies
    In billows and fringes of foam;
And the sailor in vain turns his pitiful eyes
    Towards his dear, peaceable home.

When fire lies and smothers, or gnaws thro' the beam,
    Air forces it fiercer to glow:
And engines in vain in cold torrents may stream,
    If the wind should with violence blow.

In the forest it tears up the sturdy old oak,
    That many a tempest had known;
The tall mountain's pine into splinters is broke,
    And over the precipice blown.

And yet, though it rages with fury so wild,
    On solid earth, water, or fire,
Without its assistance, the tenderest child
    Would struggle, and gasp, and expire.

Pure air, pressing into the curious clay,
    Gave life to these bodies at first;
And when in the bosom it ceases to play,
    We crumble again to our dust.

## Earth

What is it that's cover'd so richly with green,
 And gives to the forest its birth?
A thousand plants bloom on its bosom serene
 Whose bosom?—the bosom of earth.

Hidden deep in its bowels the emerald shines,
 The ruby, and amethyst blue:
And silver and gold glitter bright in the mines
 Of Mexico rich, and Peru.

Large quarries of granite and marble are spread
 In its wonderful bosom, like bones;
Chalk, gravel, and coals; salt, sulphur, and lead;
 And thousands of beautiful stones.

Beasts, savage and tame, of all colours and forms,
 Either stalk in its deserts or creep;
White bears sit and growl to the northerly storms,
 And shaggy goats bound from the steep.

The oak and the snowdrop, the cedar and rose,
 Alike on its surface are seen:
The tall fir of Norway, surrounded with snows,
 And the mountain ash scarlet and green.

Fine grass and rich mosses creep over its hills,
 Flow'rs breathe their perfumes to the gale;
Tall water-weeds dip in its murmuring rills,
 And harvests wave bright in the vale.

And when this poor body is cold and decay'd,
 And this warm throbbing heart is at rest;
My head upon thee, mother Earth, shall be laid,
 To find a long home in thy breast.

## *Water*

What is it that glitters so clear and serene,
  Or dances in billows so white?
Ships skimming along on its surface are seen—
  'Tis water that glitters so bright.

Sea-weeds wind about in its cavities wet,
  The pearl oyster quietly sleeps;
A thousand fair shells, yellow, amber, and jet;
  And coral glows red in its deeps.

Whales lash the white foam in their frolicsome wrath,
  While hoarsely the winter wind roars;
And shoals of green mackerel stretch from the north,
  And wander along by our shores.

When tempests sweep over its bosom serene,
  Like mountains its billows arise;
The ships now appear to be buried between,
  And now carried up to the skies.

It gushes out clear from the sides of the hill,
  And sparkles bright down from the steep;
Then waters the valley, and roars thro' the mill,
  And wanders in many a sweep.

The trav'ller that crosses the desert so wide,
  Hot, weary, and stifled with dust,
Longs often to stoop at some rivulet's side,
  To quench in its waters his thirst.

The stately white swan glides along on its breast,
  Nor ruffles its surface serene;
And the duckling unfledged waddles out of its nest,
  To dabble in ditch water green.

The clouds, blown about in the chilly blue sky,
   Vast cisterns of water contain;
Like snowy white feathers in winter they fly,
   In summer stream in gentle rain.

When sunbeams so bright on the falling drops shine,
   The rainbow enlivens the show'r,
And glows in the heavens, a beautiful sign
   That water shall drown us no more.

# JANE TAYLOR
## 1783–1824

### *The Star*

Twinkle, twinkle, little star,
How I wonder what you are!
Up above the world so high,
Like a diamond in the sky.

When the blazing sun is gone,
When he nothing shines upon,
Then you show your little light,
Twinkle, twinkle, all the night.

Then the traveller in the dark,
Thanks you for your tiny spark,
He could not see which way to go,
If you did not twinkle so.

In the dark blue sky you keep,
And often through my curtains peep,
For you never shut your eye,
Till the sun is in the sky.

As your bright and tiny spark,
Lights the traveller in the dark—
Though I know not what you are,
Twinkle, twinkle, little star.

# WILLIAM HOWITT
## 1792–1879

### *The Wind in a Frolic*

The wind one morning sprung up from sleep,
Saying, 'Now for a frolic! now for a leap!
Now for a mad-cap, galloping chase!
I'll make a commotion in every place!'
So it swept with a bustle right through a great town,
Creaking the signs, and scattering down
Shutters; and whisking, with merciless squalls,
Old women's bonnets and gingerbread stalls.
There never was heard a much lustier shout,
As the apples and oranges trundled about;
And the urchins, that stand with their thievish eyes
For ever on watch, ran off each with a prize.

Then away to the field it went blustering and humming,
And the cattle all wondered whatever was coming;
It plucked by their tails the grave, matronly cows,
And tossed the colts' manes all about their brows,
Till, offended at such a familiar salute,
They all turned their backs, and stood sullenly mute.
So on it went, capering and playing its pranks:
Whistling with reeds on the broad river's banks;
Puffing the birds as they sat on the spray,
Or the traveller grave on the king's highway.
It was not too nice to hustle the bags
Of the beggar, and flutter his dirty rags:
'Twas so bold, that it feared not to play its joke
With the doctor's wig, or the gentleman's cloak.
Through the forest it roared, and cried gaily, 'Now,
You sturdy old oaks, I'll make you bow!'
And it made them bow without more ado,
Or it cracked their great branches through and through.

Then it rushed like a monster on cottage and farm,
Striking their dwellers with sudden alarm;
And they ran out like bees in a midsummer swarm.
There were dames with their 'kerchiefs tied over their caps,
To see if their poultry were free from mishaps;
The turkeys they gobbled, the geese screamed aloud,
And the hens crept to roost in a terrified crowd;
There was rearing of ladders, and logs laying on
Where the thatch from the roof threatened soon to be gone.

But the wind had passed on, and had met in a lane,
With a schoolboy, who panted and struggled in vain;
For it tossed him, and twirled him, then passed, and he stood,
With his hat in a pool, and his shoe in the mud.

There was a poor man, hoary and old,
Cutting the heath on the open wold—
The strokes of his bill were faint and few,
Ere this frolicsome wind upon him blew;
But behind him, before him, about him it came,
And the breath seemed gone from his feeble frame;
So he sat him down with a muttering tone,
Saying, 'Plague on the wind! was the like ever known?
But nowadays every wind that blows
Tells one how weak an old man grows!'

But away went the wind in its holiday glee;
And now it was far on the billowy sea,
And the lordly ships felt its staggering blow,
And the little boats darted to and fro,
But lo! it was night, and it sank to rest,
On the sea-bird's rock, in the gleaming west,
Laughing to think, in its fearful fun,
How little of mischief it had done.

# ANON., English
### *c.*1820

## *One Little Boy*

I'm a little gentleman,
Play, and ride, and dance I can;
Very handsome clothes I wear,
And I live on dainty fare:
And whenever out I ride,
I've a servant by my side.

And I never, all the day,
Need do anything but play,
Nor even soil my little hand,
Because I am so very grand:
O! I'm very glad, I'm sure,
I need not labour, like the poor.

For I think I could not bear,
Such old shabby clothes to wear;
To lie upon so hard a bed,
And only live on barley bread;
And what is worse, too, ev'ry day
To have to work as hard as they.

## *Another Little Boy*

I'm a little husbandman,
Work and labour hard I can;
I'm as happy all the day
At my work as if 'twere play;
Tho' I've nothing fine to wear,
Yet for that I do not care.

When to work I go along,
Singing loud my morning song,
With my wallet at my back,
Or my waggon whip to smack;
O, I am as happy then,
As the idle gentlemen.

I've a healthy appetite,
And I soundly sleep at night,
Down I lie content, and say,
'I've been useful all the day:
I'd rather be a plough-boy, than
A useless little gentleman.'

# JOHN CLARE
## 1793–1864

### *Clock a Clay*

In the cowslips peeps I lye
Hidden from the buzzing fly
While green grass beneath me lies
Pearled wi' dew like fishes eyes
Here I lye a clock a clay
Waiting for the time o' day

While grassy forests quake surprise
And the wild wind sobs and sighs
My gold home rocks as like to fall
On its pillars green and tall
When the pattering rain drives bye
Clock a Clay keeps warm and dry

Day by day and night by night
All the week I hide from sight
In the cowslips peeps I lye
In rain and dew still warm and dry
Day and night and night and day
Red black spotted clock a clay

My home it shakes in wind and showers
Pale green pillar top't wi' flowers
Bending at the wild winds breath
Till I touch the grass beneath
Here still I live lone clock a clay
Watching for the time of day

*Clock a clay*  ladybird or ladybug

## Little Trotty Wagtail

Little trotty wagtail he went in the rain
And tittering tottering sideways he near got straight again
He stooped to get a worm and look'd up to catch a fly
And then he flew away e're his feathers they were dry

Little trotty wagtail he waddled in the mud
And left his little foot marks trample where he would
He waddled in the water pudge and waggle went his tail
And chirrup up his wings to dry upon the garden rail

Little trotty wagtail you nimble all about
And in the dimpling water pudge you waddle in and out
Your home is nigh at hand and in the warm pigsty
So little Master Wagtail I'll bid you a 'Good bye'

# SAMUEL GRISWOLD GOODRICH
## 1793–1860

### Higglety, Pigglety, Pop!

Higglety, pigglety, pop!
The dog has eaten the mop;
The pig's in a hurry,
The cat's in a flurry,
Higglety, pigglety, pop!

# JOHN KEATS
## 1795–1821

### *Meg Merrilies*

Old Meg she was a gipsy,
  And lived upon the moors;
Her bed it was the brown heath turf,
  And her house was out of doors.
Her apples were swart blackberries,
  Her currants, pods o' broom;
Her wine was dew of the wild white rose,
  Her book a churchyard tomb.

Her brothers were the craggy hills,
  Her sisters larchen trees;
Alone with her great family
  She lived as she did please.
No breakfast had she many a morn,
  No dinner many a noon,
And, 'stead of supper, she would stare
  Full hard against the moon.

But every morn, of woodbine fresh
  She made her garlanding;
And, every night, the dark glen yew
  She wove, and she would sing.
And with her fingers, old and brown,
  She plaited mats of rushes,
And gave them to the cottagers
  She met among the bushes.

Old Meg was brave as Margaret Queen,
  And tall as Amazon:
An old red blanket cloak she wore,
  A chip-hat had she on.
God rest her aged bones somewhere—
  She died full long agone!

# THOMAS HOOD
## 1799–1845

### *Choosing their Names*

Our old cat has kittens three—
What do you think their names should be?

One is tabby with emerald eyes,
    And a tail that's long and slender,
And into a temper she quickly flies
    If you ever by chance offend her.
        I think we shall call her this—
        I think we shall call her that—
Now, don't you think that Pepperpot
        Is a nice name for a cat?

One is black with a frill of white,
    And her feet are all white fur,
If you stroke her she carries her tail upright
    And quickly begins to purr.
        I think we shall call her this—
        I think we shall call her that—
Now, don't you think that Sootikin
        Is a nice name for a cat?

One is a tortoiseshell yellow and black,
    With plenty of white about him;
If you tease him, at once he sets up his back,
    He's a quarrelsome one, ne'er doubt him.
        I think we shall call him this—
        I think we shall call him that—
Now, don't you think that Scratchaway
        Is a nice name for a cat?

Our old cat has kittens three
And I fancy these their names will be:
Pepperpot, Sootikin, Scratchaway—there!
Were ever kittens with these to compare?
And we call the old mother—
    Now, what do you think?—
Tabitha Longclaws Tiddley Wink.

# SARA COLERIDGE
## 1802–1852

### *The Storm*

See lightning is flashing,
The forest is crashing,
The rain will come dashing,
    A flood will be rising anon;

The heavens are scowling,
The thunder is growling,
The loud winds are howling,
    The storm has come suddenly on!

But now the sky clears,
The bright sun appears,
Now nobody fears,
    But soon every cloud will be gone.

# HENRY WADSWORTH LONGFELLOW
## 1807–1882

### *Paul Revere's Ride*

Listen, my children, and you shall hear
Of the midnight ride of Paul Revere,
On the eighteenth of April, in Seventy-five;
Hardly a man is now alive
Who remembers that famous day and year.

He said to his friend, 'If the British march
By land or sea from the town to-night,
Hang a lantern aloft in the belfry arch
Of the North Church tower as a signal light,—
One, if by land, and two, if by sea;
And I on the opposite shore will be,
Ready to ride and spread the alarm
Through every Middlesex village and farm,
For the country folk to be up and to arm.'

Then he said, 'Goodnight!' and with muffled oar
Silently rowed to the Charlestown shore,
Just as the moon rose over the bay,
Where swinging wide at her moorings lay
The Somerset, British man-of-war;
A phantom ship, with each mast and spar
Across the moon like a prison bar,
And a huge black hulk, that was magnified
By its own reflection in the tide.

Meanwhile, his friend, through alley and street,
Wanders and watches with eager ears,
Till in the silence around him he hears
The muster of men at the barrack door,
The sound of arms, and the tramp of feet,
And the measured tread of the grenadiers,
Marching down to their boats on the shore.

Then he climbed the tower of the Old North Church,
By the wooden stairs, with stealthy tread,
To the belfry-chamber overhead,
And startled the pigeons from their perch
On the sombre rafters, that round him made
Masses and moving shapes of shade,—
By the trembling ladder, steep and tall,
To the highest window in the wall,
Where he paused to listen and look down
A moment on the roofs of the town,
And the moonlight flowing over all.

Beneath, in the churchyard, lay the dead,
In their night-encampment on the hill,
Wrapped in silence so deep and still
That he could hear, like a sentinel's tread,
The watchful night-wind, as it went
Creeping along from tent to tent,
And seeming to whisper, 'All is well!'
A moment only he feels the spell
Of the place and the hour, and the secret dread
Of the lonely belfry and the dead;
For suddenly all his thoughts are bent
On a shadowy something far away,
Where the river widens to meet the bay,—
A line of black that bends and floats
On the rising tide, like a bridge of boats.

Meanwhile, impatient to mount and ride,
Booted and spurred, with a heavy stride
On the opposite shore walked Paul Revere.
Now he patted his horse's side,
Now gazed at the landscape far and near,
Then, impetuous, stamped the earth,
And turned and tightened his saddle-girth;
But mostly he watched with eager search
The belfry-tower of the Old North Church,
As it rose above the graves on the hill,
Lonely and spectral and sombre and still.

And lo! as he looks, on the belfry's height
A glimmer, and then a gleam of light!
He springs to the saddle, the bridle he turns,
But lingers and gazes, till full on his sight
A second lamp in the belfry burns!

A hurry of hoofs in a village street,
A shape in the moonlight, a bulk in the dark,
And beneath, from the pebbles, in passing, a spark
Struck out by a steed flying fearless and fleet:
That was all! And yet, through the gloom and the light,
The fate of a nation was riding that night;
And the spark struck out by that steed, in his flight,
Kindled the land into flame with its heat.

He has left the village and mounted the steep,
And beneath him, tranquil and broad and deep,
Is the Mystic, meeting the ocean tides;
And under the alders that skirt its edge,
Now soft on the sand, now loud on the ledge,
Is heard the tramp of his steed as he rides.

It was twelve by the village clock,
When he crossed the bridge into Medford town.
He heard the crowing of the cock,
And the barking of the farmer's dog,
And felt the damp of the river fog,
That rises after the sun goes down.

It was one by the village clock,
When he galloped into Lexington.
He saw the gilded weathercock
Swim in the moonlight as he passed,
And the meeting-house windows, blank and bare,
Gaze at him with a spectral glare,
As if they already stood aghast
At the bloody work they would look upon.

It was two by the village clock,
When he came to the bridge in Concord town.
He heard the bleating of the flock,
And the twitter of birds among the trees,
And felt the breath of the morning breeze
Blowing over the meadows brown.
And one was safe and asleep in his bed
Who at the bridge would be first to fall,
Who that day would be lying dead,
Pierced by a British musket-ball.

You know the rest. In the books you have read,
How the British Regulars fired and fled,—
How the farmers gave them ball for ball,
From behind each fence and farm-yard wall,
Chasing the red-coats down the lane,
Then crossing the fields to emerge again
Under the trees at the turn of the road,
And only pausing to fire and load.

So through the night rode Paul Revere;
And so through the night went his cry of alarm
To every Middlesex village and farm,—
A cry of defiance and not of fear,
A voice in the darkness, a knock at the door,
And a word that shall echo forevermore!
For, borne on the night-wind of the Past,
Through all our history, to the last,
In the hour of darkness and peril and need,
The people will waken and listen to hear
The hurrying hoof-beats of that steed,
And the midnight message of Paul Revere.

# JOHN GREENLEAF WHITTIER
## 1807–1892

## *Hymn*

SUNG AT THE ANNIVERSARY OF THE CHILDREN'S MISSION,
BOSTON (1878)

Thine are all the gifts, O God!
   Thine the broken bread;
Let the naked feet be shod,
   And the starving fed.

Let Thy children, by Thy grace,
   Give as they abound,
Till the poor have breathing space
   And the lost are found.

Wiser than the miser's hoards
   Is the giver's choice;
Sweeter than the song of birds
   Is the thankful voice.

Welcome smiles on faces sad
   As the flowers of spring;
Let the tender hearts be glad
   With the joy they bring.

Happier for their pity's sake
   Make their sports and plays,
And from lips of childhood take
   Thy perfected praise!

# THOMAS MILLER
## 1807–1874

### *Evening*
### *(In words of one syllable)*

The day is past, the sun is set,
   And the white stars are in the sky;
While the long grass with dew is wet,
   And through the air the bats now fly.

The lambs have now lain down to sleep,
   The birds have long since sought their nests;
The air is still; and dark, and deep
   On the hill side the old wood rests.

Yet of the dark I have no fear,
   But feel as safe as when 'tis light;
For I know God is with me there,
   And He will guard me through the night.

For God is by me when I pray,
   And when I close mine eyes in sleep,
I know that He will with me stay,
   And will all night watch by me keep.

For he who rules the stars and sea,
   Who makes the grass and trees to grow,
Will look on a poor child like me,
   When on my knees I to Him bow.

He holds all things in His right hand,
   The rich, the poor, the great, the small;
When we sleep, or sit, or stand,
   Is with us, for He loves us all.

# RICHARD MONCKTON MILNES, LORD HOUGHTON

### 1809–1885

## *Lady Moon*

Lady Moon, Lady Moon, where are you roving?
    Over the sea.
Lady Moon, Lady Moon, whom are you loving?
    All that love me.

Are you not tired with rolling, and never
    Resting to sleep?
Why look so pale, and so sad, as for ever
    Wishing to weep?

Ask me not this, little child, if you love me;
    You are too bold;
I must obey my dear Father above me,
    And do as I'm told.

Lady Moon, Lady Moon, where are you roving?
    Over the sea.
Lady Moon, Lady Moon, whom are you loving?
    All that love me.

# EDGAR ALLAN POE

### 1809–1849

## *Eldorado*

Gaily bedight,
A gallant knight,
In sunshine and in shadow,
Had journeyed long,
Singing a song,
In search of Eldorado.

But he grew old—
This knight so bold—
And o'er his heart a shadow
Fell as he found
No spot of ground
That looked like Eldorado.

And, as his strength
Failed him at length,
He met a pilgrim shadow:
'Shadow,' said he,
'Where can it be,
This land of Eldorado?'

'Over the mountains
Of the Moon,
Down the valley of the Shadow,
Ride, boldly ride,'
The shade replied,
'If you seek for Eldorado.'

# ALFRED, LORD TENNYSON
### 1809–1892

## *The City Child*

Dainty little maiden, whither would you wander?
 Whither from this pretty home, the home where mother dwells?
'Far and far away,' said the dainty little maiden,
'All among the gardens, auriculas, anemones,
 Roses and lilies and Canterbury-bells.'

Dainty little maiden, whither would you wander?
 Whither from this pretty house, this city-house of ours?
'Far and far away,' said the dainty little maiden,
'All among the meadows, the clover and the clematis,
 Daisies and kingcups and honeysuckle-flowers.'

## Minnie and Winnie

Minnie and Winnie
  Slept in a shell.
Sleep, little ladies!
  And they slept well.

Pink was the shell within,
  Silver without;
Sounds of the great sea
  Wandered about.

Sleep, little ladies,
  Wake not soon!
Echo on echo
  Dies to the moon.

Two bright stars
  Peeped into the shell.
'What are they dreaming of?
  Who can tell?'

Started a green linnet
  Out of the croft;
Wake, little ladies,
  The sun is aloft!

# ROBERT BROWNING
## 1812–1889

### The Pied Piper of Hamelin

Hamelin Town's in Brunswick,
  By famous Hanover city;
The river Weser, deep and wide,
Washes its wall on the southern side;
A pleasanter spot you never spied;

But, when begins my ditty,
Almost five hundred years ago,
To see the townsfolk suffer so
   From vermin, was a pity.

   Rats!
They fought the dogs and killed the cats,
   And bit the babies in the cradles,
And ate the cheeses out of the vats,
   And licked the soup from the cooks' own ladles,
Split open the kegs of salted sprats,
Made nests inside men's Sunday hats,
And even spoiled the women's chats
     By drowning their speaking
     With shrieking and squeaking
In fifty different sharps and flats.

At last the people in a body
   To the Town Hall came flocking:
'Tis clear,' cried they, 'our Mayor's a noddy;
   And as for our Corporation—shocking
To think we buy gowns lined with ermine
For dolts that can't or won't determine
What's best to rid us of our vermin!
You hope, because you're old and obese,
To find in the furry civic robe ease?
Rouse up, sirs! Give your brains a racking
To find the remedy we're lacking,
Or, sure as fate, we'll send you packing!'
At this the Mayor and Corporation
Quaked with a mighty consternation.

An hour they sat in council,
   At length the Mayor broke silence:
'For a guilder I'd my ermine gown sell,
   I wish I were a mile hence!
It's easy to bid one rack one's brain—
I'm sure my poor head aches again,
I've scratched it so, and all in vain.

Oh for a trap, a trap, a trap!'
Just as he said this, what should hap
At the chamber door but a gentle tap?
'Bless us,' cried the Mayor, 'what's that?'
(With the Corporation as he sat,
Looking little though wondrous fat;
Nor brighter was his eye, nor moister
Than a too-long-opened oyster,
Save when at noon his paunch grew mutinous
For a plate of turtle, green and glutinous)
'Only a scraping of shoes on the mat?
Anything like the sound of a rat
Makes my heart go pit-a-pat!'

'Come in!' the Mayor cried, looking bigger:
And in did come the strangest figure!
His queer long coat from heel to head
Was half of yellow and half of red,
And he himself was tall and thin,
With sharp blue eyes, each like a pin,
And light loose hair, yet swarthy skin,
No tuft on cheek nor beard on chin,
But lips where smiles went out and in;
There was no guessing his kith and kin:
And nobody could enough admire
The tall man and his quaint attire.
Quoth one: 'It's as my great-grandsire,
Starting up at the Trump of Doom's tone,
Had walked this way from his painted tombstone!'

He advanced to the council-table:
And, 'Please your honours,' said he, 'I'm able,
By means of a secret charm, to draw
    All creatures living beneath the sun,
    That creep or swim or fly or run,
After me so as you never saw!
And I chiefly use my charm
On creatures that do people harm,
The mole and toad and newt and viper;
And people call me the Pied Piper.'

(And here they noticed round his neck
　　A scarf of red and yellow stripe,
To match with his coat of the self-same check;
　　And at the scarf's end hung a pipe;
And his fingers, they noticed, were ever straying
As if impatient to be playing
Upon this pipe, as low it dangled
Over his vesture so old-fangled.)
'Yet,' said he, 'poor piper as I am,
In Tartary I freed the Cham,
　　Last June, from his huge swarms of gnats;
I eased in Asia the Nizam
　　Of a monstrous brood of vampire-bats:
And as for what your brain bewilders,
　　If I can rid your town of rats
Will you give me a thousand guilders?'
'One? fifty thousand!'—was the exclamation
Of the astonished Mayor and Corporation.

Into the street the Piper stept,
　　Smiling first a little smile,
As if he knew what magic slept
　　In his quiet pipe the while;
Then, like a musical adept,
To blow the pipe his lips he wrinkled,
And green and blue his sharp eyes twinkled,
Like a candle-flame where salt is sprinkled;
And ere three shrill notes the pipe uttered,
You heard as if an army muttered;
And the muttering grew to a grumbling;
And the grumbling grew to a mighty rumbling;
And out of the houses the rats came tumbling,
Great rats, small rats, lean rats, brawny rats,
Brown rats, black rats, grey rats, tawny rats,
Grave old plodders, gay young friskers,
　　Fathers, mothers, uncles, cousins,
Cocking tails and pricking whiskers,
　　Families by tens and dozens,
Brothers, sisters, husbands, wives—
Followed the Piper for their lives.

From street to street he piped advancing,
And step for step they followed dancing,
Until they came to the river Weser,
   Wherein all plunged and perished!
—Save one who, stout as Julius Caesar,
Swam across and lived to carry
   (As he, the manuscript he cherished)
To Rat-land home his commentary:
Which was, 'At the first shrill notes of the pipe,
I heard a sound as of scraping tripe,
And putting apples, wondrous ripe,
Into a cider-press's gripe:
And a moving away of pickle-tub-boards,
And a leaving ajar of conserve-cupboards,
And a drawing the corks of train-oil-flasks,
And a breaking the hoops of butter-casks;
And it seemed as if a voice
   (Sweeter far than by harp or by psaltery
Is breathed) called out, "Oh rats, rejoice!
   The world is grown to one vast drysaltery!
So munch on, crunch on, take your nuncheon,
Breakfast, supper, dinner, luncheon!"
And just as a bulky sugar-puncheon,
All ready staved, like a great sun shone
Glorious scarce an inch before me,
Just as methought it said, "Come, bore me!"
—I found the Weser rolling o'er me.'

You should have heard the Hamelin people
Ringing the bells till they rocked the steeple.
'Go,' cried the Mayor 'and get long poles,
Poke out the nests and block up the holes!
Consult with carpenters and builders,
And leave in our town not even a trace
Of the rats!'—when suddenly, up the face
Of the Piper perked in the market-place,
With a 'First, if you please, my thousand guilders!'

A thousand guilders! The Mayor looked blue;
So did the Corporation too.
For council dinners made rare havoc
With Claret, Moselle, Vin-de-Grave, Hock;
And half the money would replenish
Their cellar's biggest butt with Rhenish.
To pay this sum to a wandering fellow
With a gipsy coat of red and yellow!
'Beside,' quoth the Mayor with a knowing wink,
'Our business was done at the river's brink;
We saw with our eyes the vermin sink,
And what's dead can't come to life, I think.
So, friend, we're not the folks to shrink
From the duty of giving you something for drink,
And a matter of money to put in your poke;
But as for the guilders, what we spoke
Of them, as you very well know, was in joke.
Besides, our losses have made us thrifty.
A thousand gilders! Come, take fifty!'

The Piper's face fell, and he cried
'No trifling! I can't wait, beside!
I've promised to visit by dinnertime
Baghdad, and accept the prime
Of the Head-Cook's pottage, all he's rich in,
For having left, in the Caliph's kitchen,
Of a nest of scorpions no survivor:
With him I proved no bargain-driver,
With you, don't think I'll bate a stiver!
And folks who put me in a passion
May find me pipe after another fashion.'

'How?' cried the Mayor, 'd'ye think I brook
Being worse treated than a cook?
Insulted by a lazy ribald
With idle pipe and vesture piebald?
You threaten us, fellow? Do your worst,
Blow your pipe there till you burst!'

Once more he stepped into the street
   And to his lips again
   Laid his long pipe of smooth straight cane;
And ere he blew three notes (such sweet
Soft notes as yet musician's cunning
   Never gave the enraptured air)
There was a rustling that seemed like a bustling
Of merry crowds justling at pitching and hustling
Small feet were pattering, wooden shoes clattering,
Little hands clapping and little tongues chattering,
And, like fowls in a farmyard when barley is scattering,
Out came the children running.
All the little boys and girls,
With rosy cheeks and flaxen curls,
And sparkling eyes and teeth like pearls,
Tripping and skipping, ran merrily after
The wonderful music with shouting and laughter.

The Mayor was dumb, and the Council stood
As if they were changed into blocks of wood,
Unable to move a step, or cry
To the children merrily skipping by
—Could only follow with the eye
That joyous crowd at the Piper's back.
But how the Mayor was on the rack,
And the wretched Council's bosoms beat,
As the Piper turned from the High Street
To where the Weser rolled its waters
Right in the way of their sons and daughters!
However he turned from south to west,
And to Koppelberg Hill his steps addressed,
And after him the children pressed;
Great was the joy in every breast.
'He never can cross that mighty top!
He's forced to let the piping drop,
And we shall see our children stop!'
When, lo, as they reached the mountain-side,
A wondrous portal opened wide,
As if a cavern was suddenly hollowed;
And the Piper advanced and the children followed,

And when all were in to the very last,
The door in the mountain-side shut fast.
Did I say, all? No! One was lame,
   And could not dance the whole of the way;
And in after years, if you would blame
   His sadness, he was used to say—
'It's dull in our town since my playmates left!
I can't forget that I'm bereft
Of all the pleasant sights they see,
Which the Piper also promised me.
For he led us, he said, to a joyous land,
Joining the town and just at hand,
Where waters gushed and fruit trees grew
And flowers put forth a fairer hue,
And everything was strange and new;
The sparrows were brighter than peacocks here,
And their dogs outran our fallow deer,
And honey-bees had lost their stings,
And horses were born with eagles' wings:
And just as I became assured
My lame foot would be speedily cured,
The music stopped and I stood still,
And found myself outside the hill,
Left alone against my will,
To go now limping as before,
And never hear of that country more!'

Alas, alas for Hamelin!
   There came into many a burgher's pate
   A text which says that heaven's gate
   Opes to the rich at as easy rate
As the needle's eye takes a camel in!
The Mayor sent east, west, north, and south,
To offer the Piper, by word of mouth,
   Wherever it was men's lot to find him,
Silver and gold to his heart's content,
If he'd only return the way he went,
   And bring the children behind him.

But when they saw 'twas a lost endeavour,
And Piper and dancers were gone for ever,
They made a decree that lawyers never
    Should think their records dated duly
If, after the day of the month and year,
These words did not as well appear,
'And so long after what happened here
    On the Twenty-second of July,
Thirteen hundred and seventy-six':
And the better in memory to fix
The place of the children's last retreat,
They called it the Pied Piper's Street—
Where anyone playing on pipe or tabor
Was sure for the future to lose his labour.
Nor suffered they hostelry or tavern
    To shock with mirth a street so solemn;
But opposite the place of the cavern
    They wrote the story on a column;
And on the great church-window painted
The same, to make the world acquainted
How their children were stolen away,
And there it stands to this very day.
And I must not omit to say
That in Transylvania there's a tribe
Of alien people who ascribe
The outlandish ways and dress
On which their neighbours lay such stress,
To their fathers and mothers having risen
Out of some subterraneous prison
Into which they were trepanned
Long time ago in a mighty band
Out of Hamelin town in Brunswick land,
But how or why, they don't understand.

        *     *     *

So, Willy, let you and me be wipers
Of scores out with all men—especially pipers!
And, whether they pipe us free from rats or from mice,
If we've promised them aught, let us keep our promise!

# EDWARD LEAR
## 1812–1888

### 'There was an Old Man with a beard'

There was an Old Man with a beard,
Who said, 'It is just as I feared!—
   Two Owls and a Hen,
   Four Larks and a Wren,
Have all built their nests in my beard!'

### The Owl and the Pussy-cat

The Owl and the Pussy-cat went to sea
   In a beautiful pea-green boat,
They took some honey, and plenty of money,
   Wrapped up in a five-pound note.
The Owl looked up to the stars above,
   And sang to a small guitar,
'O lovely Pussy! O Pussy, my love
   What a beautiful Pussy you are,
      You are,
      You are!
   What a beautiful Pussy you are!'

Pussy said to the Owl, 'You elegant fowl!
   How charmingly sweet you sing!
O let us be married! too long we have tarried:
   But what shall we do for a ring?'
They sailed away, for a year and a day,
   To the land where the Bong-tree grows,
And there in a wood a Piggy-wig stood
   With a ring at the end of his nose,
      His nose,
      His nose,
   With a ring at the end of his nose.

'Dear Pig, are you willing to sell for one shilling
  Your ring?' Said the Piggy, 'I will.'
So they took it away, and were married next day
  By the Turkey who lives on the hill.
They dined on mince, and slices of quince,
  Which they ate with a runcible spoon;
And hand in hand, on the edge of the sand,
  They danced by the light of the moon,
      The moon,
      The moon,
  They danced by the light of the moon.


## 'There was an Old Man who forgot'

There was an Old Man who forgot,
That his tea was excessively hot.
  When they said, 'Let it cool,'
  He answered, 'You fool!
I shall pour it back into the pot.'


## The Jumblies

They went to sea in a Sieve, they did,
  In a Sieve they went to sea:
In spite of all their friends could say,
On a winter's morn, on a stormy day,
  In a Sieve they went to sea!
And when the Sieve turned round and round,
And everyone cried, 'You'll all be drowned!'
They called aloud, 'Our Sieve ain't big,
But we don't care a button! we don't care a fig!
  In a Sieve we'll go to sea!'
    Far and few, far and few,
      Are the lands where the Jumblies live;
     Their heads are green, and their hands are blue,
      And they went to sea in a Sieve.

They sailed away in a Sieve, they did,
   In a Sieve they sailed so fast,
With only a beautiful pea-green veil
Tied with a riband by way of a sail,
   To a small tobacco-pipe mast;
And everyone said, who saw them go,
'O won't they be soon upset, you know!
For the sky is dark, and the voyage is long,
And happen what may, it's extremely wrong
   In a Sieve to sail so fast!'
     Far and few, far and few,
       Are the lands where the Jumblies live;
       Their heads are green, and their hands are blue,
       And they went to sea in a Sieve.

The water it soon came in, it did,
   The water it soon came in;
So to keep them dry, they wrapped their feet
In a pinky paper all folded neat,
   And they fastened it down with a pin.
And they passed the night in a crockery-jar,
And each of them said, 'How wise we are!
Though the sky be dark, and the voyage be long,
Yet we never can think we were rash or wrong,
   While round in our Sieve we spin!'
     Far and few, far and few,
       Are the lands where the Jumblies live;
       Their heads are green, and their hands are blue,
       And they went to sea in a Sieve.

And all night long they sailed away;
   And when the sun went down,
They whistled and warbled a moony song
To the echoing sound of a coppery gong,
   In the shade of the mountains brown.
'O Timballoo! How happy we are,
When we live in a sieve and a crockery-jar,
And all night long in the moonlight pale,
We sail away with a pea-green sail,

In the shade of the mountains brown!'
   Far and few, far and few,
     Are the lands where the Jumblies live;
    Their heads are green, and their hands are blue,
     And they went to sea in a Sieve.

They sailed to the Western Sea, they did,
  To a land all covered with trees,
And they bought an Owl, and a useful Cart,
And a pound of Rice, and a Cranberry Tart,
  And a hive of silvery Bees.
And they bought a Pig, and some green Jackdaws,
And a lovely Monkey with lollipop paws,
And forty bottles of Ring-Bo-Ree,
  And no end of Stilton Cheese.
   Far and few, far and few,
     Are the lands where the Jumblies live;
    Their heads are green, and their hands are blue,
     And they went to sea in a Sieve.

And in twenty years they all came back,
  In twenty years or more,
And everyone said, 'How tall they've grown!
For they've been to the Lakes, and the Torrible Zone,
  And the hills of the Chankly Bore';
And they drank their health, and gave them a feast
Of dumplings made of beautiful yeast;
And everyone said, 'If we only live,
We too will go to sea in a Sieve,
  To the hills of the Chankly Bore!'
   Far and few, far and few,
     Are the lands where the Jumblies live;
    Their heads are green, and their hands are blue,
     And they went to sea in a Sieve.

## The Dong with a Luminous Nose

When awful darkness and silence reign
Over the great Gromboolian plain,
 Through the long, long wintry nights;—
When the angry breakers roar
As they beat on the rocky shore;—
 When Storm-clouds brood on the towering heights
Of the Hills of the Chankly Bore:—

Then, through the vast and gloomy dark,
There moves what seems a fiery spark,
 A lonely spark with silvery rays
 Piercing the coal-black night,—
 A Meteor strange and bright:—
Hither and thither the vision strays,
 A single lurid light.

Slowly it wanders,—pauses,—creeps,—
Anon it sparkles,—flashes and leaps;
And ever as onward it gleaming goes
A light on the Bong-tree stems it throws.
And those who watch at that midnight hour
From Hall or Terrace, or lofty Tower,
Cry, as the wild light passes along,—
 'The Dong!—the Dong!
 The wandering Dong through the forest goes!
 The Dong! the Dong!
 The Dong with a luminous Nose!'

 Long years ago
 The Dong was happy and gay,
Till he fell in love with a Jumbly Girl
 Who came to those shores one day,
For the Jumblies came in a Sieve, they did,—
Landing at eve near the Zemmery Fidd
 Where the Oblong Oysters grow,
 And the rocks are smooth and gray.

And all the woods and the valleys rang
With the Chorus they daily and nightly sang,—
    *'Far and few, far and few,*
    *Are the lands where the Jumblies live;*
    *Their heads are green, and their hands are blue,*
    *And they went to sea in a Sieve.'*


  Happily, happily passed those days!
    While the cheerful Jumblies staid;
   They danced in circlets all night long,
  To the plaintive pipe of the lively Dong,
    In moonlight, shine, or shade.
For day and night he was always there
By the side of the Jumbly Girl so fair,
With her sky-blue hands, and her sea-green hair.
Till the morning came of that hateful day
When the Jumblies sailed in their Sieve away,
And the Dong was left on the cruel shore
Gazing—gazing for evermore,—
Ever keeping his weary eyes on
That pea-green sail on the far horizon,—
Singing the Jumbly Chorus still
As he sate all day on the grassy hill,—
    *'Far and few, far and few,*
    *Are the lands where the Jumblies live;*
    *Their heads are green, and their hands are blue,*
    *And they went to sea in a Sieve.'*


But when the sun was low in the West,
  The Dong arose and said;—
—'What little sense I once possessed
  Has quite gone out of my head!'—
And since that day he wanders still
By lake and forest, marsh and hill,
Singing—'O somewhere, in valley or plain
Might I find my Jumbly Girl again!
For ever I'll seek by lake and shore
Till I find my Jumbly Girl once more!'

Playing a pipe with silvery squeaks,
Since then his Jumbly Girl he seeks,
And because by night he could not see,
He gathered the bark of the Twangum Tree
   On the flowery plain that grows.
   And he wove him a wondrous Nose,—
A Nose as strange as a Nose could be!
Of vast proportions and painted red,
And tied with cords to the back of his head.
      —In a hollow rounded space it ended
      With a luminous Lamp within suspended,
        All fenced about
        With a bandage stout
        To prevent the wind from blowing it out;—
      And with holes all round to send the light,
      In gleaming rays on the dismal night.

And now each night, and all night long,
Over those plains still roams the Dong;
And above the wail of the Chimp and Snipe
You may hear the squeak of his plaintive pipe
While ever he seeks, but seeks in vain
To meet with his Jumbly Girl again;
Lonely and wild—all night he goes,—
The Dong with a luminous Nose!
And all who watch at the midnight hour,
From Hall or Terrace, or lofty Tower,
Cry, as they trace the Meteor bright,
Moving along through the dreary night,—
      'This is the hour when forth he goes,
      The Dong with a luminous Nose!
      Yonder—over the plain he goes;
        He goes!
        He goes;
      The Dong with a luminous Nose!'

## *Calico Pie*

Calico Pie,
 The little Birds fly
Down to the calico tree,
 Their wings were blue
 And they sang 'Tilly-loo!'
 Till away they flew,—
And they never came back to me!
 They never came back!
 They never came back!
They never came back to me!

Calico Jam,
 The little Fish swam,
Over the syllabub sea,
 He took off his hat,
 To the Sole and the Sprat,
 And the Willeby-wat,—
But he never came back to me!
 He never came back!
 He never came back!
He never came back to me!

Calico Ban,
 The little Mice ran,
To be ready in time for tea,
 Flippity flup,
 They drank it all up,
 And danced in the cup,—
But they never came back to me!
 They never came back!
 They never came back!
They never came back to me!

Calico Drum,
The Grasshoppers come,
The Butterfly, Beetle, and Bee,
Over the ground,
Around and round,
With a hop and a bound,—
But they never came back!
They never came back!
They never came back!
They never came back to me!


## Incidents in the Life of my Uncle Arly

O my agèd Uncle Arly!
Sitting on a heap of Barley
Thro' the silent hours of night,—
Close beside a leafy thicket:—
On his nose there was a Cricket,—
In his hat a Railway-Ticket;—
(But his shoes were far too tight).

Long ago, in youth, he squander'd
All his goods away, and wander'd
To the Tiniskoop-hills afar.
There on golden sunsets blazing,
Every evening found him gazing,—
Singing,—'Orb! You're quite amazing!
How I wonder what you are!'

Like the ancient Medes and Persians,
Always by his own exertions
He subsisted on those hills;—
Whiles,—by teaching children spelling,—
Or at times by merely yelling,—
Or at intervals by selling
Propter's Nicodemus Pills.

Later, in his morning rambles
He perceived the moving brambles—
 Something square and white disclose;—
'Twas a First-class Railway-Ticket;
But, on stooping down to pick it
Off the ground,—a pea-green Cricket
 Settled on my uncle's Nose.

Never—never more,—oh! never,
Did that Cricket leave him ever,—
 Dawn or evening, day or night;—
Clinging as a constant treasure,—
Chirping with a cheerious measure,—
Wholly to my uncle's pleasure,
 (Though his shoes were far too tight).

So for three-and-forty winters,
Till his shoes were worn to splinters,
 All those hills he wander'd o'er,—
Sometimes silent;—sometimes yelling;—
Till he came to Borley-Melling,
Near his old ancestral dwelling;—
 (But his shoes were far too tight).

On a little heap of Barley
Died my agèd Uncle Arly,
 And they buried him one night;—
Close beside the leafy thicket;—
There,—his hat and Railway-Ticket;—
There,—his ever-faithful Cricket;—
 (But his shoes were far too tight).


## 'O dear! How disgusting is life!'

O dear! How disgusting is life!
To improve it O what can we do?
Most disgusting is hustle and strife,
and of all things an ill-fitting shoe—
shoe,
O bother an ill-fitting shoe!

# CECIL FRANCES ALEXANDER
## 1818–1895

### *Dreams*

Beyond, beyond the mountain line,
   The grey-stone and the boulder,
Beyond the growth of dark green pine,
   That crowns its western shoulder,
There lies that fairy land of mine,
   Unseen of a beholder.

Its fruits are all like rubies rare,
   Its streams are clear as glasses:
There golden castles hang in air,
   And purple grapes in masses,
And noble knights and ladies fair
   Come riding down the passes.

Ah me! they say if I could stand
   Upon those mountain ledges,
I should but see on either hand
   Plain fields and dusty hedges:
And yet I know my fairy land
   Lies somewhere o'er their hedges.

# FREDERICK LOCKER-LAMPSON
## 1821–1895

### *A Terrible Infant*

I recollect a nurse called Ann,
  Who carried me about the grass,
And one fine day a fair young man
  Came up and kissed the pretty lass:
She did not make the least objection!
      Thinks I, *Aha!*
*When I can talk I'll tell Mamma!*
—And that's my earliest recollection.

# ELIZABETH ANNA HART
## 1822–1888?

### *Mother Tabbyskins*

Sitting at a window
  In her cloak and hat,
I saw Mother Tabbyskins,
  The *real* old cat!
    Very old, very old,
      Crumplety and lame;
  Teaching kittens how to scold—
    Is it not a shame?

Kittens in the garden
  Looking in her face,
Learning how to spit and swear—
  Oh, what a disgrace!
    Very wrong, very wrong,
      Very wrong, and bad;
  Such a subject for our song,
    Makes us all too sad.

Old Mother Tabbyskins,
  Sticking out her head,
Gave a howl, and then a yowl,
  Hobbled off to bed.
    Very sick, very sick,
      Very savage, too;
    Pray send for a doctor quick—
      Any one will do!

Doctor Mouse came creeping,
  Creeping to her bed;
Lanced her gums and felt her pulse,
  Whispered she was dead.
    Very sly, very sly,
      The *real* old cat
    Open kept her weather eye—
      Mouse! beware of that!

Old Mother Tabbyskins,
  Saying 'Serves him right',
Gobbled up the doctor, with
  Infinite delight.
    Very fast, very fast,
      Very pleasant, too—
    'What a pity it can't last!
      Bring another, do'

Doctor Dog comes running,
  Just to see her begs;
Round his neck a comforter,
  Trousers on his legs.
    Very grand, very grand—
      Golden-headed cane
    Swinging gaily from his hand,
      Mischief in his brain!

'Dear Mother Tabbyskins,
  And how are you now?
Let me feel your pulse—so, so;
  Show your tongue—bow, wow!
    Very ill, very ill,
      Please attempt to purr;
    Will you take a draught or pill?
      Which do you prefer?'

Ah, Mother Tabbyskins,
  Who is now afraid?
Of poor little Doctor Mouse
  You a mouthful made.
    Very nice, very nice
      Little doctor he;
    But for Doctor Dog's advice
      *You* must pay the fee.

Doctor Dog comes nearer,
  Says she must be bled;
I heard Mother Tabbyskins
  Screaming in her bed.
    Very near, very near,
      Scuffling out and in;
    Doctor Dog looks full and queer—
      Where is Tabbyskin?

I will tell the Moral
  Without any fuss:
Those who lead the young astray
  *Always* suffer thus.
    Very nice, very nice,
      Let our conduct be;
    For all doctors are not mice,
      Some are dogs, you see!

# WILLIAM BRIGHTY RANDS
## 1823–1882

### The World

Great, wide, beautiful, wonderful World,
With the wonderful water round you curled,
And the wonderful grass upon your breast—
World, you are beautifully drest.

The wonderful air is over me,
And the wonderful wind is shaking the tree,
It walks on the water, and whirls the mills,
And talks to itself on the tops of the hills.

You friendly Earth, how far do you go,
With the wheatfields that nod and the rivers that flow,
With cities and gardens, and cliffs, and isles,
And people upon you for thousands of miles?

Ah, you are so great, and I am so small,
I tremble to think of you, World, at all;
And yet, when I said my prayers today,
A whisper inside me seemed to say,
'You are more than the Earth, though you are such a dot:
You can love and think, and the Earth cannot.'

### The Cat of Cats

I am the cat of cats. I am
    The everlasting cat!
Cunning, and old, and sleek as jam,
    The everlasting cat!
I hunt the vermin in the night—
    The everlasting cat!
For I see best without the light—
    The everlasting cat!

# WILLIAM ALLINGHAM
## 1824−1889

### *The Fairies*

Up the airy mountain,
  Down the rushy glen,
We daren't go a-hunting
  For fear of little men;
Wee folk, good folk,
  Trooping all together;
Green jacket, red cap,
  And white owl's feather!

Down along the rocky shore
  Some make their home,
They live on crispy pancakes
  Of yellow tide-foam;
Some in the reeds
  Of the black mountain-lake,
With frogs for their watchdogs,
  All night awake.

High on the hill-top
  The old King sits;
He is now so old and grey
  He's nigh lost his wits.
With a bridge of white mist
  Columbkill he crosses,
On his stately journeys
  From Slieveleague to Rosses;
Or going up with music
  On cold starry nights,
To sup with the Queen
  Of the gay Northern Lights.

They stole little Bridget
　For seven years long;
When she came down again
　Her friends were all gone.
They took her lightly back,
　Between the night and morrow,
They thought that she was fast asleep,
　But she was dead with sorrow.
They have kept her ever since
　Deep within the lake,
On a bed of flag-leaves,
　Watching till she wake.

By the craggy hillside,
　Through the mosses bare,
They have planted thorn trees
　For pleasure, here and there.
Is any man so daring
　As dig them up in spite,
He shall find their sharpest thorns
　In his bed at night.

Up the airy mountain,
　Down the rushy glen,
We daren't go a-hunting
　For fear of little men;
Wee folk, good folk,
　Trooping all together;
Green jacket, red cap,
　And white owl's feather!

# LUCY LARCOM
## 1824–1893

### *The Brown Thrush*

There's a merry brown thrush sitting up in the tree;
'He's singing to me! he's singing to me!'
And what does he say, little girl, little boy?
'Oh, the world's running over with joy!
　　　Don't you hear? Don't you see?
　　　Hush! look! in my tree!
　　　I'm as happy as happy can be!'

And the brown thrush keeps singing, 'A nest do you see,
And five eggs hid by me in the juniper-tree?
Don't meddle! don't touch! little girl, little boy,
Or the world will lose some of its joy!
　　　Now I'm glad! now I'm free!
　　　And I always shall be,
　　　If you never bring sorrow to me.'

So the merry brown thrush sings away in the tree,
To you and to me, to you and to me;
And he sings all the day, little girl, little boy,
'Oh, the world's running over with joy!
　　　But long it won't be,
　　　Don't you know? don't you see?
　　　Unless we are as good as can be!'

# GEORGE MacDONALD
## 1824–1905

### *The Wind and the Moon*

Said the Wind to the Moon, 'I will blow you out;
    You stare
    In the air
    Like a ghost in a chair,
Always looking what I am about—
I hate to be watched; I'll blow you out.'

The Wind blew hard, and out went the Moon.
    So deep
    On a heap
    Of clouds to sleep,
Down lay the Wind, and slumbered soon,
Muttering low, 'I've done for that Moon.'

He turned in his bed; she was there again!
    On high
    In the sky,
    With her one ghost eye,
The Moon shone white and alive and plain.
Said the Wind, 'I will blow you out again.'

The Wind he took to his revels once more;
    On down,
    In town,
    Like a merry-mad clown,
He leaped and hallooed with whistle and roar—
'What's that?' the glimmering thread once more!

He flew in a rage—he danced and blew;
    But in vain
    Was the pain
    Of his bursting brain;
For still the broader the Moon-scrap grew,
The broader he swelled his big cheeks and blew.

Slowly she grew—till she filled the night,
  And shone
  On her throne
  In the sky alone,
A matchless, wonderful silvery light,
Radiant and lovely, the queen of the night.

The Wind blew hard, and the Moon grew dim.
  'With my sledge
  And my wedge,
  I have knocked off her edge!
If only I blow right fierce and grim,
The creature will soon be dimmer than dim.'

He blew and he blew, and she thinned to a thread.
  'One puff
  More's enough
  To blow her to snuff!
One good puff more where the last was bred,
And glimmer, glimmer, glum will go the thread.'

He blew a great blast, and the thread was gone.
  In the air
  Nowhere
  Was a moonbeam bare;
Far off and harmless the shy stars shone—
Sure and certain the Moon was gone!

Said the Wind: 'What a marvel of power am I!
  With my breath,
  God faith!
  I blew her to death—
First blew her away right out of the sky—
Then blew her in; what strength have I!'

But the Moon she knew nothing about the affair;
  For high
  In the sky,
  With her one white eye,
Motionless, miles above the air,
She had never heard the great Wind blare.

### *A Baby-Sermon*

The lightning and thunder
They go and they come;
But the stars and the stillness
Are always at home.


# D'ARCY WENTWORTH THOMPSON
## 1829–1902

### *That Dear Little Cat*

Who's that ringing at our door-bell?
'I'm a little black cat, and I'm not very well.'
'Then rub your little nose with a little mutton-fat,
And that's the best cure for a little pussy cat.'


# EMILY DICKINSON
## 1830–1886

### *'A little Dog that wags his tail'*

A little Dog that wags his tail
And knows no other joy
Of such a little Dog am I
Reminded by a Boy

Who gambols all the living Day
Without an earthly cause
Because he is a little Boy
I honestly suppose—

The Cat that in the Corner dwells
Her martial Day forgot
The Mouse but a Tradition now
Of her desireless Lot

Another class remind me
Who neither please nor play
But not to make a 'bit of noise'
Beseech each little Boy—


### 'The Butterfly upon the Sky'

The Butterfly upon the Sky,
That doesn't know its Name
And hasn't any tax to pay
And hasn't any Home

Is just as high as you and I,
And higher, I believe,
So soar away and never sigh
And that's the way to grieve—


### 'Not at Home to Callers'

Not at Home to Callers
Says the Naked Tree—
Bonnet due in April—
Wishing you Good Day—


# CHRISTINA ROSSETTI
## 1830–1894

### Goblin Market

Morning and evening
Maids heard the goblins cry:
'Come buy our orchard fruits,
Come buy, come buy:
Apples and quinces,
Lemons and oranges,
Plump unpecked cherries,

Melons and raspberries,
Bloom-down-cheeked peaches,
Swart-headed mulberries,
Wild free-born cranberries,
Crab-apples, dewberries,
Pine-apples, blackberries,
Apricots, strawberries;—
All ripe together
In summer weather,—
Morns that pass by,
Fair eves that fly;
Come buy, come buy:
Our grapes fresh from the vine,
Pomegranates full and fine,
Dates and sharp bullaces,
Rare pears and greengages,
Damsons and bilberries,
Taste them and try:
Currants and gooseberries,
Bright-fire-like barberries,
Figs to fill your mouth,
Citrons from the South,
Sweet to tongue and sound to eye;
Come buy, come buy.'

Evening by evening
Among the brookside rushes,
Laura bowed her head to hear,
Lizzie veiled her blushes:
Crouching close together
In the cooling weather,
With clasping arms and cautioning lips,
With tingling cheeks and finger tips.
'Lie close,' Laura said,
Pricking up her golden head:
'We must not look at goblin men,
We must not buy their fruits:
Who knows upon what soil they fed
Their hungry thirsty roots?'
'Come buy,' call the goblins
Hobbling down the glen.

'Oh,' cried Lizzie. 'Laura, Laura,
You should not peep at goblin men.'
Lizzie covered up her eyes,
Covered close lest they should look;
Laura reared her glossy head,
And whispered like the restless brook:
'Look, Lizzie, look, Lizzie,
Down the glen tramp little men.
One hauls a basket,
One bears a plate,
One lugs a golden dish
Of many pounds' weight.
How fair the vine must grow
Whose grapes are so luscious;
How warm the wind must blow
Through those fruit bushes.'
'No,' said Lizzie: 'No, no, no;
Their offers should not charm us,
Their evil gifts would harm us.'
She thrust a dimpled finger
In each ear, shut eyes and ran:
Curious Laura chose to linger
Wondering at each merchant man.
One had a cat's face,
One whisked a tail,
One tramped at a rat's pace,
One crawled like a snail,
One like a wombat prowled obtuse and furry,
One like a ratel tumbled hurry skurry.
She heard a voice like voice of doves
Cooing all together:
They sounded kind and full of loves
In the pleasant weather.

Laura stretched her gleaming neck
Like a rush-imbedded swan,
Like a lily from the beck,
Like a moonlit poplar branch,
Like a vessel at the launch
When its last restraint is gone.

Backwards up the mossy glen
Turned and trooped the goblin men,
With their shrill repeated cry,
'Come buy, come buy.'
When they reached where Laura was
They stood stock still upon the moss,
Leering at each other,
Brother with queer brother;
Signalling each other,
Brother with sly brother.
One set his basket down,
One reared his plate;
One began to weave a crown
Of tendrils, leaves, and rough nuts brown
(Men sell not such in any town);
One heaved the golden weight
Of dish and fruit to offer her:
'Come buy, come buy,' was still their cry.
Laura stared but did not stir,
Longed but had no money.
The whisk-tailed merchant bade her taste
In tones as smooth as honey,
The cat-faced purr'd,
The rat-paced spoke a word
Of welcome, and the snail-paced even was heard;
One parrot-voiced and jolly
Cried 'Pretty Goblin' still for 'Pretty Polly';
One whistled like a bird.

But sweet-tooth Laura spoke in haste:
'Good Folk, I have no coin;
To take were to purloin:
I have no copper in my purse,
I have no silver either,
And all my gold is on the furze
That shakes in windy weather
Above the rusty heather.'
'You have much gold upon your head.'
They answered all together:
'Buy from us with a golden curl.'

She clipped a precious golden lock.
She dropped a tear more rare than pearl,
Then sucked their fruit globes fair or red.
Sweeter than honey from the rock,
Stronger than man-rejoicing wine,
Clearer than water flowed that juice;
She never tasted such before,
How should it cloy with length of use?
She sucked and sucked and sucked the more
Fruits which that unknown orchard bore;
She sucked until her lips were sore;
Then flung the emptied rinds away
But gathered up one kernel stone,
And knew not was it night or day
As she turned home alone.

Lizzie met her at the gate
Full of wise upbraidings:
'Dear, you should not stay so late,
Twilight is not good for maidens;
Should not loiter in the glen
In the haunts of goblin men.
Do you not remember Jeanie,
How she met them in the moonlight,
Took their gifts both choice and many,
Ate their fruits and wore their flowers
Plucked from bowers
Where summer ripens at all hours?
But ever in the noonlight
She pined and pined away;
Sought them by night and day,
Found them no more, but dwindled and grew grey;
Then fell with the first snow,
While to this day no grass will grow
Where she lies low:
I planted daisies there a year ago
That never blow.
You should not loiter so.'
'Nay, hush,' said Laura:
'Nay, hush, my sister:

I ate and ate my fill,
Yet my mouth waters still:
Tomorrow night I will
Buy more;' and kissed her.
'Have done with sorrow;
I'll bring you plums to-morrow
Fresh on their mother twigs,
Cherries worth getting;
You cannot think what figs
My teeth have met in,
What melons icy-cold
Piled on a dish of gold
Too huge for me to hold,
What peaches with a velvet nap,
Pellucid grapes without one seed:
Odorous indeed must be the mead
Whereon they grow, and pure the wave they drink
With lilies at the brink,
And sugar-sweet their sap.'

Golden head by golden head,
Like two pigeons in one nest
Folded in each other's wings,
They lay down in their curtained bed:
Like two blossoms on one stem,
Like two flakes of new-fall'n snow,
Like two wands of ivory
Tipped with gold for awful kings.
Moon and stars gazed in at them,
Wind sang to them lullaby,
Lumbering owls forebore to fly,
Not a bat flapped to and fro
Round their nest:
Cheek to cheek and breast to breast
Locked together in one nest.

Early in the morning
When the first cock crowed his warning,
Neat like bees, as sweet and busy,
Laura rose with Lizzie:
Fetched in honey, milked the cows,
Aired and set to rights the house,
Kneaded cakes of whitest wheat,
Cakes for dainty mouths to eat,
Next churned butter, whipped up cream,
Fed their poultry, sat and sewed;
Talked as modest maidens should:
Lizzie with an open heart,
Laura in an absent dream,
One content, one sick in part;
One warbling for the mere bright day's delight,
One longing for the night.

At length slow evening came:
They went with pitchers to the reedy brook;
Lizzie most placid in her look,
Laura most like a leaping flame.
They drew the gurgling water from its deep.
Lizzie plucked purple and rich golden flags,
Then turning homeward said: 'The sunset flushes
Those furthest loftiest crags;
Come, Laura, not another maiden lags.
No wilful squirrel wags.
The beasts and birds are fast asleep.'
But Laura loitered still among the rushes,
And said the bank was steep.

And said the hour was early still,
The dew not fall'n, the wind not chill;
Listening ever, but not catching
The customary cry,
'Come buy, come buy,'
With its iterated jingle
Of sugar-baited words:
Not for all her watching
Once discerning even one goblin

Racing, whisking, tumbling, hobbling—
Let alone the herds
That used to tramp along the glen,
In groups or single,
Of brisk fruit-merchant men.

Till Lizzie urged, 'O Laura, come;
I hear the fruit-call, but I dare not look:
You should not loiter longer at this brook:
Come with me home.
The stars rise, the moon bends her arc,
Each glow-worm winks her spark,
Let us get home before the night grows dark:
For clouds may gather
Though this is summer weather,
Put out the lights and drench us through;
Then if we lost our way what should we do?'

Laura turned cold as stone
To find her sister heard that cry alone,
That goblin cry,
'Come buy our fruits, come buy.'
Must she then buy no more such dainty fruit?
Must she no more such succous pasture find,
Gone deaf and blind?
Her tree of life drooped from the root:
She said not one word in her heart's sore ache:
But peering thro' the dimness, nought discerning,
Trudged home, her pitcher dripping all the way;
So crept to bed, and lay
Silent till Lizzie slept;
Then sat up in a passionate yearning,
And gnashed her teeth for baulked desire, and wept
As if her heart would break.

Day after day, night after night,
Laura kept watch in vain
In sullen silence of exceeding pain.

*succous* juicy

She never caught again the goblin cry,
'Come buy, come buy';—
She never spied the goblin men
Hawking their fruits along the glen:
But when the noon waxed bright
Her hair grew thin and grey;
She dwindled, as the fair full moon doth turn
To swift decay and burn
Her fire away.

One day remembering her kernel-stone
She set it by a wall that faced the south;
Dewed it with tears, hoped for a root,
Watched for a waxing shoot,
But there came none.
It never saw the sun,
It never felt the trickling moisture run:
While with sunk eyes and faded mouth
She dreamed of melons, as a traveller sees
False waves in desert drouth
With shade of leaf-crowned trees,
And burns the thirstier in the sandful breeze.

She no more swept the house,
Tended the fowls or cows,
Fetched honey, kneaded cakes of wheat,
Brought water from the brook:
But sat down listless in the chimney-nook
And would not eat.

Tender Lizzie could not bear
To watch her sister's cankerous care,
Yet not to share.

She night and morning
Caught the goblins' cry:
'Come buy our orchard fruits,
Come buy, come buy:'—
Beside the brook, along the glen,
She heard the tramp of goblin men,

The voice and stir
Poor Laura could not hear;
Longed to buy fruit to comfort her,
But feared to pay too dear.
She thought of Jeanie in her grave,
Who should have been a bride;
But who for joys brides hope to have
Fell sick and died
In her gay prime,
In earliest winter time,
With the first glazing rime,
With the first snow-fall of crisp winter time.

Till Laura dwindling
Seemed knocking at Death's door.
Then Lizzie weighed no more
Better and worse;
But put a silver penny in her purse,
Kissed Laura, crossed the heath with clumps of furze
At twilight, halted by the brook:
And for the first time in her life
Began to listen and look.

Laughed every goblin
When they spied her peeping:
Came towards her hobbling,
Flying, running, leaping,
Puffing and blowing,
Chuckling, clapping, crowing,
Clucking and gobbling,
Mopping and mowing,
Full of airs and graces,
Pulling wry faces,
Demure grimaces,
Cat-like and rat-like,
Ratel- and wombat-like,
Snail-paced in a hurry,
Parrot-voiced and whistler,
Helter skelter, hurry skurry,

Chattering like magpies,
Fluttering like pigeons,
Gliding like fishes,—
Hugged her and kissed her:
Squeezed and caressed her:
Stretched up their dishes,
Panniers, and plates:
'Look at our apples
Russet and dun,
Bob at our cherries,
Bite at our peaches,
Citrons and dates,
Grapes for the asking,
Pears red with basking
Out in the sun,
Plums on their twigs;
Pluck them and suck them,—
Pomegranates, figs.'

'Good folk,' said Lizzie,
Mindful of Jeanie:
'Give me much and many:'
Held out her apron,
Tossed them her penny.
'Nay, take a seat with us,
Honour and eat with us,'
They answered grinning:
'Our feast is but beginning.
Night yet is early,
Warm and dew-pearly,
Wakeful and starry:
Such fruits as these
No man can carry;
Half their bloom would fly,
Half their dew would dry,
Half their flavour would pass by.
Sit down and feast with us,
Be welcome guest with us,
Cheer you and rest with us.'—

'Thank you,' said Lizzie: 'But one waits
At home alone for me:
So without further parleying,
If you will not sell me any
Of your fruits though much and many,
Give me back my silver penny
I tossed you for a fee.'—
They began to scratch their pates,
No longer wagging, purring,
But visibly demurring,
Grunting and snarling.
One called her proud,
Cross-grained, uncivil;
Their tones waved loud,
Their looks were evil.
Lashing their tails
They trod and hustled her,
Elbowed and jostled her,
Clawed with their nails,
Barking, mewing, hissing, mocking,
Tore her gown and soiled her stocking,
Twitched her hair out by the roots,
Stamped upon her tender feet,
Held her hands and squeezed their fruits
Against her mouth to make her eat.

White and golden Lizzie stood,
Like a lily in a flood,—
Like a rock of blue-veined stone
Lashed by tides obstreperously,—
Like a beacon left alone
In a hoary roaring sea,
Sending up a golden fire,—
Like a fruit-crowned orange-tree
White with blossoms honey-sweet
Sore beset by wasp and bee,—
Like a royal virgin town
Topped with gilded dome and spire
Close beleaguered by a fleet
Mad to tug her standard down.

One may lead a horse to water,
Twenty cannot make him drink.
Though the goblins cuffed and caught her,
Coaxed and fought her,
Bullied and besought her,
Scratched her, pinched her black as ink,
Kicked and knocked her,
Mauled and mocked her,
Lizzie uttered not a word;
Would not open lip from lip
Lest they should cram a mouthful in:
But laughed in heart to feel the drip
Of juice that syruped all her face,
And lodged in dimples of her chin,
And streaked her neck which quaked like curd.
At last the evil people,
Worn out by her resistance,
Flung back her penny, kicked their fruit
Along whichever road they took,
Not leaving root or stone or shoot;
Some writhed into the ground,
Some dived into the brook
With ring and ripple,
Some scudded on the gale without a sound,
Some vanished in the distance.

In a smart, ache, tingle,
Lizzie went her way;
Knew not was it night or day;
Sprang up the bank, tore thro' the furze,
Threaded copse and dingle,
And heard her penny jingle
Bouncing in her purse,—
Its bounce was music to her ear.
She ran and ran
As if she feared some goblin man
Dogged her with gibe or curse
Or something worse:

But not one goblin skurried after,
Nor was she pricked by fear;
The kind heart made her windy-paced
That urged her home quite out of breath with haste
And inward laughter.

She cried, 'Laura,' up the garden,
'Did you miss me?
Come and kiss me.
Never mind my bruises,
Hug me, kiss me, suck my juices
Squeezed from goblin fruits for you,
Goblin pulp and goblin dew.
Eat me, drink me, love me;
Laura, make much of me;
For your sake I have braved the glen
And had to do with goblin merchant men.'

Laura started from her chair,
Flung her arms up in the air,
Clutched her hair:
'Lizzie, Lizzie, have you tasted
For my sake the fruit forbidden?
Must your light like mine be hidden,
Your young life like mine be wasted,
Undone in mine undoing,
And ruined in my ruin,
Thirsty, cankered, goblin-ridden?'—
She clung about her sister,
Kissed and kissed and kissed her:
Tears once again
Refreshed her shrunken eyes,
Dropping like rain
After long sultry drouth;
Shaking with aguish fear, and pain,
She kissed and kissed her with a hungry mouth.

Her lips began to scorch,
That juice was wormwood to her tongue,
She loathed the feast:
Writhing as one possessed she leaped and sung,
Rent all her robe, and wrung
Her hands in lamentable haste,
And beat her breast.
Her locks streamed like the torch
Borne by a racer at full speed,
Or like the mane of horses in their flight,
Or like an eagle when she stems the light
Straight toward the sun,
Or like a caged thing freed,
Or like a flying flag when armies run.

Swift fire spread through her veins, knocked at her heart,
Met the fire smouldering there
And overbore its lesser flame;
She gorged on bitterness without a name:
Ah fool, to choose such part
Of soul-consuming care!
Sense failed in the mortal strife:
Like the watch-tower of a town
Which an earthquake shatters down,
Like a lightning-stricken mast,
Like a wind-uprooted tree
Spun about,
Like a foam-topped waterspout
Cast down headlong in the sea.
She fell at last;
Pleasure past and anguish past,
Is it death or is it life?

Life out of death.
That night long Lizzie watched by her,
Counted her pulse's flagging stir,
Felt for her breath,
Held water to her lips, and cooled her face
With tears and fanning leaves.
But when the first birds chirped about their eaves,

And early reapers plodded to the place
Of golden sheaves,
And dew-wet grass
Bowed in the morning winds so brisk to pass,
And new buds with new day
Opened of cup-like lilies on the stream.
Laura awoke as from a dream,
Laughed in the innocent old way,
Hugged Lizzie but not twice or thrice;
Her gleaming locks showed not one thread of grey,
Her breath was sweet as May,
And light danced in her eyes.

Days, weeks, months, years
Afterwards, when both were wives
With children of their own;
Their mother-hearts beset with fears,
Their lives bound up in tender lives;
Laura would call the little ones
And tell them of her early prime,
Those pleasant days long gone
Of not-returning time;
Would talk about the haunted glen,
The wicked quaint fruit-merchant men,
Their fruits like honey to the throat
But poison in the blood
(Men sell not such in any town):
Would tell them how her sister stood
In deadly peril to do her good,
And win the fiery antidote:
Then joining hands to little hands
Would bid them cling together,—
'For there is no friend like a sister
In calm or stormy weather;
To cheer one on the tedious way,
To fetch one if one goes astray,
To lift one if one totters down,
To strengthen whilst one stands.'

## *Minnie and Mattie*

Minnie and Mattie
    And fat little May,
Out in the country,
    Spending a day.

Such a bright day,
    With the sun glowing,
And the trees half in leaf,
    And the grass growing.

Pinky white pigling
    Squeals through his snout,
Woolly white lambkin
    Frisks all about.

Cluck! cluck! the nursing hen
    Summons her folk,—
Ducklings all downy soft,
    Yellow as yolk.

Cluck! cluck! the mother hen
    Summons her chickens
To peck the dainty bits
    Found in her pickings.

Minne and Mattie
    And May carry posies,
Half of sweet violets,
    Half of primroses.

Give the sun time enough,
    Glowing and glowing,
He'll rouse the roses
    And bring them blowing.

Don't wait for roses
   Losing today,
O Minnie, Mattie,
   And wise little May.

Violets and primroses
   Blossom to-day
For Minnie and Mattie
And fat little May.


## *If I Were a Queen*

'If I were a Queen,
   What would I do?
I'd make you King,
   And I'd wait for you.'

'If I were a King,
   What would I do?
I'd make you Queen,
   For I'd marry you.'


# LEWIS CARROLL
## 1832–1898

## *Brother and Sister*

'Sister, sister go to bed!
Go and rest your weary head.'
Thus the prudent brother said.

'Do you want a battered hide,
Or scratches to your face applied?'
Thus his sister calm replied.

'Sister, do not raise my wrath.
I'd make you into mutton broth
As easily as kill a moth!'

The sister raised her beaming eye
And looked on him indignantly
And sternly answered, 'Only try!'

Off to the cook he quickly ran.
'Dear Cook, please lend a frying-pan
To me as quickly as you can.'

'And wherefore should I lend it you?'
'The reason, Cook, is plain to view.
I wish to make an Irish stew.'

'What meat is in that stew to go?'
'My sister'll be the contents!'
                                    'Oh!'
'You'll lend the pan to me, Cook?'
                                    'No!'

*Moral:* Never stew your sister.

### *The Mouse's Tale*

'Fury said to
a mouse, That
   he met in the
     house, "Let
      us both go
       to law: *I*
        will prose-
       cute *you*. —
      Come, I'll
     take no de-
    nial: We
   must have
  the trial;
 For really
this morn-
ing I've
nothing
to do."
Said the
 mouse to
  the cur,
   "Such a
    trial, dear
     sir, With
      no jury
       or judge,
        would
       be wast-
      ing our
     breath."
    "I'll be
   judge,
  I'll be
 jury,"
said
cun-
 ning
  old
   Fury:
    "I'll
     try
     the
    whole
   cause,
  and
con-
 demn
you to
death."'

## A Lullaby

Speak roughly to your little boy,
    And beat him when he sneezes:
He only does it to annoy,
    Because he knows it teases.

      Wow! wow! wow!

I speak severely to my boy,
    I beat him when he sneezes;
For he can thoroughly enjoy
    The pepper when he pleases!

      Wow! wow! wow!


## Jabberwocky

'Twas brillig, and the slithy toves
    Did gyre and gimble in the wabe:
All mimsy were the borogoves,
    And the mome raths outgrabe.

'Beware the Jabberwock, my son!
    The jaws that bite, the claws that catch!
Beware the Jubjub bird, and shun
    The frumious Bandersnatch!'

He took his vorpal sword in hand:
    Long time the manxome foe he sought—
So rested he by the Tumtum tree,
    And stood awhile in thought.

And as in uffish thought he stood,
    The Jabberwock, with eyes of flame,
Came whiffling through the tulgey wood,
    And burbled as it came!

One, two! One, two! And through and through
  The vorpal blade went snicker-snack!
He left it dead, and with its head
  He went galumphing back.

'And hast thou slain the Jabberwock?
  Come to my arms, my beamish boy!
O frabjous day! Callooh! Callay!'
  He chortled in his joy.

'Twas brillig, and the slithy toves
  Did gyre and gimble in the wabe:
All mimsy were the borogoves,
  And the mome raths outgrabe.


# CELIA THAXTER
## 1835–1894

### *Chanticleer*

I wake! I feel the day is near;
  I hear the red cock crowing!
He cries, ''Tis dawn!' How sweet and clear
His cheerful call comes to my ear,
  While light is slowly growing!
The white snow gathers flake on flake;
  I hear the red cock crowing!
Is anybody else awake
To see the winter morning break,
  While thick and fast 'tis snowing?
I think the world is all asleep;
  I hear the red cock crowing!
Out of the frosty pane I peep;
The drifts are piled so wide and deep,
  And the wild wind is blowing!
Nothing I see has shape or form;
  I hear the red cock crowing!

But that dear voice comes through the storm
To greet me in my nest so warm,
    As if the sky were glowing!
A happy little child, I lie
    And hear the red cock crowing.
The day is dark. I wonder why
His voice rings out so brave and high,
    With gladness overflowing.

# W. S. GILBERT
## 1836–1911

### 'There was an old man of St Bees'

There was an old man of St Bees,
    Who was stung in the arm by a wasp.
        When asked 'Does it hurt?'
        He replied, 'No, it doesn't,
    I'm so glad it wasn't a hornet.'

# BRET HARTE
## 1836–1902

### Miss Edith's Modest Request

My papa knows you, and he says you're a man who makes reading for
        books;
But I never read nothing you wrote, nor did papa—I know by his
        looks.
So I guess you're like me when I talk, and I talk, and I talk all the day,
And they only say: 'Do stop that child!' or, 'Nurse, take Miss Edith
        away.'

But papa said if I was good I could ask you—alone by myself—
If you wouldn't write me a book like that little one up on the shelf.
I don't mean the pictures, of course, for to make *them* you've got to be
    smart;
But the reading that runs all around them, you know—just the easiest
    part.

You needn't mind what it's about, for no one will see it but me
And Jane—that's my nurse—and John—he's the coachman—just only
    us three.
You're to write of a bad little girl, that was wicked and bold and all
    that;
And then you are to write, if you please, something good—very
    good—of a cat!

This cat she was virtuous and meek, and kind to her parents and mild,
And careful and neat in her ways, though her mistress was such a bad
    child;
And hours she would sit and would gaze when her mistress—that's
    me—was so bad,
And blink, just as if she would say: 'O Edith! you make my heart sad.'

And yet, you would scarcely believe it, that beautiful angelic cat
Was blamed by the servants for stealing whatever, they said, she'd
    get at.
And when John drank my milk—don't you tell me!—I know just the
    way it was done—
They said 'twas the cat—and she sitting and washing her face in
    the sun!

And then there was Dick, my canary. When I left its cage open
    one day,
They all made believe that she ate it, though I know that the bird flew
    away.
And why? Just because she was playing with a feather she found on the
    floor,
As if cats couldn't play with a feather without people thinking 'twas
    more.

Why, once we were romping together, when I knocked down a vase
    from the shelf,
That cat was as grieved and distressed as if she had done it herself;
And she walked away sadly and hid herself, and never came out until
    tea—
So they say, for they sent *me* to bed, and she never came even to me.

No matter whatever happened, it was laid at the door of that cat.
Why, once when I tore my apron—she was wrapped in it, and I called,
    'Rat!'—
Why, they blamed that on *her*. I shall never—no, not to my dying
    day—
Forget the pained look that she gave me when they slapped *me* and
    took me away.

Of course, you know just what comes next, when a child is as lovely
    as that:
She wasted quite slowly away—it was goodness was killing that cat.
I know it was nothing she ate, for her taste was exceedingly nice;
But they said she stole Bobby's ice cream, and caught a bad cold from
    the ice.

And you'll promise to make me a book like that little one up on the
    shelf,
And you'll call her 'Naomi,' because it's a name that she just gave
    herself;
For she'd scratch at my door in the morning, and whenever I'd call
    out. 'Who's there?'
She would answer, 'Naomi! Naomi!' like a Christian I vow and declare.

And you'll put me and her in a book. And, mind, you're to say I
    was bad;
And I might have been badder than that but for the example I had.
And you'll say that she was a Maltese, and—what's that you asked? 'Is
    she dead?'
Why, please sir, *there ain't any cat!* You're to make one up out of
    your head!

# PALMER COX
## 1840–1924

### *The Mouse's Lullaby*

Oh, rock-a-by, baby mouse, rock-a-by, so!
When baby's asleep to the baker's I'll go,
And while he's not looking I'll pop from a hole,
And bring to my baby a fresh penny roll.

# CHARLES E. CARRYL
## 1841–1920

### *The Camel's Complaint*

Canary-birds feed on sugar and seed,
  Parrots have crackers to crunch;
And as for the poodles, they tell me the noodles
  Have chicken and cream for their lunch.
    But there's never a question
    About *my* digestion—
      *Anything* does for me.

Cats, you're aware, can repose in a chair,
  Chickens can roost upon rails;
Puppies are able to sleep in a stable,
  And oysters can slumber in pails,
    But no one supposes
    A poor camel dozes—
      *Any place* does for me.

Lambs are enclosed where it's never exposed,
  Coops are constructed for hens;
Kittens are treated to houses well heated,
  And pigs are protected by pens.
    But a camel comes handy
    Wherever it's sandy—
      *Anywhere* does for me.

People would laugh if you rode a giraffe,
  Or mounted the back of an ox;
It's nobody's habit to ride on a rabbit,
  Or try to bestraddle a fox.
    But as for a camel, he's
    Ridden by families—
      *Any load* does for me.

A snake is as round as a hole in the ground,
  And weasels are wavy and sleek;
And no alligator could ever be straighter
  Than lizards that live in a creek.
    But a camel's all lumpy
    And bumpy and humpy—
      *Any shape* does for me.

## The Sleepy Giant

My age is three hundred and seventy-two,
  And I think, with the deepest regret,
How I used to pick up and voraciously chew
  The dear little boys whom I met.

I've eaten them raw, in their holiday suits;
  I've eaten them curried with rice;
I've eaten them baked, in their jackets and boots,
  And found them exceedingly nice.

But now that my jaws are too weak for such fare,
  I think it exceedingly rude
To do such a thing, when I'm quite well aware
  Little boys do not like to be chewed.

And so I contentedly live upon eels,
    And try to do nothing amiss,
And I pass all the time I can spare from my meals
    In innocent slumber—like this.


# CHARLES HENRY ROSS
### *c.*1842–1897

## *Jack*

That's Jack;
Lay a stick on his back!
What's he done? I cannot say.
We'll find out tomorrow,
And beat him today.


# ELIZABETH T. CORBETT
### fl. 1878

## *Three Wise Old Women*

Three wise old women were they, were they,
Who went to walk on a winter day:
One carried a basket to hold some berries,
One carried a ladder to climb for cherries,
The third, and she was the wisest one,
Carried a fan to keep off the sun.

But they went so far, and they went so fast,
They quite forgot their way at last,
So one of the wise women cried in a fright,
'Suppose we should meet a bear tonight!
Suppose he should eat me!' 'And me!!' 'And me!!!'
'What is to be done?' cried all the three.

'Dear, dear!' said one, 'we'll climb a tree,
There out of the way of the bears we'll be.'
But there wasn't a tree for miles around;
They were too frightened to stay on the ground,
So they climbed their ladder up to the top,
And sat there screaming 'We'll drop! We'll drop!'

But the wind was strong as wind could be,
And blew their ladder right out to sea;
So the three wise women were all afloat
In a leaky ladder instead of a boat,
And every time the waves rolled in,
Of course the poor things were wet to the skin.

Then they took their basket, the water to bale,
They put up their fan instead of a sail:
But what became of the wise women then,
Whether they ever sailed home again,
Whether they saw any bears, or no,
You must find out, for I don't know.

# KATE GREENAWAY

## 1846–1901

### *Three Little Girls*

Three little girls were sitting on a rail,
    Sitting on a rail,
    Sitting on a rail;
Three little girls were sitting on a rail,
   On a fine hot day in September.

What did they talk about that fine day,
    That fine day,
    That fine day?
What did they talk about that fine day,
   That fine hot day in September?

The crows and the corn they talked about,
    Talked about,
    Talked about;
But nobody knows what was said by the crows,
    On that fine hot day in September.


# JAMES WHITCOMB RILEY
## 1849–1916

### *Jack the Giant-Killer*

BAD BOY'S VERSION

Tell you a story—an' it's a fac':—
Wunst wuz a little boy, name wuz Jack,
An' he had sword an' buckle an' strap
Maked of gold, an' a "visibul cap';
An' he killed Gi'nts 'at et whole cows—
Th' horns an' all —an' pigs an' sows!
But Jack, his golding sword wuz, oh!
So awful sharp 'at he could go
An' cut th' ole Gi'nts clean in two
'Fore 'ey knowed what he wuz goin' to do!
An' *one* ole Gi'nt, he had four
Heads, an' name wuz 'Bumblebore'—
An' he wuz feared o' Jack—'cause he,
*Jack*, he killed six—five—ten—three,
An' all o' th' uther ole Gi'nts but him:
An' thay wuz a place Jack haf to swim
'Fore he could git t' ole 'Bumblebore'—
Nen thay wuz 'griffuns' at the door:
But Jack, he thist plunged in an' swum
Clean acrost; an' when he come
To th' uther side, he thist put on
His "visibul cap,' an' nen, dog-gone!
You couldn't see him at all!—An' so
He slewed the 'griffuns'—*boff*, you know!

Nen wuz a horn hunged over his head,
High on th' wall, an' words 'at read,—
'Whoever kin this trumpet blow
Shall cause the Gi'nt's overth'ow!'
An' Jack, he thist reached up an' blowed
The stuffin' out of it! an' th'owed
Th' castul gates wide open, an'
Nen tuk his gold sword in his han',
An' thist marched in t' ole 'Bumblebore',
An', 'fore he knowed, he put 'bout four
Heads on him—an' chopped 'em off, too!—
Wisht 'at *I'd* been Jack!—don't you?


## A Nonsense Rhyme

Ringlety-jing!
     And what will we sing?
Some little crinkety-crankety thing
     That rhymes and chimes,
     And skips, sometimes,
As though wound up with a kink in the spring.

          Grunkety-krung!
     And chunkety-plung!
Sing the song that the bullfrog sung,—
     A song of the soul
     Of a mad tadpole
That met his fate in a leaky bowl:
And it's O for the first false wiggle he made
In a sea of pale pink lemonade!
          And it's O for the thirst
               Within him pent,
          And the hopes that burst
               As his reason went—
When his strong arm failed and his strength was spent!

Sing, O sing
Of the things that cling,
And the claws that clutch and the fangs that sting—
Till the tadpole's tongue
And his tail upflung
Quavered and failed with a song unsung!
O the dank despair in the rank morass,
Where the crawfish crouch in the cringing grass,
And the long limp rune of the loon wails on
For the mad, sad soul
Of a bad tadpole
Forever lost and gone!

Jinglety-jee!
And now we'll see
What the last of the lay shall be,
As the dismal tip of the tune, O friends,
Swoons away and the long tale ends.
And it's O and alack!
For the tangled legs
And the spangled back
Of the green grig's eggs,
And the unstrung strain
Of the strange refrain
That the winds wind up like a strand of rain!

And it's O,
Also,
For the ears wreathed low,
Like a laurel-wreath on the lifted brow
Of the frog that chants of the why and how,
And the wherefore too, and the thus and so
Of the wail he weaves in a woof of woe!
Twangle, then, with your wrangling strings,
The tinkling links of a thousand things!
And clang the pang of a maddening moan
Till the Echo, hid in a land unknown,
Shall leap as he hears, and hoot and hoo
Like the wretched wraith of a Whoopty-Doo!

## *The Nine Little Goblins*

They all climbed up on a high board-fence—
　Nine little goblins, with green-glass eyes—
Nine little goblins that had no sense,
　　And couldn't tell coppers from cold mince pies;
　　　And they all climbed up on the fence, and sat—
　　　And I asked them what they were staring at.

And the first one said, as he scratched his head
　With a queer little arm that reached out of his ear
And rasped its claws in his hair so red—
　　'This is what this little arm is fer!'
　　　And he scratched and stared, and the next one said,
　　　'How on earth do *you* scratch your head?'

And he laughed like the screech of a rusty hinge—
　Laughed and laughed till his face grew black;
And when he choked, with a final twinge
　　Of his stifling laughter, he thumped his back
　　　With a fist that grew on the end of his tail
　　　Till the breath came back to his lips so pale.

And the third little goblin leered round at me—
　And there were no lids on his eyes at all,—
And he clucked one eye, and he says, says he,
　　'What is the style of your socks this fall?'
　　　And he clapped his heels—and I sighed to see
　　　That he had hands where his feet should be.

Then a bald-faced goblin, gray and grim,
　Bowed his head, and I saw him slip
His eyebrows off, as I looked at him,
　　And paste them over his upper lip;
　　　And then he moaned in remorseful pain—
　　　'Would—Ah, would I'd me brows again!'

And then the whole of the goblin band
  Rocked on the fence-top to and fro,
And clung, in a long row, hand in hand,
    Singing the songs that they used to know—
      Singing the songs that their grandsires sung
      In the goo-goo days of the goblin-tongue.

And ever they kept their green-glass eyes
  Fixed on me with a stony stare—
Till my own grew glazed with a dread surmise,
    And my hat whooped up on my lifted hair,
      And I felt the heart in my breast snap to,
      As you've heard the lid of a snuff-box do.

And they sang: 'You're asleep! There is no board-fence,
  And never a goblin with green-glass eyes!—
'Tis only a vision the mind invents
    After a supper of cold mince pies.—
      And you're doomed to dream this way,' they said,—
      *'And you shan't wake up till you're clean plum dead!'*


## A Few of the Bird-Family

The Old Bob-white and Chipbird;
  The Flicker, and Chewink,
And little hopty-skip bird
  Along the river-brink.

The Blackbird, and Snowbird,
  The Chicken-hawk, and Crane;
The glossy old black Crow-bird,
  And Buzzard down the lane.

The Yellowbird, and Redbird,
  The Tomtit, and the Cat;
The Thrush, and that Red*head*-bird
  The rest's all pickin' at!

The Jay-bird, and the Bluebird
  The Sapsuck, and the Wren—
The Cockadoodle-doo-bird,
  And our old Settin'-hen!


## *The King of Oo-Rinktum-Jing*

Dainty Baby Austin!
Your Daddy's gone to Boston
  To see the King
  Of Oo-Rinktum-Jing
And the whale he rode acrost on!

Boston Town's a city:
But O it's such a pity!—
  They'll greet the King
  Of Oo-Rinktum-Jing
With never a nursery ditty!

But me and you and Mother
Can stay with Baby-brother,
  And sing of the King
  Of Oo-Rinktum-Jing
And laugh at one another!

So what cares Baby Austin
If Daddy *has* gone to Boston
  To see the King
  Of Oo-Rinktum-Jing
And the whale he rode acrost on?

# ROBERT LOUIS STEVENSON
## 1850—1894

### *Pirate Story*

Three of us afloat in the meadow by the swing,
Three of us aboard in the basket on the lea.
Winds are in the air, they are blowing in the spring,
And waves are on the meadows like the waves there are at sea.

Where shall we adventure, today that we're afloat,
Wary of the weather and steering by a star?
Shall it be to Africa, a-steering of a boat,
To Providence, or Babylon, or off to Malabar?

Hi! But here's a squadron a-rowing on the sea—
Cattle on the meadow a-charging with a roar!
Quick, and we'll escape them, they're as mad as they can be.
The wicket is the harbour and the garden is the shore.

### *Where Go the Boats?*

Dark brown is the river,
  Golden is the sand.
It flows along for ever,
  With trees on either hand.

Green leaves a-floating,
  Castles of the foam,
Boats of mine a-boating—
  Where will all come home?

On goes the river,
  And out past the mill,
Away down the valley,
  Away down the hill.

Away down the river,
  A hundred miles or more,
Other little children
  Shall bring my boats ashore.

## The Moon

The moon has a face like the clock in the hall;
She shines on thieves on the garden wall,
On streets and fields and harbour quays,
And birdies asleep in the forks of the trees.

The squalling cat and the squeaking mouse,
The howling dog by the door of the house,
The bat that lies in bed at noon,
All love to be out by the light of the moon.

But all of the things that belong to the day
Cuddle to sleep to be out of her way;
And flowers and children close their eyes
Till up in the morning the sun shall rise.

## The Swing

How do you like to go up in a swing,
  Up in the air so blue?
Oh, I do think it the pleasantest thing
  Ever a child can do!

Up in the air and over the wall,
  Till I can see so wide,
Rivers and trees and cattle and all
  Over the countryside—

Till I look down on the garden green,
  Down on the roof so brown—
Up in the air I go flying again,
  Up in the air and down!

## Block City

What are you able to build with your blocks?
Castle and palaces, temples and docks.
Rain may keep raining, and others go roam,
But I can be happy and building at home.

Let the sofa be mountains, the carpet be sea,
There I'll establish a city for me:
A kirk and a mill and a palace beside,
And a harbour as well where my vessels may ride.

Great is the palace with pillar and wall,
A sort of tower on the top of it all,
And steps coming down in an orderly way
To where my toy vessels lie safe in the bay.

This one is sailing and that one is moored:
Hark to the song of the sailors on board!
And see on the steps of my palace, the kings
Coming and going with presents and things!

## Autumn Fires

In the other gardens
    And all up the vale,
From the autumn bonfires
    See the smoke trail!

Pleasant summer over
    And all the summer flowers,
The red fire blazes,
    The grey smoke towers.

Sing a song of seasons!
    Something bright in all!
Flowers in the summer,
    Fires in the fall!

# EUGENE FIELD
### 1850–1895

## *Wynken, Blynken, and Nod*

Wynken, Blynken, and Nod one night
  Sailed off in a wooden shoe—
Sailed on a river of crystal light,
  Into a sea of dew.
  'Where are you going, and what do you wish?'
  The old moon asked the three.
  'We have come to fish for the herring fish
  That live in this beautiful sea;
  Nets of silver and gold have we!'
      Said Wynken,
      Blynken,
      And Nod.

The old moon laughed and sang a song,
  As they rocked in the wooden shoe,
And the wind that sped them all night long
  Ruffled the waves of dew.
The little stars were the herring fish
  That lived in that beautiful sea—
  'Now cast your nets wherever you wish—
  Never afeard are we';
  So cried the stars to the fishermen three:
      Wynken,
      Blynken,
      And Nod.

All night long their nets they threw
  To the stars in the twinkling foam—
Then down from the skies came the wooden shoe,
  Bringing the fishermen home;

'Twas all so pretty a sail it seemed
  As if it could not be,
And some folks thought 'twas a dream they'd dreamed
  Of sailing that beautiful sea—
  But I shall name you the fishermen three:
      Wynken,
      Blynken,
      And Nod.

Wynken and Blynken are two little eyes,
  And Nod is a little head,
And the wooden shoe that sailed the skies
  Is the wee one's trundle-bed.
So shut your eyes while mother sings
  Of wonderful sights that be,
And you shall see the beautiful things
  As you rock in the misty sea,
  Where the old shoe rocked the fishermen three:
      Wynken,
      Blynken,
      And Nod.

## *The Duel*

The gingham dog and the calico cat
Side by side on the table sat;
'Twas half-past twelve, and (what do you think!)
Nor one nor t' other had slept a wink!
  The old Dutch clock and the Chinese plate
  Appeared to know so sure as fate
There was going to be a terrible spat.
  *(I wasn't there; I simply state*
  *What was told to me by the Chinese plate!)*

The gingham dog went 'bow-wow-wow!'
And the calico cat replied 'mee-ow!'
The air was littered, an hour or so,
With bits of gingham and calico,
　　While the old Dutch clock in the chimney-place
　　Up with its hands before its face,
For it always dreaded a family row!
　　(*Now mind: I'm only telling you*
　　*What the old Dutch clock declares is true!*)

The Chinese plate looked very blue,
And wailed, 'Oh, dear! what shall we do!'
But the gingham dog and the calico cat
Wallowed this way and tumbled that,
　　Employing every tooth and claw
　　In the awfullest way you ever saw—
And, oh! how the gingham and calico flew!
　　(*Don't fancy I exaggerate—*
　　*I got my news from the Chinese plate!*)

Next morning, where the two had sat
They found no trace of dog or cat;
And some folks think unto this day
That burglars stole that pair away!
　　But the truth about the cat and pup
　　Is this: they ate each other up!
Now what do you really think of that!
　　(*The old Dutch clock it told me so,*
　　*And that is how I came to know.*)

# LAURA E. RICHARDS
## 1850–1943

### *Eletelephony*

Once there was an elephant,
Who tried to use the telephant—
No! No! I mean an elephone
Who tried to use the telephone—
(Dear me! I am not certain quite
That even now I've got it right.)

Howe'er it was, he got his trunk
Entangled in the telephunk;
The more he tried to get it free,
The louder buzzed the telephee—
(I fear I'd better drop the song
Of elephop and telephong!)

### *Why Does It Snow?*

'Why does it snow? Why does it snow?'
The children come crowding around me to know.
I said to my nephew, I said to my niece,
'It's just the old woman a-plucking her geese.'

  With her riddle cum dinky dido,
  With her riddle cum dinky dee.

The old woman sits on a pillowy cloud,
She calls to her geese, and they come in a crowd;
A cackle, a wackle, a hiss and a cluck,
And then the old woman begins for to pluck.

  With her riddle cum dinky dido,
  With her riddle cum dinky dee.

The feathers go fluttering up in the air,
Until the poor geese are entirely bare;
A toddle, a waddle, a hiss and a cluck,
'You may grow some more if you have the good luck!'

   With your riddle cum dinky dido,
   With your riddle cum dinky dee.

The feathers go swirling, around and around,
Then whirlicking, twirlicking, sink to the ground;
The farther they travel, the colder they grow,
And when they get down here, they're turned into snow.

   With their riddle cum dinky dido,
   With their riddle cum dinky dee.


# E. NESBIT

## 1858–1924

### *Child's Song in Spring*

The silver birch is a dainty lady,
   She wears a satin gown;
The elm tree makes the old churchyard shady,
   She will not live in town.

The English oak is a sturdy fellow,
   He gets his green coat late;
The willow is smart in a suit of yellow,
   While brown the beech trees wait.

Such a gay green gown God gives the larches—
   As green as He is good!
The hazels hold up their arms for arches,
   When Spring rides through the wood.

*E. Nesbit*

The chestnut's proud and the lilac's pretty,
　The poplar's gentle and tall,
But the plane tree's kind to the poor dull city—
　I love him best of all!

# A. E. HOUSMAN
## 1859–1936

## *The African Lion*

To meet a bad lad on the African waste
　Is a thing that a lion enjoys;
But he rightly and strongly objects to the taste
　Of good and uneatable boys.

When he bites off a piece of a boy of that sort
　He spits it right out of his mouth,
And retires with a loud and dissatisfied snort
　To the east, or the west, or the south.

So lads of good habits, on coming across
　A lion, need feel no alarm,
For they know they are sure to escape with the loss
　Of a leg, or a head, or an arm.

## *Purple William*

### OR, THE LIAR'S DOOM

The hideous hue which William is
Was not originally his:
So long as William told the truth
He was a usual-coloured youth.

He now is purple. One fine day
His tender father chanced to say
'What colour is a whelp, and why?'
'Purple' was William's false reply.

'Pooh' said his Pa, 'You silly elf,
'It's no more purple than yourself
'Dismiss the notion from your head.'
'I, too, am purple' William said.

And he *was* purple. With a yell
His mother off the sofa fell
Exclaiming 'William's purple! Oh!'
William replied 'I told you so.'

His parents, who could not support
The pungency of this retort,
Died with a simultaneous groan.
The purple orphan was alone.

# HENRY CHARLES BEECHING
## 1859–1919

### *Going Down Hill on a Bicycle*

A BOY'S SONG

With lifted feet, hands still,
I am poised, and down the hill
Dart, with heedful mind;
The air goes by in a wind.

Swifter and yet more swift,
Till the heart with a mighty lift
Makes the lungs laugh, the throat cry:—
'O bird, see; see, bird, I fly.

'Is this, is this your joy?
O bird, then I, though a boy,
For a golden moment share
Your feathery life in air!'

Say, heart, is there aught like this
In a world that is full of bliss?
'Tis more than skating, bound
Steel-shod to the level ground.

Speed slackens now, I float
Awhile in my airy boat;
Till, when the wheels scarce crawl,
My feet to the treadles fall.

Alas, that the longest hill
Must end in a vale; but still,
Who climbs with toil, wheresoe'er,
Shall find wings waiting there.

# KENNETH GRAHAME
## 1859–1932

### *Ducks' Ditty*

All along the backwater,
Through the rushes tall,
Ducks are a-dabbling,
Up tails all!

Ducks' tails, drakes' tails,
Yellow feet a-quiver,
Yellow bills all out of sight
Busy in the river!

Slushy green undergrowth
Where the roach swim—
Here we keep our larder,
Cool and full and dim.

Every one for what he likes!
*We* like to be
Heads down, tails up,
Dabbling free!

High in the blue above
Swifts whirl and call—
*We* are down a-dabbling
Up tails all!

## Song of Mr Toad

The world has held great Heroes,
  As history-books have showed;
But never a name to go down to fame
  Compared with that of Toad!

The clever men at Oxford
  Know all that there is to be knowed.
But they none of them know one half as much
  As intelligent Mr Toad!

The animals sat in the Ark and cried,
  Their tears in torrents flowed.
Who was it said, 'There's land ahead'?
  Encouraging Mr Toad!

The Army all saluted
  As they marched along the road,
Was it the King? Or Kitchener?
  No. It was Mr Toad!

The Queen and her Ladies-in-waiting
  Sat in the window and sewed.
She cried, 'Look! who's that *handsome* man?'
  They answered, 'Mr Toad.'

# L. LESLIE BROOKE
## 1862–1940

### *Johnny Crow's Garden*

Johnny Crow
Would dig and sow
Till he made a little Garden.

And the Lion
Had a green and yellow Tie on
In Johnny Crow's Garden.

And the Rat
Wore a Feather in his Hat
But the Bear
Had nothing to wear
In Johnny Crow's Garden.

So the Ape
Took his Measure with a Tape
In Johnny Crow's Garden.

Then the Crane
Was caught in the Rain
In Johnny Crow's Garden.

And the Beaver
Was afraid he had a Fever
But the Goat
Said:
'It's nothing but his Throat'
In Johnny Crow's Garden.

And the Pig
Danced a Jig
In Johnny Crow's Garden.

Then the Stork
Gave a Philosophic Talk
Till the Hippopotami
Said: 'Ask no further "What am I?"'
While the Elephant
Said something quite irrelevant
In Johnny Crow's Garden.

And the Goose—
Well,
The Goose *was* a Goose
In Johnny Crow's Garden.

And the Mouse
Built himself a little House
Where the Cat
Sat down beside the Mat
In Johnny Crow's Garden.

And the Whale
Told a very long Tale
In Johnny Crow's Garden.

And the Owl
Was a funny old Fowl
And the Fox
Put them all in the Stocks
In Johnny Crow's Garden.

But Johnny Crow
He let them go
And they all sat down
To their dinner in a row
In Johnny Crow's Garden!

# EDWARD ABBOTT PARRY
## 1863–1943

### *'I would like you for a comrade'*

I would like you for a comrade,
  For I love you, that I do,
I never met a little girl
  As amiable as you;
I would teach you how to dance and sing,
  And how to talk and laugh,
If I were not a little girl
  And you were not a calf.

I would like you for a comrade,
  You should share my barley meal,
And butt me with your little horns
  Just hard enough to feel;
We would lie beneath the chestnut trees
  And watch the leaves uncurl,
If I were not a clumsy calf
  And you a little girl.

# KATHARINE PYLE
## 1863–1938

### *The Toys Talk of the World*

'I should like,' said the vase from the china-store,
'To have seen the world a little more.

When they carried me here I was wrapped up tight,
But they say it is really a lovely sight.'

'Yes,' said a little plaster bird,
'That is exactly what *I* have heard;

'There are thousands of trees, and oh, what a sight
It must be when the candles are all alight.'

The fat top rolled on his other side:
'It is not in the least like that,' he cried.

'Except myself and the kite and ball,
None of you know of the world at all.

'There are houses, and pavements hard and red,
And everything spins around,' he said;

'Sometimes it goes slowly, and sometimes fast,
And often it stops with a bump at last.'

The wooden donkey nodded his head:
'I had heard the world was like that,' he said.

The kite and the ball exchanged a smile,
But they did not speak; it was not worth while.


# ESTHER W. BUXTON
## fl. *c.*1910

### *Putting the World to Bed*

The little snow people are hurrying down
    From their home in the clouds overhead;
They are working as hard as ever they can,
    Putting the world to bed.

Every tree in a soft fleecy nightgown they clothe;
    Each part has its night-cap of white.
And o'er the cold ground a thick cover they spread
    Before they say good-night.

And so they come eagerly sliding down,
  With a swift and silent tread,
Always as busy as busy can be,
  Putting the world to bed.

# RUDYARD KIPLING
## 1865–1936

### *Mowgli's Song Against People*

I will let loose against you the fleet-footed vines—
I will call in the Jungle to stamp out your lines!
  The roofs shall fade before it,
    The house-beams shall fall;
  And the *Karela*, the bitter *Karela*,
    Shall cover it all!

In the gates of these your councils my people shall sing.
In the doors of these your garners the Bat-folk shall cling;
  And the snake shall be your watchman,
    By a hearthstone unswept;
  For the *Karela*, the bitter *Karela*,
    Shall fruit where ye slept!

Ye shall not see my strikers; ye shall hear them and guess.
By night, before the moon-rise, I will send for my cess,
  And the wolf shall be your herdsman
    By a landmark removed;
  For the *Karela*, the bitter *Karela*,
    Shall seed where ye loved!

I will reap your fields before you at the hands of a host.
Ye shall glean behind my reapers for the bread that is lost;
  And the deer shall be your oxen
    On a headland untilled;
  For the *Karela*, the bitter *Karela*,
    Shall leaf where ye build!

I have untied against you the club-footed vines—
I have sent in the Jungle to swamp out your lines!
    The trees—the trees are on you!
    The house-beams shall fall;
    And the *Karela*, the bitter *Karela*,
    Shall cover you all!

*Karela*  a wild melon

## The Hump

The Camel's hump is an ugly lump
    Which well you may see at the Zoo;
But uglier yet is the hump we get
    From having too little to do.

Kiddies and grown-ups too-oo-oo,
If we haven't enough to do-oo-oo,
    We get the hump—
    Cameelious hump—
The hump that is black and blue!

We climb out of bed with a frouzly head,
    And a snarly-yarly voice.
We shiver and scowl and we grunt and we growl
    At our bath and our boots and our toys;

And there ought to be a corner for me
(And I know there is one for you)
    When we get the hump—
    Cameelious hump—
The hump that is black and blue!

The cure for this ill is not to sit still,
    Or frowst with a book by the fire;
But to take a large hoe and a shovel also,
    And dig till you gently perspire;

And then you will find that the sun and the wind,
And the Djinn of the Garden too,
    Have lifted the hump—
    The horrible hump—
The hump that is black and blue!

I get it as well as you-oo-oo—
If I haven't enough to do-oo-oo!
    We all get hump—
    Cameelious hump—
Kiddies and grown-ups too!

## Merrow Down

### I

There runs a road by Merrow Down—
    A grassy track today it is—
An hour out of Guildford town,
    Above the river Wey it is.

Here, when they heard the horse-bells ring,
    The ancient Britons dressed and rode
To watch the dark Phœnicians bring
    Their goods along the Western Road.

Yes, here, or hereabouts, they met
    To hold their racial talks and such—
To barter beads for Whitby jet,
    And tin for gay shell torques and such.

But long and long before that time
    (When bison used to roam on it)
Did Taffy and her Daddy climb
    That Down, and had their home on it.

Then beavers built in Broadstonebrook
    And made a swamp where Bramley stands;
And bears from Shere would come and look
    For Taffimai where Shamley stands.

The Wey, that Taffy called Wagai,
    Was more than six times bigger then;
And all the Tribe of Tegumai
    They cut a noble figure then!

### II

Of all the Tribe of Tegumai
    Who cut that figure, none remain,—
On Merrow Down the cuckoos cry—
    The silence and the sun remain.

But as the faithful years return
    And hearts unwounded sing again,
Comes Taffy dancing through the fern
    To lead the Surrey spring again.

Her brows are bound with bracken-fronds,
    And golden elf-locks fly above;
Her eyes are bright as diamonds
    And bluer than the sky above.

In mocassins and deer-skin cloak,
    Unfearing, free and fair she flits,
And lights her little damp-wood smoke
    To show her Daddy where she flits.

For far—oh, very far behind,
    So far she cannot call to him,
Comes Tegumai alone to find
    The daughter that was all to him!

## The Way through the Woods

They shut the road through the woods
Seventy years ago.
Weather and rain have undone it again,
And now you would never know
There was once a road through the woods
Before they planted the trees.
It is underneath the coppice and heath,
And the thin anemones.
Only the keeper sees
That, where the ring-dove broods,
And the badgers roll at ease,
There was once a road through the woods.

Yet, if you enter the woods
Of a summer evening late,
When the night-air cools on the trout-ringed pools
Where the otter whistles his mate,
(They fear not men in the woods,
Because they see so few.)
You will hear the beat of a horse's feet,
And the swish of a skirt in the dew,
Steadily cantering through
The misty solitudes,
As though they perfectly knew
The old lost road through the woods . . .
But there is no road through the woods.

## 'Cities and Thrones and Powers'

Cities and Thrones and Powers
  Stand in Time's eye,
Almost as long as flowers,
  Which daily die:
But, as new buds put forth
  To glad new men,
Out of the spent and unconsidered Earth
  The Cities rise again.

This season's Daffodil,
  She never hears
What change, what chance, what chill,
  Cut down last year's;
But with bold countenance,
  And knowledge small,
Esteems her seven days' continuance
  To be perpetual.

So Time that is o'er-kind
  To all that be,
Ordains us e'en as blind,
  As bold as she:
That in our very death,
  And burial sure,
Shadow to shadow, well persuaded, saith,
  'See how our works endure!'

# W. B. YEATS
## 1865–1939

### *A Cradle Song*

The angels are stooping
Above your bed;
They weary of trooping
With the whimpering dead.

God's laughing in Heaven
To see you so good;
The Sailing Seven
Are gay with His mood.

I sigh that kiss you,
For I must own
That I shall miss you
When you have grown.

# CHARLOTTE MEW
## 1869–1928

### *The Pedlar*

Lend me, a little while, the key
  That locks your heavy heart, and I'll give you back—
Rarer than books and ribbons and beads bright to see,
  This little Key of Dreams out of my pack.

The road, the road, beyond men's bolted doors,
  There shall I walk and you go free of me,
For yours lies North across the moors,
  And mine South. To what sea?

How if we stopped and let our solemn selves go by,
    While my gay ghost caught and kissed yours, as ghosts don't do,
And by the wayside this forgotten you and I
    Sat, and were twenty-two?

Give me the key that locks your tired eyes,
    And I will lend you this one from my pack,
Brighter than coloured beads and painted books that make men wise:
    Take it. No, give it back!

## The Changeling

Toll no bell for me, dear Father, dear Mother,
        Waste no sighs;
There are my sisters, there is my little brother
    Who plays in the place called Paradise
Your children all, your children for ever;
        But I, so wild,
Your disgrace, with the queer brown face, was never,
    Never, I know, but half your child!

In the garden at play, all day, last summer,
        Far and away I heard
The sweet 'tweet-tweet' of a strange new-comer,
    The dearest, clearest call of a bird.
It lived down there in the deep green hollow,
    My own old home, and the fairies say
The word of a bird is a thing to follow,
    So I was away a night and a day.

One evening, too, by the nursery fire,
    We snuggled close and sat round so still,
When suddenly as the wind blew higher,
    Something scratched on the window-sill.
A pinched brown face peered in—I shivered;
    No one listened or seemed to see;
The arms of it waved and the wings of it quivered,
    Whoo—I knew it had come for me;
    Some are as bad as bad can be!

All night long they danced in the rain,
Round and round in a dripping chain,
Threw their caps at the window-pane,
  Tried to make me scream and shout
  And fling the bedclothes all about:
I meant to stay in bed that night,
And if only you had left a light
  They would never have got me out.

  Sometimes I wouldn't speak, you see,
  Or answer when you spoke to me,
Because in the long, still dusks of Spring
You can hear the whole world whispering;
  The shy green grasses making love,
  The feathers grow on the dear, grey dove,
  The tiny heart of the redstart beat,
  The patter of the squirrel's feet,
The pebbles pushing in the silver streams,
The rushes talking in their dreams,
  The swish-swish of the bat's black wings,
  The wild-wood bluebell's sweet ting-tings,
    Humming and hammering at your ear,
    Everything there is to hear
In the heart of hidden things,
  But not in the midst of the nursery riot,
  That's why I wanted to be quiet,
    Couldn't do my sums, or sing,
    Or settle down to anything.
  And when, for that, I was sent upstairs
  I *did* kneel down to say my prayers;
But the King who sits on your high church steeple
Has nothing to do with us fairy people!

'Times I pleased you, dear Father, dear Mother,
  Learned all my lessons and liked to play,
And dearly I loved the little pale brother
  Whom some other bird must have called away.

Why did They bring me here to make me
  Not quite bad and not quite good,
Why, unless They're wicked, do They want, in spite, to take me
  Back to their wet, wild wood?
Now, every night I shall see the windows shining,
  The gold lamp's glow, and the fire's red gleam,
While the best of us are twining twigs and the rest of us are whining
    In the hollow by the stream.
Black and chill are Their nights on the wold;
  And They live so long and They feel no pain:
I shall grow up, but never grow old,
I shall always, always be very cold,
  I shall never came back again!


# ANON., African American

## *The Origin of the Snake*

Up the hill and down the level!
Up the hill and down the level!
Granny's puppy treed the Devil.

Puppy howl, and Devil shake!
Puppy howl, and Devil shake!
Devil leave, and there's your snake.

Mash his head: the sun shine bright!
Mash his head: the sun shine bright!
Tail don't die until it's night.

Night come on, and spirits groan!
Night come on, and spirits groan!
Devil come and gets his own.

# ANON., American

## *The Frog*

What a wonderful bird the frog are—
When he sit, he stand almost;
When he hop, he fly almost.
He ain't got no sense hardly;
He ain't got no tail hardly either.
When he sit, he sit on what he ain't got—almost.

# HILAIRE BELLOC
## 1870–1953

## *The Frog*

Be kind and tender to the Frog,
   And do not call him names,
As 'Slimy skin', or 'Polly-wog',
   Or likewise 'Ugly James',
Or 'Gape-a-grin', or 'Toad-gone-wrong',
   Or 'Billy Bandy-knees':
The Frog is justly sensitive
   To epithets like these.
No animal will more repay
   A treatment kind and fair;
At least so lonely people say
Who keep a frog (and, by the way,
   They are extremely rare).

## Jim
### Who Ran Away from his Nurse, and Was Eaten by a Lion

There was a boy whose name was Jim;
His friends were very good to him.
They gave him tea, and cakes, and jam,
And slices of delicious ham,
And chocolate with pink inside,
And little tricycles to ride,
And read him stories through and through,
And even took him to the Zoo—
But there it was the dreadful fate
Befell him, which I now relate.

You know—at least you *ought* to know,
For I have often told you so—
That children never are allowed
To leave their nurses in a crowd;
Now this was Jim's especial foible,
He ran away when he was able,
And on this inauspicious day
He slipped his hand and ran away!
He hadn't gone a yard when—Bang!
With open jaws, a lion sprang,
And hungrily began to eat
The boy: beginning at his feet.

Now, just imagine how it feels
When first your toes and then your heels,
And then by gradual degrees,
Your shins and ankles, calves and knees,
Are slowly eaten, bit by bit.
No wonder Jim detested it!
No wonder that he shouted 'Hi!'
The honest keeper heard his cry,
Though very fat he almost ran
To help the little gentleman.

'Ponto!' he ordered as he came
(For Ponto was the lion's name),
'Ponto!' he cried, with angry frown.
'Let go, Sir! Down, Sir! Put it down!'

The lion made a sudden stop,
He let the dainty morsel drop,
And slunk reluctant to his cage,
Snarling with disappointed rage.
But when he bent him over Jim,
The honest keeper's eyes were dim.
The lion having reached his head,
The miserable boy was dead!

When Nurse informed his parents, they
Were more concerned than I can say:—
His Mother, as she dried her eyes,
Said, 'Well—it gives me no surprise,
He would not do as he was told!'
His Father, who was self-controlled,
Bade all the children round attend
To James's miserable end,
And always keep a-hold of Nurse
For fear of finding something worse.

# W. H. DAVIES
## 1871–1940

### *To W.S.—On his Wonderful Toys*

Lend me your precious toys,
    But for one day and night;
I'll take them under my orchard boughs,
    And nurse them out of sight;
Till my two hands, all warm with love,
Fill them with breath, and make them move!

And when Night comes, a grey-haired child
   Shall hobble off to bed;
With rabbits, mice and little birds
   Around his face and head;
Where in your toys his secret lies—
To keep his childhood till he dies.

# WALTER DE LA MARE
## 1873–1956

### *The Silver Penny*

'Sailorman, I'll give to you
   My bright silver penny,
If out to sea you'll sail me
   And my dear sister Jenny.'

'Get in, young sir, I'll sail ye
   And your dear sister Jenny,
But pay she shall her golden locks
   Instead of your penny.'

They sail away, they sail away,
   O fierce the winds blew!
The foam flew in clouds
   And dark the night grew!

And all the green sea-water
   Climbed steep into the boat;
Back to the shore again
   Sail they will not.

Drowned is the sailorman,
   Drowned is sweet Jenny,
And drowned in the deep sea
   A bright silver penny.

## Hi!

Hi! handsome hunting man
Fire your little gun,
Bang! Now the animal
Is dead and dumb and done.
Nevermore to peep again, creep again, leap again,
Eat or sleep or drink again, Oh, what fun!

## The Storm

First there were two of us, then there were three of us,
Then there was one bird more,
Four of us—wild white sea-birds,
Treading the ocean floor;
And the *wind* rose, and the *sea* rose,
To the angry billows' roar—
With one of us—two of us—three of us—four of us
Sea-birds on the shore.

Soon there were five of us, soon there were nine of us,
And lo! in a trice sixteen!
And the yeasty surf curdled over the sands,
The gaunt grey rocks between;
And the tempest raved, and the lightning's fire
Struck blue on the spindrift hoar—
And on four of us—ay, and on four times four of us
Sea-birds on the shore.

And our sixteen waxed to thirty-two,
And they to past three score—
A wild, white welter of winnowing wings,
And ever more and more;
And the winds lulled, and the sea went down,
And the sun streamed out on high,
Gilding the pools and the spume and the spars
'Neath the vast blue deeps of the sky;

And the isles and the bright green headlands shone,
  As they'd never shone before,
Mountains and valleys of silver cloud,
  Wherein to swing, sweep, soar—
A host of screeching, scolding, scrabbling
  Sea-birds on the shore—
A snowy, silent, sun-washed drift
  Of sea-birds on the shore.


## *The Listeners*

'Is there anybody there?' said the Traveller,
  Knocking on the moonlit door;
And his horse in the silence champed the grasses
  Of the forest's ferny floor:
And a bird flew up out of the turret,
  Above the Traveller's head:
And he smote upon the door again a second time;
  'Is there anybody there?' he said.
But no one descended to the Traveller;
  No head from the leaf-fringed sill
Leaned over and looked into his grey eyes,
  Where he stood perplexed and still.
But only a host of phantom listeners
  That dwelt in the lone house then
Stood listening in the quiet of the moonlight
  To that voice from the world of men:
Stood thronging the faint moonbeams on the dark stair,
  That goes down to the empty hall,
Hearkening in an air stirred and shaken
  By the lonely Traveller's call.
And he felt in his heart their strangeness,
  Their stillness answering his cry,
While his horse moved, cropping the dark turf,
  'Neath the starred and leafy sky;
For he suddenly smote on the door, even
  Louder, and lifted his head:—
'Tell them I came, and no one answered,
  That I kept my word,' he said.

Never the least stir made the listeners,
   Though every word he spake
Fell echoing through the shadowiness of the still house
   From the one man left awake:
Ay, they heard his foot upon the stirrup,
   And the sound of iron on stone,
And how the silence surged softly backward,
   When the plunging hoofs were gone.

# ROBERT FROST
## 1874–1963

### *The Pasture*

I'm going out to clean the pasture spring;
I'll only stop to rake the leaves away
(And wait to watch the water clear, I may):
I shan't be gone long.—You come too.

I'm going out to fetch the little calf
That's standing by the mother. It's so young
It totters when she licks it with her tongue.
I shan't be gone long.—You come too.

### *The Last Word of a Bluebird*

AS TOLD TO A CHILD

As I went out a Crow
In a low voice said, 'Oh,
I was looking for you.
How do you do?
I just came to tell you
To tell Lesley (will you?)
That her little Bluebird
Wanted me to bring word

That the north wind last night
That made the stars bright
And made ice on the trough
Almost made him cough
His tail feathers off.

He just had to fly!
But he sent her Good-by,
And said to be good,
And wear her red hood,
And look for skunk tracks
In the snow with an ax—
And do everything!
And perhaps in the spring
He would come back and sing.'

# HARRY GRAHAM
## 1874–1936

### *Tender-Heartedness*

Billy, in one of his nice new sashes,
Fell in the fire and was burnt to ashes;
Now, although the room grows chilly,
I haven't the heart to poke poor Billy.

# GERTRUDE STEIN
## 1874–1946

### *'The teachers taught her that the world was round'*

The teachers taught her
That the world was round
That the sun was round
That the moon was round
That the stars were round
And that they were all going around and around
And not a sound.
It was sad it almost made her cry
But then she did not believe it
Because the mountains were so high,
And so she thought she had better sing
And then a dreadful thing was happening
She remembered when she had been young
That one day she had sung,
And there was a looking glass in front of her
And as she sang her mouth was round and was going around and
around.
Oh dear oh dear was everything just to be round and go around and
around.
What could she do but try and remember the mountains were so
high they could stop anything.
But she could not keep on remembering and forgetting of course
not but she could sing of course she could sing and she could cry of
course she could cry.
Oh my.

# HUGHES MEARNS
## 1875–1965

### The Little Man

As I was walking up the stair
I met a man who wasn't there;
He wasn't there again today.
I wish, I wish he'd stay away.

# ROSE FYLEMAN
## 1877–1957

### Punch and Judy

'Punch,' said Judy,
'You're looking moody.'
'Judy,' said Punch,
'*I want my lunch.*'

### The Cat

There was a cat in Egypt, in Egypt, in Egypt;
There was a cat in Egypt, it's many a long year;
It wore a gold ear-ring, an ear-ring, an ear-ring,
It wore a gold ear-ring hanging in its ear.

It wore a gold ear-ring, an ear-ring, an ear-ring,
It wore a gold ear-ring hanging in its ear.
That's all that I can tell you, can tell you, can tell you—
There was a cat in Egypt, it's many a long year.

### Solo with Chorus

I am a book with a cover of blue,
We are the children that read it through.

I am a ship with a wooden mast,
We are the waves that go rolling past.

I am a barn with a creaking door,
We are the mice that live under the floor.

I am a street in a great big town,
We are the people that walk up and down.

I am a wood, all green in the spring,
We are the birds that sing, that sing.

# H. D. C. PEPLER
## 1878–1951

### Concerning Dragons

#### CHILD

Are *all* the dragons fled?
Are all the *goblins dead*?
Am I *quite* safe in bed?

#### NURSE

Thou art quite safe in bed
Dragons and goblings all are dead.

#### CHILD

Are there no witches here?
Nor any giants near,
So that I need not fear?

NURSE

Who puts such nonsense in thy head—
Witches and giants all are dead.


CHILD

Nurse, have you seen the Ghost
Which comes to Jacob's Post?
I *nearly* did—almost!


NURSE

Hush! do not talk so wild;
There are no ghosts my child.


CHILD

When Michael's angels fought
The dragon, was it caught?
Did it jump and *roar*?
[Oh! Nurse, don't shut the door.]
And did it try to *bite*?
[Nurse, don't blow out the light.]


NURSE

Hush, thou knowest what I said,
Saints and dragons all are dead.


FATHER
(to himself)

O child, nurse lies to thee,
For Dragons thou shalt see.
Please God that on that day
Thou may'st a dragon slay.
And if thou do'st not faint
God shall not want a Saint.

# CARL SANDBURG
### 1878–1967

## *'Little girl, be careful what you say'*

Little girl, be careful what you say
when you make talk with words, words—
for words are made of syllables
and syllables, child, are made of air—
and air is so thin—air is the breath of God—
air is finer than fire or mist,
finer than water or moonlight,
finer than spider-webs in the moon,
finer than water-flowers in the morning:
   and words are strong, too,
   stronger than rocks or steel
stronger than potatoes, corn fish, cattle,
and soft, too, soft as little pigeon-eggs,
soft as the music of hummingbird wings.
   So little girl, when you speak greetings,
when you tell jokes, make wishes or prayers,
   be careful, be careless, be careful,
   be what you wish to be.


## *We Must Be Polite*

### (LESSONS FOR CHILDREN ON HOW TO BEHAVE UNDER PECULIAR CIRCUMSTANCES)

1

If we meet a gorilla
what shall we do?

Two things we may do
if we so wish to do.

Speak to the gorilla,
very, very respectfully,
'How do you do, sir?'

Or, speak to him with less
distinction of manner,
'Hey, why don't you go back
where you came from?'

2

If an elephant knocks on your door
and asks for something to eat,
there are two things to say:

Tell him there are nothing but cold
victuals in the house and he will do
better next door.

Or say: We have nothing but six bushels
of potatoes—will that be enough for
your breakfast, sir?

## Be Ready

Be land ready
for you shall go back to land.

Be sea ready
for you have been nine-tenths water
and the salt taste shall cling to your mouth.

Be sky ready
for air, air, has been so needful to you—
you shall go back, back to the sky.

## Auctioneer

Now I go down here and bring up a moon.
How much am I bid for the moon?
You see it a bright moon and brand-new.
What can I get to start it? how much?
What! who ever ever heard such a bid for a moon?
    Come now, gentlemen, come.
This is a solid guaranteed moon.
You may never have another chance
    to make a bid on such a compact
    eighteen-carat durable gold moon.
You could shape a thousand wedding rings
    out of this moongold.
I can guarantee the gold and the weddings
    will last forever
    and then a thousand years more.
Come gentlemen, no nonsense, make me a bid.

## Stars

The stars are too many to count.
The stars make sixes and sevens.
The stars tell nothing—and everything.
The stars look scattered.
Stars are so far away they never speak
    when spoken to.

# VACHEL LINDSAY
## 1879–1931

## *The Moon's the North Wind's Cooky*

(WHAT THE LITTLE GIRL SAID)

The Moon's the North Wind's cooky.
He bites it, day by day,
Until there's but a rim of scraps
That crumble all away.

The South Wind is a baker.
He kneads clouds in his den,
And bakes a crisp new moon *that . . . greedy
North . . . Wind . . . eats . . . again!*


## *The Little Turtle*

(A RECITATION FOR MARTHA WAKEFIELD,
THREE YEARS OLD)

There was a little turtle.
He lived in a box.
He swam in a puddle.
He climbed on the rocks.

He snapped at a mosquito.
He snapped at a flea.
He snapped at a minnow.
And he snapped at me.

He caught the mosquito.
He caught the flea.
He caught the minnow.
But he didn't catch me.

# HAROLD MONRO
## 1879–1932

### *Overheard on a Saltmarsh*

Nymph, nymph, what are your beads?

Green glass, goblin. Why do you stare at them?

Give them me.

      No.

Give them me. Give them me.

         No.

Then I will howl all night in the reeds,
Lie in the mud and howl for them.

Goblin, why do you love them so?

They are better than stars or water,
Better than voices of winds that sing,
Better than any man's fair daughter,
Your green glass beads on a silver ring.

Hush, I stole them out of the moon.

Give me your beads, I want them.

         No.

I will howl in a deep lagoon
For your green glass beads, I love them so.
Give them me. Give them.

      No.

# ALFRED NOYES
## 1880–1959

### *The Highwayman*

#### PART ONE

The wind was a torrent of darkness among the gusty trees,
The moon was a ghostly galleon tossed upon cloudy seas,
The road was a ribbon of moonlight over the purple moor,
And the highwayman came riding—
      Riding—riding—
The highwayman came riding, up to the old inn-door.

He'd a French cocked-hat on his forehead, a bunch of lace at his chin,
A coat of the claret velvet, and breeches of brown doeskin:
They fitted with never a wrinkle; his boots were up to the thigh!
And he rode with a jewelled twinkle,
      His pistol butts a-twinkle,
His rapier hilt a-twinkle, under the jewelled sky.

Over the cobbles he clattered and clashed in the dark inn-yard,
And he tapped with his whip on the shutters, but all was locked and
    barred:
He whistled a tune to the window; and who should be waiting there
But the landlord's black-eyed daughter
      Bess, the landlord's daughter,
Plaiting a dark red love-knot into her long black hair.

And dark in the dark old inn-yard a stable-wicket creaked
Where Tim, the ostler, listened; his face was white and peaked,
His eyes were hollows of madness, his hair like mouldy hay;
But he loved the landlord's daughter,
      The landlord's red-lipped daughter:
Dumb as a dog he listened, and he heard the robber say—

'One kiss, my bonny sweetheart, I'm after a prize tonight,
But I shall be back with the yellow gold before the morning light.
Yet if they press me sharply, and harry me through the day,
Then look for me by moonlight,
     Watch for me by moonlight:
I'll come to thee by moonlight, though Hell should bar the way.'

He rose upright in the stirrups, he scarce could reach her hand;
But she loosened her hair i' the casement! His face burnt like a brand
As the black cascade of perfume came tumbling over his breast;
And he kissed its waves in the moonlight,
     (Oh, sweet black waves in the moonlight)
Then he tugged at his reins in the moonlight, and galloped away to the
    West.

### PART TWO

He did not come in the dawning; he did not come at noon;
And out of the tawny sunset, before the rise o' the moon,
When the road was a gypsy's ribbon, looping the purple moor,
A red-coat troop came marching—
     Marching—marching—
King George's men came marching, up to the old inn-door.

They said no word to the landlord, they drank his ale instead;
But they gagged his daughter and bound her to the foot of her narrow
    bed.
Two of them knelt at her casement, with muskets at the side!
There was death at every window;
     And Hell at one dark window;
For Bess could see, through her casement, the road that *he* would ride.

They had tied her up to attention, with many a sniggering jest:
They had bound a musket beside her, with the barrel beneath her
    breast!
'Now keep good watch!' and they kissed her.
     She heard the dead man say—
*Look for me by moonlight;*
    *Watch for me by moonlight;*
*I'll come to thee by moonlight, though Hell should bar the way!*

She twisted her hands behind her; but all the knots held good!
She writhed her hands till her fingers were wet with sweat or blood!
They stretched and strained in the darkness, and the hours crawled by
    like years;
Till, now, on the stroke of midnight,
      Cold, on the stroke of midnight,
The tip of one finger touched it! The trigger at least was hers!

The tip of one finger touched it; she strove no more for the rest!
Up, she stood up to attention, with the barrel beneath her breast,
She would not risk their hearing; she would not strive again;
For the road lay bare in the moonlight,
      Blank and bare in the moonlight;
And the blood of her veins in the moonlight throbbed to her Love's
    refrain.

*Tlot-tlot, tlot-tlot!* Had they heard it? The horse-hoofs ringing clear—
*Tlot-tlot, tlot-tlot*, in the distance? Were they deaf that they did not
    hear?
Down the ribbon of moonlight, over the brow of the hill,
The highwayman came riding,
      Riding, riding!
The red-coats looked to their priming! She stood up straight and still!

*Tlot-tlot*, in the frosty silence! *Tlot-tlot* in the echoing night!
Nearer he came and nearer! Her face was like a light!
Her eyes grew wide for a moment; she drew one last deep breath,
Then her finger moved in the moonlight,
      Her musket shattered the moonlight,
Shattered her breast in the moonlight and warned him—with her
    death.

He turned; he spurred him westward; he did not know who stood
Bowed with her head o'er the musket, drenched with her own red
    blood!
Not till the dawn he heard it, and slowly blanched to hear
How Bess, the landlord's daughter,
      The landlord's black-eyed daughter,
Had watched for her Love in the moonlight, and died in the darkness
    there.

Back, he spurred like a madman, shrieking a curse to the sky,
With the white road smoking behind him, and his rapier brandished
    high!
Blood-red were his spurs i' the golden noon; wine-red was his velvet
    coat;
When they shot him down on the highway,
      Down like a dog on the highway,
And he lay in his blood on the highway, with the bunch of lace at his
    throat.

          \*    \*    \*

*And still of a winter's night, they say, when the wind is in the trees,*
*When the moon is a ghostly galleon tossed upon cloudy seas,*
*When the road is a ribbon of moonlight over the purple moor,*
*A highwayman comes riding—*
      *Riding—riding—*
*A highwayman comes riding, up to the old inn-door.*

*Over the cobbles he clatters and clangs in the dark inn-yard;*
*And he taps with his whip on the shutters, but all is locked and barred:*
*He whistles a tune to the window, and who should be waiting there*
*But the landlord's black-eyed daughter,*
      *Bess, the landlord's daughter,*
*Plaiting a dark red love-knot into her long black hair.*

### Daddy Fell into the Pond

Everyone grumbled. The sky was gray.
We had nothing to do and nothing to say.
We were nearing the end of a dismal day,
And there seemed to be nothing beyond,
    THEN
    *Daddy fell into the pond!*

And everyone's face grew merry and bright,
And Timothy danced for sheer delight.
'Give me the camera, quick, oh quick!
He's crawling out of the duckweed.' *Click!*

Then the gardener suddenly slapped his knee,
And doubled up, shaking silently,
And the ducks all quacked as if they were daft
And it sounded as if the old drake laughed.

Oh, there wasn't a thing that didn't respond
  WHEN
  *Daddy fell into the pond!*


# ELEANOR FARJEON
## 1881–1965

### *The Tide in the River*

The tide in the river,
The tide in the river,
The tide in the river runs deep.
  I saw a shiver
  Pass over the river
As the tide turned in its sleep.


### *Good Night*

Now good night.
Fold up your clothes
As you were taught,
Fold your two hands,
Fold up your thought;
Day is the plough-land,
Night is the stream,
Day is for doing
And night is for dream.
  Now good night.

# ELIZABETH MADOX ROBERTS
## 1881–1941

### *Christmas Morning*

If Bethlehem were here to-day,
Or this were very long ago,
There wouldn't be a winter time
Nor any cold or snow.

I'd run out through the garden gate,
And down along the pasture walk;
And off beside the cattle barns
I'd hear a kind of gentle talk.

I'd move the heavy iron chain
And pull away the wooden pin;
I'd push the door a little bit
And tiptoe very softly in.

The pigeons and the yellow hens
And all the cows would stand away;
Their eyes would open wide to see
A lady in the manger hay,

If this were very long ago
And Bethlehem were here to-day.

And Mother held my hand and smiled—
I mean the lady would—and she
Would take the woolly blankets off
Her little boy so I could see.

His shut-up eyes would be asleep,
And he would look like our John,
And he would be all crumpled too,
And have a pinkish colour on.

I'd watch his breath go in and out.
His little clothes would all be white.
I'd slip my finger in his hand
To feel how he could hold it tight.

And she would smile and say, 'Take care',
The mother, Mary, would, 'Take care';
And I would kiss his little hand
And touch his hair.

While Mary put the blankets back
The gentle talk would soon begin.
And when I'd tiptoe softly out
I'd meet the wise men going in.


## The People

The ants are walking under the ground,
And the pigeons are flying over the steeple,
And in between are the people.


# A. A. MILNE
## 1882–1956

### Happiness

John had
Great Big
Waterproof
Boots on;
John had a
Great Big
Waterproof
Hat;

John had a
Great Big
Waterproof
Mackintosh—
And that
(Said John)
   Is
   That.


## *Disobedience*

James James
Morrison Morrison
Weatherby George Dupree
Took great
Care of his Mother,
Though he was only three.
James James
Said to his Mother,
'Mother,' he said, said he;
'You must never go down to the end of the town,
   if you don't go down with me.'


James James
Morrison's Mother
Put on a golden gown,
James James
Morrison's Mother
Drove to the end of the town.
James James
Morrison's Mother
Said to herself, said she:
'I can get right down to the end of the town and be
   back in time for tea.'

King John
Put up a notice,
'LOST or STOLEN or STRAYED!
JAMES JAMES
MORRISON'S MOTHER
SEEMS TO HAVE BEEN MISLAID.
LAST SEEN
WANDERING VAGUELY:
QUITE OF HER OWN ACCORD,
SHE TRIED TO GET DOWN TO THE END OF THE
TOWN—**FORTY SHILLINGS REWARD!**'

James James
Morrison Morrison
(Commonly known as Jim)
Told his
Other relations
Not to go blaming *him*.
James James
*Said* to his Mother,
'Mother,' he said, said he:
'You must *never* go down to the end of the town
   without consulting me.'

James James
Morrison's mother
Hasn't been heard of since.
King John
Said he was sorry,
So did the Queen and Prince.
King John
(Somebody told me)
Said to a man he knew:
'If people go down to the end of the town, well,
   what can *anyone do*?'

(*Now then, very softly*)
    J.J.
    M.M.
    W. G. Du P.
    Took great
    C/o his M*****
    Though he was only 3.
    J.J.
    Said to his M*****
    'M*****,' he said, said he:
'You-must-never-go-down-to-the-end-of-the-town-
    if-you-don't-go-down-with ME!'

## Bad Sir Brian Botany

Sir Brian had a battleaxe with great big knobs on;
    He went among the villagers and blipped them on the head.
On Wednesday and on Saturday, but mostly on the latter day,
    He called at all the cottages, and this is what he said:
      'I am Sir Brian!' (*ting-ling*)
       'I am Sir Brian!' (*rat-tat*)
      'I am Sir Brian, as bold as a lion—
        Take *that!*—and *that!*—and *that!*'

Sir Brian had a pair of boots with great big spurs on,
    A fighting pair of which he was particularly fond.
On Tuesday and on Friday, just to make the street look tidy,
    He'd collect the passing villagers and kick them in the pond.
      'I am Sir Brian!' (*sper-lash!*)
       'I am Sir Brian!' (*sper-losh!*)
      'I am Sir Brian, as bold as a lion—
        Is anyone else for a wash?'

Sir Brian woke one morning, and he couldn't find his battleaxe;
   He walked into the village in his second pair of boots.
He had gone a hundred paces, when the street was full of faces,
   And the villagers were round him with ironical salutes.
      'You are Sir Brian? Indeed!
        You are Sir Brian? Dear, dear!
      You are Sir Brian, as bold as a lion?
        Delighted to meet you here!'

Sir Brian went on a journey, and he found a lot of duckweed:
   They pulled him out and dried him, and they blipped him on the head.
They took him by the breeches, and they hurled him into ditches,
   And they pushed him under waterfalls, and this is what they said:
      'You are Sir Brian—don't laugh,
        You are Sir Brian—don't cry;
      You are Sir Brian, as bold as a lion—
        Sir Brian, the lion, good-bye!'

Sir Brian struggled home again, and chopped up his battleaxe,
   Sir Brian took his fighting boots, and threw them in the fire.
He is quite a different person now he hasn't got his spurs on,
   And he goes about the village as B. Botany, Esquire.
      'I am Sir Brian? Oh, *no!*
        I am Sir Brian? Who's he?
      *I* haven't got any title, I'm Botany—
        Plain Mr Botany (B).'


# ANNA WICKHAM

## 1884–1947

### *Letter to a Boy at School*

George and me
We'll sing to one another
Like two birds upon a tree.
And that has seldom happened
With a boy and his own Mother.

That George and me
Both write poetry
Shows there's a sympathy
More than in every family
Between George and me.

I first wrote poetry to please my Dad
Who wanted to write novels and was sad;
He never could write more than the first pages,
And then he wrote so slowly that it took him ages.

But I wrote easily
Although in poetry;
And when I was a girl at school,
When I learned grammar and was taught a rule
Or I was taught the meaning of a word such as inanimate,
I'd write a poem out upon my slate,
With all I knew of words and grammar to that date.

But when I wrote for my dear father,
I always used to worry rather
And think that for a girl it might be waste of time
To spend her life and love in making rhyme;
And I thought, maybe
I should be better knitting for my baby.

And now my dear and youngest son
Has brains enough to find my verses fun;
And so my head's no longer in a whirl
Wondering if I ought to write them, being born a girl.

And so I'll make
For George's sake,
As soon as I have time,
The very finest thing I can in rhyme;
And everything I know
And dream and hope will go
Into this book,
Which will be a good pie,
Since I write better than I cook.

And George and me
Will sit and sing to one another
Like two birds upon a tree.
And in our pie
I'll not write 'George and I',
Though both are in the nominative case;
Our poetry will be a pleasant place,
Where grammar is most right when it is wrong,
In ways that sound well, in a song.

## Nursery Song

Too-well-done
Has blown out the sun;
She made curdy puddings
Till milk there was none:

And the baby starved
For all he was clean
And the cat ate my thrush
And still looked lean.

Such ugly confusion
There never was seen
Since Too-well-done
Has blown out the sun.

# ANON., English

## Three Little Ghostesses

Three little ghostesses,
Sitting on postesses,
Eating buttered toastesses,
Greasing their fistesses,
Up to the wristesses,
Oh, what beastesses
To make such feastesses!

# SARA TEASDALE
## 1884–1933

### *Night*

Stars over snow
  And in the west a planet
Swinging below a star—
  Look for a lovely thing and you will find it,
It is not far—
  It never will be far.

# EZRA POUND
## 1885–1972

### *A Girl*

The tree has entered my hands,
The sap has ascended my arms,
The tree has grown in my breast—
Downward,
The branches grow out of me, like arms

Tree you are,
Moss you are,
You are violets with wind above them.
A child—*so* high—you are,
And all this is folly to the world.

# HUMBERT WOLFE
## 1885–1940

### *The Blackbird*

In the far corner,
Close by the swings,
Every morning
A blackbird sings.

His bill's so yellow,
His coat's so black,
That he makes a fellow
Whistle back.

Ann, my daughter,
Thinks that he
Sings for us two
Especially.

# FRANCES CORNFORD
## 1886–1960

### *A Child's Dream*

I had a little dog, and my dog was very small;
He licked me in the face, and he answered to my call;
Of all the treasures that were mine, I loved him most of all.

His nose was fresh as morning dew and blacker than the night;
I thought that it could even snuff the shadows and the light;
And his tail he held bravely, like a banner in a fight.

His body covered thick with hair was very good to smell;
His little stomach underneath was pink as any shell;
And I loved him and honoured him, more than words can tell.

We ran out in the morning, both of us, to play,
Up and down across the fields for all that sunny day;
But he ran so swiftly—he ran right away.

I looked for him, I called for him, entreatingly. Alas,
The dandelions could not speak, though they had seen him pass,
And nowhere was his waving tail among the waving grass.

I called him in a thousand ways and yet he did not come;
The pathways and the hedges were horrible and dumb.
I prayed to God who never heard. My desperate soul grew numb.

The sun sank low. I ran; I prayed: 'If God has not the power
To find him, let me die. I cannot bear another hour.'
When suddenly I came upon a great yellow flower.

And all among its petals, such was Heaven's grace,
In that golden hour, in that golden place,
All among its petals, was his hairy face.

# ELIZABETH GODLEY
## fl. 1931

### *Ninety-Nine*

| | |
|---|---|
| THE DOCTOR. | Good morning, and How do you do? |
| | Pray what is the matter with you? |
| THE PATIENT. | I've a cough and a sneeze |
| | And two very bad knees |
| | And a toe that is bothering, too. |
| THE DOCTOR. | Hum, hum. I'll run over your chest— |
| | Will you kindly unbutton your vest? |
| | Now say '*Ninety-nine.*' |
| | Can you sleep? Can you dine? |
| | You say you're not feeling your best? |
| THE PATIENT. | I'm feeling exceedingly ill. |

| | |
|---|---|
| THE DOCTOR. | Hum, hum. Can you swallow a pill? |
| THE PATIENT. | No, no. |
| THE DOCTOR. | Speak up louder! |
| THE PATIENT. | NO, NO! |
| THE DOCTOR. | A grey powder . . . |
| | Let's see . . . In some jam. |

THE PATIENT (*who likes jam*). As you will.

THE DOCTOR. Ha, ha! Tra-la-la! Tootle-oo.
Now I'll tell you a thing that is true:
You can say 'Ninety-nine,'
You can sleep, you can dine—
*There's nothing the matter with you!*

THE PATIENT (*in a loud voice*). Nothing the matter with me?
How can that possibly be?
I've a sneeze and a cough,
And a toe nearly off,
And a horrible—

THE DOCTOR. Fiddle-de-dee!

(*They glare at one another.*)

THE DOCTOR. And now there is business to do.

(*Pause.*)

THE PATIENT (*in a very feeble voice*). I have only a penny or two . . .
If you speak of your fees—

THE DOCTOR. Fifty pounds, if you please!
There's nothing the matter with you.

# BEATRICE CURTIS BROWN
## fl. 1936

### *Jonathan Bing*

Poor old Jonathan Bing
Went out in his carriage to visit the King,
But everyone pointed and said, 'Look at that!
Jonathan Bing has forgotten his hat!'
(He'd forgotten his hat!)

Poor old Jonathan Bing
Went home and put on a new hat for the King,
But by the palace a soldier said, 'Hi!
You can't see the King; you've forgotten your tie!'
(He'd forgotten his tie!)

Poor old Jonathan Bing,
He put on a beautiful tie for the King,
But when he arrived, an Archbishop said, 'Ho!
You can't come to court in pyjamas, you know!'
(He'd come in pyjamas!)

Poor old Jonathan Bing
Went home and addressed a short note to the King:
'If you please will excuse me, I won't come to tea;
For home's the best place for all people like me!'


# HUGH LOFTING
## 1886–1947

### *Picnic*

Ella, fell a
Maple tree.
Hilda, build a
Fire for me.

Teresa, squeeze a
Lemon, so.
Amanda, hand a
Plate to Flo.

Nora, pour a
Cup of tea.
Fancy, Nancy,
What a spree!

# EDITH SITWELL
## 1887–1964

### 'The King of China's daughter'

The King of China's daughter,
She never would love me,
Though I hung my cap and bells upon
Her nutmeg tree.
For oranges and lemons,
The stars in bright blue air
(I stole them long ago, my dear)
Were dangling there.
The Moon did give me silver pence,
The Sun did give me gold,
And both together softly blew
And made my porridge cold;
But the King of China's daughter
Pretended not to see
When I hung my cap and bells upon
The nutmeg tree.

The King of China's daughter
So beautiful to see
With her face like yellow water, left
Her nutmeg tree.
Her little rope for skipping
She kissed and gave it me—

Made of painted notes of singing-birds
Among the fields of tea.
I skipped across the nutmeg grove,—
I skipped across the sea;
But neither sun nor moon, my dear,
Has yet caught me.

## Trams

Castles of crystal,
Castles of wood,
Moving on pulleys
Just as you should!
See the gay people
Flaunting like flags,
Bells in the steeple,
Sky all in rags.
Bright as a parrot
Flaunts the gay heat—
Songs in the garret,
Fruit in the street;
Plump as a cherry,
Red as a rose,
Old Mother Berry—
Blowing her nose!

# SUSAN MILES

1887–?

## Plumbers

I knew that in winter it would snow,
For my brother had told me.
I knew that snow was white
And soft
And altogether wonderful;
But how white and soft and wonderful
I did not know,

Being too young to remember
Winter.
One day snow fell;
And the garden
Was a new garden;
The trees were new trees.
There were icicles.

I marvelled that my brother
Had forgotten to tell me
That there would be icicles.
How could a child see icicles
And not remember?
Or frost on wire-netting,
And not tell?
I was happier than on my birthday;
I was happier than on Christmas morning.
'Selfish little pig,'
Said Nurse.
'You don't think of the poor plumbers;
Nor you don't think of their poor children.
No breakfast for them, poor lambs!
No nice porridge,
No bacon fat;
Not when the poor plumbers
Can't work
On account of the frost.
No fun in the snow,
Not for them.
They wouldn't have the heart.
No more would you have the heart,
Not without you were a selfish little pig.'
And my bacon fat choked me,
Because of the bitter knowledge
That one couldn't love icicles
Nor frost on wire-netting,
Because of people called plumbers:
—Not without one was a selfish
Little pig.

# T. S. ELIOT
## 1888–1965

### *Mr Mistoffelees*

You ought to know Mr Mistoffelees!
The Original Conjuring Cat—
(There can be no doubt about that).
Please listen to me and don't scoff. All his
Inventions are off his own bat.
There's no such Cat in the metropolis;
He holds all the patent monopolies
For performing surprising illusions
And creating eccentric confusions.
  At prestidigitation
    And at legerdemain
  He'll defy examination
    And deceive you again.
The greatest magicians have something to learn
From Mr Mistoffelees' Conjuring Turn.
Presto!
  Away we go!
    And we all say: OH!
      Well I never!
      Was there ever
      A Cat so clever
        As Magical Mr Mistoffelees!

He is quiet and small, he is black
From his ears to the top of his tail;
He can creep through the tiniest crack
He can walk on the narrowest rail.

He can pick any card from a pack,
He is equally cunning with dice;
He is always deceiving you into believing
That he's only hunting for mice.
    He can play any trick with a cork
    Or a spoon and a bit of fish-paste;
    If you look for a knife or a fork
        And you think it is merely misplaced—
    You have seen it one moment, and then it is *gawn*!
    But you'll find it next week lying out on the lawn.
        And we all say: OH!
            Well I never!
            Was there ever
            A Cat so clever
                As Magical Mr Mistoffelees!

His manner is vague and aloof,
You would think there was nobody shyer—
But his voice has been heard on the roof
When he was curled up by the fire.
And he's sometimes been heard by the fire
When he was about on the roof—
(At least we all *heard* that somebody purred)
Which is incontestable proof
    Of his singular magical powers:
        And I have known the family to call
    Him in from the garden for hours,
        While he was asleep in the hall.
And not long ago this phenomenal Cat
Produced *seven kittens* right out of a hat!
    And we all said: OH!
        Well I never!
        Did you ever
        Know a Cat so clever
            As Magical Mr Mistoffelees!

# W. J. TURNER
### 1889–1946

## *Romance*

When I was but thirteen or so
  I went into a golden land;
Chimborazo, Cotopaxi
  Took me by the hand.

My father died, my brother too,
  They passed like fleeting dreams.
I stood where Popocatapetl
  In the sunlight gleams.

I dimly heard the master's voice
  And boys far off at play.
Chimborazo, Cotopaxi
  Had stolen me away.

I walked in a great golden dream
  To and fro from school—
Shining Popocatapetl
  The dusty streets did rule.

I walked home with a gold dark boy,
  And never a word I'd say,
Chimborazo, Cotopaxi
  Had taken my speech away:

I gazed entranced upon his face
  Fairer than any flower—
O shining Popocatapetl,
  It was thy magic hour:

The houses, people, traffic seemed
  Thin fading dreams by day,
Chimborazo, Cotopaxi
  They had stolen my soul away.

# IRENE McLEOD
## 1891–?

### *Lone Dog*

I'm a lean dog, a keen dog, a wild dog and lone,
I'm a rough dog, a tough dog, hunting on my own!
I'm a bad dog, a mad dog, teasing silly sheep;
I love to sit and bay the moon and keep fat souls from sleep.

I'll never be a lap dog, licking dirty feet,
A sleek dog, a meek dog, cringing for my meat.
Not for me the fireside, the well-filled plate;
But shut door and sharp stone and cuff and kick and hate.

Not for me the other dogs, running by my side,
Some have run a short while, but none of them would bide.
O mine is still the lone trail, the hard trail, the best
Wide wind and wild stars and the hunger of the quest.

# EDNA ST VINCENT MILLAY
## 1892–1950

### *The Bean-Stalk*

Ho, Giant! This is I!
I have built me a bean-stalk into your sky!
La,—but it's lovely, up so high!

This is how I came,—I put
Here my knee, there my foot,
Up and up, from shoot to shoot—
And the blessèd bean-stalk thinning
Like the mischief all the time,
Till it took me rocking, spinning,
In a dizzy, sunny circle,
Making angles with the root,

Far and out above the cackle
Of the city I was born in,
Till the little dirty city
In the light so sheer and sunny
Shone as dazzling bright and pretty
As the money that you find
In a dream of finding money—
What a wind! What a morning!—

Till the tiny, shiny city,
When I shot a glance below,
Shaken with a giddy laughter,
Sick and blissfully afraid,
Was a dew-drop on a blade,
And a pair of moments after
Was the whirling guess I made,—
And the wind was like a whip
Cracking past my icy ears,
And my hair stood out behind,
And my eyes were full of tears,
Wide-open and cold,
More tears than they could hold,
The wind was blowing so,
And my teeth were in a row,
Dry and grinning,
And I felt my foot slip,
And I scratched the wind and whined,
And I clutched the stalk and jabbered,
With my eyes shut blind,—
What a wind! What a wind!

Your broad sky, Giant,
Is the shelf of a cupboard;
I make bean-stalks, I'm
A builder, like yourself,
But bean-stalks is my trade,
I couldn't make a shelf,
Don't know how they're made,
Now, a bean-stalk is more pliant—
La, what a climb!

## Counting-out Rhyme

Silver bark of beech, and sallow
Bark of yellow birch and yellow
  Twig of willow.

Stripe of green in moosewood maple,
Colour seen in leaf of apple,
  Bark of popple.

Wood of popple pale as moonbeam,
Wood of oak for yoke and barn-beam,
  Wood of hornbeam.

Silver bark of beech, and hollow
Stem of elder, tall and yellow
  Twig of willow.


## From a Very Little Sphinx

### I

Come along in then, little girl!
Or else stay out!
But in the open door she stands,
And bites her lip and twists her hands,
And stares upon me, trouble-eyed:
'Mother,' she says, 'I can't decide!
I can't decide!'

### II

Oh, burdock, and you other dock,
That have ground coffee for your seeds,
And lovely long thin daisies, dear—
She said that you are weeds!
She said, 'Oh, what a fine bouquet!'
But afterwards I heard her say,
'She's always dragging in those weeds.'

### III

Everybody but just me
Despises burdocks. Mother, she
Despises 'em the most because
They stick so to my socks and drawers.
But father, when he sits on some,
Can't speak a decent word for 'em.

### IV

I know a hundred ways to die.
I've often thought I'd try one:
Lie down beneath a motor, truck
Some day when standing by one.

Or throw myself from off a bridge—
Except such things must be
So hard upon the scavengers
And men that clean the sea.

I know some poison I could drink.
I've often thought I'd taste it.
But mother bought it for the sink,
And drinking it would waste it.

### V

Look, Edwin! Do you see that boy
Talking to the other boy?
No, over there by those two men—
Wait, don't look now—now look again.
No, not the one in navy-blue;
That's the one he's talking to.
Sure you see him? Stripèd pants?
Well, *he was born in Paris, France.*

### VI

All the grown-up people say,
'What, those ugly thistles?
Mustn't touch them! Keep away!
Prickly! Full of bristles!'

Yet they never make me bleed
Half so much as roses!
Must be purple is a weed,
And pink and white is posies.

### VII

Wonder where this horseshoe went.
Up and down, up and down,
Up and past the monument,
Maybe into town.

Wait a minute. 'Horseshoe,
How far have you been?'
*Says it's been to Salem*
*And halfway to Lynn.*

Wonder who was in the team.
Wonder what they saw.
Wonder if they passed a bridge—
Bridge with a draw.

*Says it went from one bridge*
*Straight upon another.*
*Says it took a little girl*
*Driving with her mother.*


# J. R. R. TOLKIEN
### 1892–1973

## *Oliphaunt*

Grey as a mouse,
Big as a house,
Nose like a snake,
I make the earth shake,
As I tramp through the grass;
Trees crack as I pass.

With horns in my mouth
I walk in the South,
Flapping big ears.
Beyond count of years
I stump round and round,
Never lie on the ground,
Not even to die.
Oliphaunt am I,
Biggest of all,
Huge, old, and tall.
If ever you'd met me,
You wouldn't forget me.
If you never do,
You won't think I'm true;
But Old Oliphaunt am I,
And I never lie.

# ELIZABETH COATSWORTH
## 1893–1986

### *The Mouse*

I heard a mouse
Bitterly complaining
In a crack of moonlight
Aslant on the floor—

'Little I ask
And that little is not granted.
There are few crumbs
In this world any more.

'The bread-box is tin
And I cannot get in.

'The jam's in a jar
My teeth cannot mar.

'The cheese sits by itself
On the pantry shelf—

'All night I run
Searching and seeking,
All night I run
About on the floor,

'Moonlight is there
And a bare place for dancing,
But no little feast
Is spread any more.'


# FRANK COLLYMORE
## 1893–1980

### *Ballad of an Old Woman*

There was an old woman who never was wed;
Of twenty-one children was she brought to bed,
      Singing Glory to God.

She gave them all her poor means could afford
And brought them all up in the Fear of the Lord,
      Singing Glory to God.

As soon as they grew up, each sailed away,
One after the other to the great U.S.A.,
      Singing Glory to God.

Sometimes they thought of her, sometimes they wrote,
Sometimes they sent her a five dollar note:
      Singing Glory to God.

And when in the course of the long waiting years
The letters ceased coming, she dried her tears,
      Singing Glory to God.

And when the old shed-roof collapsed from decay
She went to the Almshouse and walked all the way,
    Singing Glory to God.

And there she mothered many motherless brats
Who slept on her shoulder and pulled at her plaits,
    Singing Glory to God.

Then one day she sickened and next day she died;
They brought out the hearse and put her inside
    Singing Glory to God.

Only weeds and nettles spring up from her clay
Who is one with the Night and the Light of the Day.
    Singing Glory to God.


# ANON., American

## *Poor Old Lady*

Poor old lady, she swallowed a fly.
I don't know why she swallowed a fly.
Poor old lady, I think she'll die.

Poor old lady, she swallowed a spider.
It squirmed and wriggled and turned inside her.
She swallowed the spider to catch the fly.
I don't know why she swallowed a fly.
Poor old lady, I think she'll die.

Poor old lady, she swallowed a bird.
How absurd! She swallowed a bird.
She swallowed the bird to catch the spider,
She swallowed the spider to catch the fly,
I don't know why she swallowed a fly.
Poor old lady, I think she'll die.

Poor old lady, she swallowed a cat.
Think of that! She swallowed a cat.
She swallowed the cat to catch the bird.
She swallowed the bird to catch the spider,
She swallowed the spider to catch the fly,
I don't know why she swallowed a fly.
Poor old lady, I think she'll die.

Poor old lady, she swallowed a dog.
She went the whole hog when she swallowed the dog.
She swallowed the dog to catch the cat,
She swallowed the cat to catch the bird,
She swallowed the bird to catch the spider.
She swallowed the spider to catch the fly,
I don't know why she swallowed a fly.
Poor old lady, I think she'll die.

Poor old lady, she swallowed a cow.
I don't know how she swallowed the cow.
She swallowed the cow to catch the dog,
She swallowed the dog to catch the cat,
She swallowed the cat to catch the bird,
She swallowed the bird to catch the spider,
She swallowed the spider to catch the fly,
I don't know why she swallowed a fly.
Poor old lady, I think she'll die.

Poor old lady, she swallowed a horse.
She died, of course.

# WILFRED OWEN
## 1893–1918

### *Sonnet*

#### TO A CHILD

Sweet is your antique body, not yet young.
Beauty withheld from youth that looks for youth.
Fair only for your father. Dear among
Masters in art. To all men else uncouth
Save me, who know your smile comes very old,
Learnt of the happy dead that laughed with gods;
For earlier suns than ours have lent you gold,
Sly fauns and trees have given you jigs and nods.

But soon your heart, hot-beating like a bird's,
Shall slow down. Youth shall lop your hair,
And you must learn wry meanings in our words.
Your smile shall dull, because too keen aware;
And when for hopes your hand shall be uncurled,
Your eyes shall close, being opened to the world.


# LOIS LENSKI
## 1893–1974

### *Sing a Song of People*

Sing a song of people
   Walking fast or slow;
People in the city,
   Up and down they go.

People on the sidewalk,
People on the bus;
People passing, passing,
In back and front of us.
People on the subway
Underneath the ground;
People riding taxis
Round and round and round.

People with their hats on,
Going in the doors;
People with umbrellas
When it rains and pours.
People in tall buildings
And in stores below;
Riding elevators
Up and down they go.

People walking singly,
People in a crowd,
People saying nothing,
People talking loud.
People laughing, smiling,
Grumpy people too;
People who just hurry
And never look at you!

Sing a song of people
　　Who like to come and go;
Sing of city people
　　You see but never know!

# GENEVIEVE TAGGARD
## 1894–1948

### *Millions of Strawberries*

Marcia and I went over the curve,
Eating our way down
Jewels of strawberries we didn't deserve,
Eating our way down
Till our hands were sticky, and our lips painted.
And over us the hot day fainted,
And we saw snakes,
And got scratched,
And a lust overcame us for the red unmatched
Small buds of berries,
Till we lay down—
Eating our way down—
And rolled in the berries like two little dogs,
Rolled
In the late gold.
And gnats hummed,
And it was cold,
And home we went, home without a berry,
Painted red and brown,
Eating our way down.

# E. E. CUMMINGS
## 1894–1962

### *in Just-*

in Just-
spring　when the world is mud-
luscious the little
lame balloonman

whistles　far　and wee

and eddieandbill come
running from marbles and
piracies and it's
spring

when the world is puddle-wonderful

the queer
old balloonman whistles
far　and　wee
and bettyandisbel come dancing

from hop-scotch and jump-rope and

it's
spring
and
　　the

　　　　goat-footed

balloonMan　whistles
far
and
wee

### hist whist

hist   whist
little ghostthings
tip-toe
twinkle-toe

little twitchy
witches and tingling
goblins
hob-a-nob   hob-a-nob

little hoppy happy
toad in tweeds
tweeds
little itchy mousies

with scuttling
eyes   rustle and run   and
hidehidehide
whisk

whisk   look out for the old woman
with the wart on her nose
what she'll do to yer
nobody knows

for she knows the devil   ooch
the devil   ouch
the devil
ach   the great

green
dancing
devil
devil

devil
devil

wheeEEE

## *maggie and milly and molly and may*

maggie and milly and molly and may
went down to the beach (to play one day)

and maggie discovered a shell that sang
so sweetly she couldn't remember her troubles, and

milly befriended a stranded star
whose rays five languid fingers were;

and molly was chased by a horrible thing
which raced sideways while blowing bubbles: and

may came home with a smooth round stone
as small as a world and as large as alone.

For whatever we lose (like a you or a me)
it's always ourselves we find in the sea


# RACHEL FIELD
## 1894–1942

### *Skyscrapers*

Do Skyscrapers ever grow tired
    Of holding themselves up high?
Do they ever shiver on frosty nights
    With their tops against the sky?
Do they feel lonely sometimes,
    Because they have grown so tall?
Do they ever wish they could just lie down
    And never get up at all?

# ROBERT GRAVES
## 1895–1985

### *Henry and Mary*

Henry was a young king,
  Mary was his queen;
He gave her a snowdrop
  On a stalk of green.

Then all for his kindness
  And all for his care
She gave him a new-laid egg
  In the garden there.

'Love, can you sing?'
                    'I cannot sing.'
  'Or tell a tale?'
                    'Not one I know.'
'Then let us play at queen and king
  As down the garden walks we go.'

### *Love without Hope*

Love without hope, as when the young bird-catcher
Swept off his tall hat to the Squire's own daughter,
So let the imprisoned larks escape and fly
Singing about her head, as she rode by.

## *Vain and Careless*

Lady, lovely lady,
 Careless and gay!
Once, when a beggar called,
 She gave her child away.

The beggar took the baby,
 Wrapped it in a shawl—
'Bring him back,' the lady said,
 'Next time you call.'

Hard by lived a vain man,
 So vain and so proud
He would walk on stilts
 To be seen by the crowd,

Up above the chimney pots,
 Tall as a mast—
And all the people ran about
 Shouting till he passed.

'A splendid match surely,'
 Neighbours saw it plain,
'Although she is so careless,
 Although he is so vain.'

But the lady played bobcherry,
 Did not see or care,
As the vain man went by her,
 Aloft in the air.

This gentle-born couple
 Lived and died apart—
Water will not mix with oil,
 Nor vain with careless heart.

## The Mirror

Mirror mirror tell me
Am I pretty or plain?
Or am I downright ugly,
And ugly to remain?

Shall I marry a gentleman?
Shall I marry a clown?
Or shall I marry
Old Knives and Scissors
Shouting through the town?

## Warning to Children

Children, if you dare to think
Of the greatness, rareness, muchness,
Fewness of this precious only
Endless world in which you say
You live, you think of things like this:
Blocks of slate enclosing dappled
Red and green, enclosing tawny
Yellow nets, enclosing white
And black acres of dominoes,
Where a neat brown paper parcel
Tempts you to untie the string.
In the parcel a small island,
On the island a large tree,
On the tree a husky fruit.
Strip the husk and pare the rind off:
In the kernel you will see
Blocks of slate enclosed by dappled
Red and green, enclosed by tawny
Yellow nets, enclosed by white
And black acres of dominoes,
Where the same brown paper parcel—
Children, leave the string untied!
For who dares undo the parcel

Finds himself at once inside it,
On the island, in the fruit,
Blocks of slate about his head,
Finds himself enclosed by dappled
Green and red, enclosed by yellow
Tawny nets, enclosed by black
And white acres of dominoes,
With the same brown paper parcel
Still untied upon his knee.

And, if he then should dare to think
Of the fewness, muchness, rareness,
Greatness of this endless only
Precious world in which he says
He lives—he then unties the string.

# DAVID McCORD
## 1897–

### *Five Chants*

#### I

Every time I climb a tree
Every time I climb a tree
Every time I climb a tree
I scrape a leg
Or skin a knee
And every time I climb a tree
I find some ants
Or dodge a bee
And get the ants
All over me

And every time I climb a tree
Where have you been?
They say to me
But don't they know that I am free
Every time I climb a tree?
I like it best
To spot a nest
That has an egg
Or maybe three

And then I skin
The other leg
But every time I climb a tree
I see a lot of things to see
Swallows rooftops and TV
And all the fields and farms there be
Every time I climb a tree
Though climbing may be good for ants
It isn't awfully good for pants
But still it's pretty good for me
Every time I climb a tree

II

Monday morning back to school
Fool fool fool fool
Monday morning back we go
No No No No
Monday morning summer's gone
John John John John
Monday morning what a pain
Jane Jane Jane Jane

III

The pickety fence
The pickety fence
Give it a lick it's
The pickety fence
Give it a lick it's
A clickety fence
Give it a lick it's
A lickety fence
Give it a lick
Give it a lick
Give it a lick
With a rickety stick
Pickety
Pickety
Pickety
Pick

IV

The cow has a cud
The turtle has mud
The rabbit has a hutch
But I haven't much

The ox has a yoke
The frog has a croak
The toad has a wart
So he's not my sort

The mouse has a hole
The polecat a pole
The goose has a hiss
And it goes like this

The duck has a pond
The bird has beyond
The hen has a chick
But I feel sick

The horse has hay
The dog has his day
The bee has a sting
And a queen not a king

The robin has a worm
The worm has a squirm
The squirrel has a nut
Every wheel has a rut

The pig has a pen
The bear has a den
The trout has a pool
While I have school

The crow has a nest
The hawk has a guest
The owl has a mate
Doggone! I'm late!

v

Thin ice
Free advice
Heavy snow
Out you go
Nice slush
Lush lush
Wet feet
Fever heat
Stuffy head
Stay in bed
Who's ill?
Me? A pill?

## *Father and I in the Woods*

'Son,'
My father used to say,
'Don't run.'

'Walk,'
My father used to say,
'Don't talk.'

'Words,'
My father used to say,
'Scare birds.'

So be:
It's sky and brook and bird
And tree.

# STEPHEN VINCENT BENÉT
## 1898–1943

## *A Sad Song*

*Rosemary, Rosemary,*
*There's a Pig in your garden,*
*With silk bristles frizzy*
*And tushers of snow!*
But Rosemary was cautious,
She said, 'Beg your pardon!
I'm really too busy
To look down below.'

*Rosemary, Rosemary,*
*There's a Bird in your kitchen!*
*His voice is gold water,*
*He says, 'Pretty Poll!'*
But Rosemary heard nothing,
Putting stitch after stitch in
The dress of a daughter,
Her thirty-sixth doll.

*Rosemary, Rosemary,*
*A silver-winged Rabbit!*
*He bridles and gentles*
*And wants you astride!*
'I prefer,' said Rosemary,
'To ride a Good Habit.'
She went buying black lentils—
She did till she died.

## A Nonsense Song

Rosemary, Rosemary, let down your hair!
The cow's in the hammock, the crow's in the chair!
I was making you songs out of sawdust and silk,
But they came in to call and they spilt them like milk.

The cat's in the coffee, the wind's in the east,
He screams like a peacock and whines like a priest
And the saw of his voice makes my blood turn to mice—
So let down your long hair and shut off his advice!

Pluck out the thin hairpins and let the waves stream,
Brown-gold as brook-waters that dance through a dream,
Gentle-curled as young cloudlings, sweet-fragrant as bay,
Till it takes all the fierceness of living away.

Oh, when you are with me, my heart is white steel.
But the bat's in the belfry, the mold's in the meal,
And I think I hear skeletons climbing the stair!
—Rosemary, Rosemary, let down your bright hair!

# FRANK HORNE
## 1899–

### *Kid Stuff*

DECEMBER, 1942

The wise guys
tell me
that Christmas
is Kid Stuff . . .
Maybe they've got
something there—
Two thousand years ago
three wise guys
chased a star
across a continent
to bring
frankincense and myrrh
to a Kid
born in a manger
with an idea in his head . . .

And as the bombs
crash
all over the world
today
the real wise guys
know
that we've all
got to go chasing stars
again
in the hope
that we can get back
some of that
Kid Stuff
born two thousand years ago.

# LAURA RIDING
### 1901–1991

## *Toward the Corner*

One, two, three.
Coming, Old Trouble, coming.
The organ-grinder is turning,
The children are sing-songing,
The organ grinder is stopping,
The children are hum-coming,
Coming, Old Trouble, coming,

One, two three.
Coming, Old Trouble, coming.
The bakeshop is sugar-crusting,
The children are window-tasting,
The bakeshop is shop-shutting,
The children are sugar-dreaming,
The children are sugar-stealing,
Coming, Old Trouble, coming.

One, two three.
Coming, Old Trouble, coming.
Father Bell is evening-praying,
The night is empty-falling,
The rats are out,
The birds are in,
Coming, Old Trouble, coming.

One, two, three.
One, two, three.
Coming, Old Trouble, coming.
Somebody's dead, who can it be?
Old Trouble is it you?

Then say so, say so.
One, two, three,
Into the great rag-bag you go.
Going, Old Trouble, going.

# LANGSTON HUGHES
## 1902–1967

### *My People*

The night is beautiful,
So the faces of my people.

The stars are beautiful,
So the eyes of my people.

Beautiful, also, is the sun.
Beautiful, also, are the souls of my people.


### *I, Too*

I too, sing America.

I am the darker brother.
They send me to eat in the kitchen
When company comes,
But I laugh,
And eat well,
And grow strong.

Tomorrow,
I'll be at the table
When company comes.
Nobody'll dare
Say to me,
'Eat in the kitchen,'
Then.

Besides,
They'll see how beautiful I am
And be ashamed—

I, too, am America.

## Children's Rhymes

By what sends
the white kids
I ain't sent:
I know I can't
be President.

What don't bug
them white kids
sure bugs me:
We know everybody
ain't free.

Lies written down
for white folks
ain't for us a-tall:
*Liberty And Justice*—
Huh!—*For All?*


## Ultimatum: Kid to Kid

Go home, stupid,
And wash your dirty face.
Go home, stupid,
This is not your place.

Go home, stupid,
You don't belong here.
If you don't go,
I will pull your ear.

I ask you if you'd like to play.
'Huh?' is all you know to say,
Standing 'round here
In the way.

So go home, stupid!
I'll spit in your eye!
Stupid, go home—
Before I cry.


## Tambourines

Tambourines!
Tambourines!
Tambourines!
To the glory of God!
Tambourines
To glory!

A gospel shout
And a gospel song:
Life is short
*But God is long!*

Tambourines!
Tambourines!
Tambourines
To glory!


## April Rain Song

Let the rain kiss you.
Let the rain beat upon your head with silver liquid drops.
Let the rain sing you a lullaby.

The rain makes still pools on the sidewalk.
The rain makes running pools in the gutter.
The rain plays a little sleep-song on our roof at night—

And I love the rain.

# OGDEN NASH

## 1902–1971

### *The Eel*

I don't mind eels
Except at meals,
And the way they feels.


### *Adventures of Isabel*

Isabel met an enormous bear,
Isabel, Isabel, didn't care;
The bear was hungry, the bear was ravenous,
The bear's big mouth was cruel and cavernous.
The bear said, Isabel, glad to meet you,
How do, Isabel, now I'll eat you!
Isabel, Isabel, didn't worry,
Isabel didn't scream or scurry.
She washed her hands and she straightened her hair up,
Then Isabel quietly ate the bear up.

Once in a night as black as pitch
Isabel met a wicked old witch.
The witch's face was cross and wrinkled,
The witch's gums with teeth were sprinkled.
Ho ho, Isabel! the old witch crowed,
I'll turn you into an ugly toad!
Isabel, Isabel, didn't worry,
Isabel didn't scream or scurry,
She showed no rage and she showed no rancour,
But she turned the witch into milk and drank her.

Isabel met a hideous giant,
Isabel continued self-reliant.
The giant was hairy, the giant was horrid,
He had one eye in the middle of his forehead.

Good morning, Isabel, the giant said,
I'll grind your bones to make my bread.
Isabel, Isabel, didn't worry,
Isabel didn't scream or scurry.
She nibbled the zwieback that she always fed off,
And when it was gone, she cut the giant's head off.

Isabel met a troublesome doctor,
He punched and he poked till he really shocked her.
The doctor's talk was of coughs and chills
And the doctor's satchel bulged with pills.
The doctor said unto Isabel,
Swallow this, it will make you well.
Isabel, Isabel, didn't worry,
Isabel didn't scream or scurry.
She took those pills from the pill concocter,
And Isabel calmly cured the doctor.


# STEVIE SMITH
## 1902–1971

### Fairy Story

I went into the wood one day
And there I walked and lost my way

When it was so dark I could not see
A little creature came to me

He said if I would sing a song
The time would not be very long

But first I must let him hold my hand tight
Or else the wood would give me a fright

I sang a song, he let me go
But now I am home again there is nobody I know.

# COUNTEE CULLEN
## 1903–1946

### Incident

Once riding in old Baltimore,
  Heart-filled, head-filled with glee,
I saw a Baltimorean
  Keep looking straight at me.

Now I was eight and very small,
  And he was no whit bigger,
And so I smiled, but he poked out
  His tongue, and called me, 'Nigger.'

I saw the whole of Baltimore
  From May until December,
Of all the things that happened there
  That's all that I remember.

# CHRISTOPHER ISHERWOOD
## 1904–1986

### The Common Cormorant

The common cormorant or shag
Lays eggs inside a paper bag
The reason you will see no doubt
It is to keep the lightning out.
But what these unobservant birds
Have never noticed is that herds
Of wandering bears may come with buns
And steal the bags to hold the crumbs.

# ANON., English

## *'A muvver was barfin' 'er biby one night'*

A muvver was barfin' 'er biby one night,
The youngest of ten and a tiny young mite,
The muvver was poor and the biby was thin,
Only a skelington covered in skin;
The muvver turned rahnd for the soap off the rack,
She was but a moment, but when she turned back,
The biby was gorn; and in anguish she cried,
'Oh, where is my biby?'—The angels replied:

'Your biby 'as fell dahn the plug-'ole,
Your biby 'as gorn dahn the plug;
The poor little thing was so skinny and thin
'E oughter been barfed in a jug;
Your biby is perfeckly 'appy,
'E won't need a barf any more,
Your biby 'as fell dahn the plug-'ole,
Not lorst, but gorn before.'

# LEONARD CLARK
## 1905–1981

## *Singing in the Streets*

I had almost forgotten the singing in the streets,
Snow piled up by the houses, drifting
Underneath the door into the warm room,
Firelight, lamplight, the little lame cat
Dreaming in soft sleep on the hearth, mother dozing,
Waiting for Christmas to come, the boys and me
Trudging over blanket fields waving lanterns to the sky.
I had almost forgotten the smell, the feel of it all,
The coming back home, with girls laughing like stars,

Their cheeks, holly berries, me kissing one,
Silent-tongued, soberly, by the long church wall;
Then back to the kitchen table, supper on the white cloth,
Cheese, bread, the home-made wine,
Symbols of the night's joys, a holy feast.
And I wonder now, years gone, mother gone,
The boys and girls scattered, drifted away with the snowflakes,
Lamplight done, firelight over,
If the sounds of our singing in the streets are still there,
Those old tunes, still praising;
And now, a lifetime of Decembers away from it all,
A branch of remembering holly stabs my cheeks,
And I think it may be so;
Yes, I believe it may be so.


# AILEEN FISHER

## 1906–

### *Fair Exchange*

I'll give a candle
or a spangle
or a bangle
or a nice shiny handle
or some rolled-up string,

I'll give a buckle
or a pickle
or a nickel
or a sprig of honeysuckle
or a copper ring . . .

If you will only let me see
your swelled-up hornet sting.

# LYDIA PENDER
## 1907–

### *The Lizard*

There on the sun-hot stone
Why do you wait, alone
And still, so still?
Neck arched, head high, tense and alert, but still,
Still as the stone?

Still is your delicate head,
Like the head of an arrow;
Still is your delicate throat,
Rounded and narrow;
Still is your delicate back,
Patterned in silver and black,
And bright with the burnished sheen that the gum-tips share.
Even your delicate feet
Are still, still as the heat,
With a stillness alive, and awake, and intensely aware.

Why do I catch my breath,
Held by your spell?
Listening, waiting—for what?
Will you not tell?
More alive in your quiet than ever the locust can be,
Shrilling his clamorous song from the shimmering tree;
More alive in your motionless grace, as the slow minutes die,
Than the scurrying ants that go hurrying busily by.
I know, if my shadow but fall by your feet on the stone,
In the wink of an eye,
Let me try—
Ah!
He's gone!

# J. K. ANNAND
1908—

## Mavis

Mavis, mavis,
  Rinnin owre the gress,
Cock your lug, gie a tug,
  Ae worm less!

Sing a sang at dawnin
  On the highest tree,
Sing again at gloamin
  A bonnie wee sang for me.

Sing it aince for pleisure,
  Sing it twice for joy,
Sing it thrice to shaw us
  That ye're the clever wee boy.

*mavis* song thrush     *gress* grass     *lug* ear     *ae* one
              *gloamin* dusk     *wee* little

## Heron

A humphy-backit heron
Nearly as big as me
Stands at the waterside
Fishin for his tea.
His skinnie-ma-linkie lang legs
Juist like reeds
Cheats aa the puddocks
Sooming 'mang the weeds.
Here's ane comin,
Grup it by the leg!
It sticks in his thrapple
Then slides doun his craig.

Neist comes a rottan,
A rottan soomin past,
Oot gangs the lang neb
And has the rottan fast.
He jabs it, he stabs it,
Sune it's in his wame,
Flip-flap in the air
Heron flees hame.

| *humphy-backit* hunch-backed | *skinnie-ma-linkie* skinny | *aa* all |
| *puddocks* frogs | *soomin* swimming | *thrapple* throat | *craig* neck |
| *neist* next | *rottan* rat | *neb* beak | *wame* belly | *hame* home |

## I Winna Let On

Gif ye kip the schule
And come wi me
I winna let on.
Gif ye douk in the burn
And sclim the tree
I winna let on.
We'll herrie bees-bykes
And feast on neeps,
I winna let on.
For ye and me
Are billies for keeps,
Your faither may speir
Your mither may fleetch
But I winna let on,
I winna let on.

*gif* if        *kip* play truant from        *schule* school        *winna* won't
*douk* bathe        *burn* stream        *sclim* climb        *herrie* steal (honey) from
*bees-bykes* beehives        *neeps* turnips        *billies* (best) friends
*speir* ask questions        *fleetch* coax or cajole

# THEODORE ROETHKE
## 1908–1963

### *Child on Top of a Greenhouse*

The wind billowing out the seat of my britches,
My feet crackling splinters of glass and dried putty,
The half-grown chrysanthemums staring up like accusers,
Up through the streaked glass, flashing with sunlight,
A few white clouds all rushing eastward,
A line of elms plunging and tossing like horses,
And everyone, everyone pointing up and shouting!


### *My Papa's Waltz*

The whiskey on your breath
Could make a small boy dizzy;
But I hung on like death:
Such waltzing was not easy.

We romped until the pans
Slid from the kitchen shelf;
My mother's countenance
Could not unfrown itself.

The hand that held my wrist
Was battered on one knuckle;
At every step you missed
My right ear scraped a buckle.

You beat time on my head
With a palm caked hard by dirt,
Then waltzed me off to bed
Still clinging to your shirt.

## The Serpent

There was a Serpent who had to sing.
There was. There was.
He simply gave up Serpenting.
Because. Because.

He didn't like his Kind of Life;
He couldn't find a proper Wife;
He was a Serpent with a soul;
He got no Pleasure down his Hole.
And so, of course, he had to Sing,
And Sing he did, like Anything!
The Birds, they were, they were Astounded;
And various Measures Propounded
To stop the Serpent's Awful Racket:
They bought a Drum. He wouldn't Whack it.
They sent,—you always send,—to Cuba
And got a Most Commodious Tuba;
They got a Horn, they got a Flute,
But Nothing would suit.
He said, 'Look, Birds, all this is futile:
I do *not* like to Bang or Tootle.'
And then he cut loose with a Horrible Note
That practically split the Top of his Throat.
'You *see*,' he said, with a Serpent's Leer,
'I'm Serious about my Singing Career!'
And the Woods Resounded with many a Shriek
As the Birds flew off to the End of Next Week.

## The Lizard

The Time to Tickle a Lizard,
Is Before, or Right After, a Blizzard.
Now the place to begin
Is just under his Chin—
And here's more Advice:
Don't Poke more than Twice
At an Intimate Place like his Gizzard.

# JAMES REEVES
## 1909–1978

### Slowly

Slowly the tide creeps up the sand,
Slowly the shadows cross the land.
Slowly the cart-horse pulls his mile,
Slowly the old man mounts the stile.

Slowly the hands move round the clock,
Slowly the dew dries on the dock.
Slow is the snail—but slowest of all
The green moss spreads on the old brick wall.

### Cows

Half the time they munched the grass, and all the time they lay
Down in the water-meadows, the lazy month of May,
    A-chewing,
    A-mooing,
To pass the hours away.

  'Nice weather,' said the brown cow.
    'Ah,' said the white.
  'Grass is very tasty.'
    'Grass is all right.'

Half the time they munched the grass, and all the time they lay
Down in the water-meadows, the lazy month of May,
    A-chewing
    A-mooing,
To pass the hours away.

  'Rain coming,' said the brown cow.
    'Ah,' said the white.
  'Flies is very tiresome.'
    'Flies bite.'

Half the time they munched the grass, and all the time they lay
Down in the water-meadows, the lazy month of May,
  A-chewing,
  A-mooing,
To pass the hours away.

  'Time to go,' said the brown cow.
  'Ah,' said the white.
  'Nice chat.' 'Very pleasant.'
  'Night.' 'Night.'

Half the time they munched the grass, and all the time they lay
Down in the water-meadows, the lazy month of May,
  A-chewing,
  A-mooing,
To pass the hours away.

## The Sea

The sea is a hungry dog,
Giant and grey.
He rolls on the beach all day.
With his clashing teeth and shaggy jaws
Hour upon hour he gnaws
The rumbling, tumbling stones,
And 'Bones, bones, bones, bones!'
The giant sea-dog moans,
Licking his greasy paws.

And when the night wind roars
And the moon rocks in the stormy cloud,
He bounds to his feet and snuffs and sniffs,
Shaking his wet sides over the cliffs,
And howls and hollos long and loud.

But on quiet days in May and June,
When even the grasses on the dune
Play no more their reedy tune,
With his head between his paws
He lies on the sandy shores,
So quiet, so quiet, he scarcely snores.

## W

The King sent for his wise men all
    To find a rhyme for W;
When they had thought a good long time
But could not think of a single rhyme,
    'I'm sorry,' said he, 'to trouble you.'

### Giant Thunder

Giant Thunder, striding home,
Wonders if his supper's done.

'Hag wife, hag wife, bring me my bones!'
'They are not done,' the old hag moans.

'Not done? not done?' the giant roars
And heaves his old wife out of doors.

Cries he 'I'll have them, cooked or not!'
But overturns the cooking-pot.

He flings the burning coals about;
See how the lightning flashes out!

Upon the gale the old hag rides,
The cloudy moon for terror hides.

All the world with thunder quakes;
Forest shudders, mountain shakes;
From the cloud the rainstorm breaks;
Village ponds are turned to lakes;
Every living creature wakes.

Hungry Giant, lie you still!
Stamp no more from hill to hill—
Tomorrow you shall have your fill.

# NORMAN NICHOLSON

## 1910–1987

### *Carol for the Last Christmas Eve*

The first night, the first night,
 The night that Christ was born,
His mother looked in his eyes and saw
 Her maker in her son.

The twelfth night, the twelfth night,
 After Christ was born,
The Wise Men found the child and knew
 Their search had just begun.

Eleven thousand, two fifty nights,
 After Christ was born,
A dead man hung in the child's light
 And the sun went down at noon.

Six hundred thousand or thereabout nights,
 After Christ was born,
I look at you and you look at me
But the sky is too dark for us to see
 And the world waits for the sun.

But the last night, the last night,
    Since ever Christ was born,
What his mother knew will be known again,
And what was found by the Three Wise Men,
And the sun will rise and so may we,
    On the last morn, on Christmas Morn,
Umpteen hundred and eternity.


# ELIZABETH BISHOP
## 1911–1979

### *Manners*

FOR A CHILD OF 1918

My grandfather said to me
as we sat on the wagon seat,
'Be sure to remember to always
speak to everyone you meet.'

We met a stranger on foot.
My grandfather's whip tapped his hat.
'Good day, sir. Good day. A fine day.'
And I said it and bowed where I sat.

Then we overtook a boy we knew
with his big pet crow on his shoulder.
'Always offer everyone a ride;
don't forget that when you get older,'

my grandfather said. So Willy
climbed up with us, but the crow
gave a 'Caw!' and flew off. I was worried.
How would he know where to go?

But he flew a little way at a time
from fence post to fence post, ahead;
and when Willy whistled he answered.
'A fine bird,' my grandfather said,

'and he's well brought up. See, he answers
nicely when he's spoken to.
Man or beast, that's good manners.
Be sure that you both always do.'

When automobiles went by,
the dust hid the people's faces,
but we shouted 'Good day! Good day!
Fine day!' at the top of our voices.

When we came to Hustler Hill,
he said that the mare was tired,
so we all got down and walked,
as our good manners required.


# MERVYN PEAKE
## 1911–1968

### *'I cannot give the reasons'*

I cannot give the reasons,
I only sing the tunes:
the sadness of the seasons
the madness of the moons.

I cannot be didactic
or lucid, but I can
be quite obscure and practic-
ally marzipan

In gorgery and gushness
and all that's squishified,
my voice has all the lushness
of what I can't abide

And yet it has a beauty
most proud and terrible
denied to those whose duty
is to be cerebral.

Among the antlered mountains
I make my viscous way
and watch the sepia fountains
throw up their lime-green spray.

## 'O here it is! And there it is!'

O here it is! And there it is!
And no one knows whose share it is
Nor dares to stake a claim—
But we have seen it in the air
A fairy like a William Pear—
With but itself to blame.

A thug it is—and smug it is
And like a floating pug it is
Above the orchard trees.
It has no right—no right at all
To soar above the orchard wall
With chilblains on its knees.

# JOHN WALSH
## 1911–1972

### *'I've Got an Apple Ready'*

My hair's tightly plaited;
I've a bright blue bow;
I don't want my breakfast,
And now I must go.

My satchel's on my shoulder;
Nothing's out of place;
And I've got an apple ready,
Just in case.

So it's 'Good-bye, Mother!'
And off down the street;
Briskly at first
On pit-a-pat feet,

But slow and more slow
As I reach the tarred
Trackway that runs
By Hodson's Yard;

For it's there sometimes
Bill Craddock waits for me
To snatch off my beret
And throw it in a tree.

Bill Craddock leaning
On Hodson's rails;
Bill with thin hands
And dirty nails;

Bill with a front tooth
Broken and bad;
His dark eyes cruel,
And somehow sad.

Often there are workmen,
And then he doesn't dare;
But this morning I feel
He'll be there.

At the corner he will pounce . . .
But quickly I'll say
'Hallo, Bill! have an apple!'—
In an ordinary way.

I'll push it in his hand
And walk right on;
And when I'm round the corner
I'll run!

# ROLAND ROBINSON
## 1912–

### *Jarrangulli*
#### RELATED BY PERCY MUMBULLA

Hear that tree-lizard singin' out,
Jarrangulli.
He's singin' out for rain.
He's in a hole up in that tree.
He wants the rain to fill that hole right up
an' cover him with rain.
That water will last him till
the drought comes on again.

It's comin' dry when he sings out,
Jarrangulli.
Soon as ever he sings out,
Jarrangulli,
he's sure to bring the rain.
That feller, he's the real rain-lizard.
He's just the same as them black cockatoos,
they're the fellers for the rain.

He's deadly poison. He's
Jarrangulli.
He'll bite you sure enough.
You climb that tree an' put your hand
over that hole, he'll bite you sure enough.
He's black an' painted with white stripes.
Jarrangulli.
He's singin' out for rain.

# MAY SARTON
## 1912–

### *Nursery Rhyme*

FOR POLLY, WHOSE EYES ARE TIRED

Shut your eyes then
And let us slip
Out of the city rain
Into a special ship,
Call her The Pilgrim,
Set sail and go
Over the world's rim
To where Rousseau
Discovered a jungle
Of indigo trees,
A marvelous tangle:
Precise oranges,
Tigers with dreaming eyes,
Larger and larger flowers,
Leaves of gigantic size—
Wander for hours
Under a crimson sun
In a pale milky sky
With a vermilion
Lizard near by,
And over it all
The strangeness that hovers
Like a green pall,
Envelops and covers
In a warm still suspense
All of the landscape
Like a sixth sense—
Till there is no escape,
Till in the grasses
(Two people Rousseau
Saw through his glasses
And wanted to know)

You who have shut your eyes
And I who brought you here
Are to our great surprise
Part of the atmosphere,
Part of the painter's dream,
Of his most intent seeing
In a place where things seem
Instead of being,
No longer living, no longer mortal,
Fabulous ladies,
Unreal, immortal—
Shut then your open eyes
Let us go softly home,
Back to the sleeping ship
Over the emerald foam,
Over the edge and slip
Out of the Rousseau world
Into the world of men,
Sails all bound up and furled:
Open your eyes again.

# IAN SERRAILLIER

## 1912–

### *Anne and the Field-Mouse*

We found a mouse in the chalk quarry today
In a circle of stones and empty oil drums
By the fag ends of a fire. There had been
A picnic there; he must have been after the crumbs.

Jane saw him first, a flicker of brown fur
In and out of the charred wood and chalk-white.
I saw him last, but not till we'd turned up
Every stone and surprised him into flight,

Though not far—little zigzag spurts from stone
To stone. Once, as he lurked in his hiding-place,
I saw his beady eyes uplifted to mine.
I'd never seen such terror in so small a face.

I watched, amazed and guilty. Beside us suddenly
A heavy pheasant whirred up from the ground,
Scaring us all; and, before we knew it, the mouse
Had broken cover, skimming away without a sound,

Melting into the nettles. We didn't go
Till I'd chalked in capitals on a rusty can:
THERE'S A MOUSE IN THOSE NETTLES. LEAVE
HIM ALONE. NOVEMBER 15th. ANNE.

# GEORGE BARKER

## 1913–1991

### *'How many apples grow on the tree?'*

How many apples grow on the tree?
    said Jenny.
O many many more than you can see!
    said Johnny.
Even more than a hundred and three?
    said Jenny.
Enough, said Johnny, for you and me
and all who eat apples from the tree
    said Johnny.

How many fish swim in the sea?
    said Jenny.
More than apples that grow on the tree
    said Johnny.
Even more than a thousand and three?
    said Jenny.
Enough, said Johnny, for you and me
and all who fish in the big blue sea
    said Johnny.

# DELMORE SCHWARTZ
## 1913–1966

## *I Am Cherry Alive*

'I am cherry alive,' the little girl sang,
'Each morning I am something new:
I am apple, I am plum, I am just as excited
As the boys who made the Hallowe'en bang:
I am tree, I am cat, I am blossom too:
When I like, if I like, I can be someone new,
Someone very old, a witch in a zoo:
I can be someone else whenever I think who,
And I want to be everything sometimes too:
And the peach has a pit and I know that too,
And I put it in along with everything
To make the grown-ups laugh whenever I sing:
And I sing: *It is true; It is untrue;*
I know, I know, the true is untrue,
The peach has a pit,
The pit has a peach:
And both may be wrong
When I sing my song,
But I don't tell the grown-ups: because it is sad,
And I want them to laugh just like I do
Because they grew up
And forgot what they knew
And they are sure
I will forget it some day too.
They are wrong. They are wrong.
When I sang my song, I knew, I knew!
I am red, I am gold,
I am green, I am blue,
I will always be me,
I will always be new!'

## *O Child, Do Not Fear the Dark and*
## *Sleep's Dark Possession*

O child, when you go down to sleep and sleep's secession,
You become more and other than you are, you become the procession
Of bird and beast and tree: you are a chorus,
A pony among horses, a sapling in a dark forest,
Lifting your limbs and boughs to the sky, leafing.
And then you are one with the beaver, one
With the little animals warm in the sun
Resting and hidden when it is white winter:
     And in sleep's river you sleep
     Like the river's self and the marine
     Beings who mouth as they glide, nosing
       And sliding lithely and smoothly
         Gleaming serenely and sleekly.


# JOHN CIARDI
## 1916–

## *All about Boys and Girls*

I know all about boys, I do,
And I know all about little girls, too.
I know what they eat. I know what they drink.
I know what they like. I know what they think.

And so I'm writing this to say,
Don't let children out to play.
It makes them sad. They'd rather go
To school or to the dentist. Oh,

I know they're bashful about saying
How much it hurts to be out playing
When they could go to school and spell
And mind their manners. They won't tell

How tired they are of games and toys.
But I know girls, and I know boys.
They like to sweep floors, chop the wood,
And practice being very good.

They'd rather sit and study hard
Than waste the whole day in the yard.
What good is fun and making noise?
That's not for girls! That's not for boys!

### Sometimes Even Parents Win

There was a young lady from Gloucester
Who complained that her parents both bossed her,
    So she ran off to Maine.
    Did her parents complain?
Not at all—they were glad to have lost her.

# GAVIN EWART

## 1916–1995

### Who Likes the Idea of Guide Cats?

Of course, we have Guide Dogs For The Blind,
and we also have Girl Guides—
but why do Guide *Cats* never come to mind?
There would be protests on all sides

if we ever let *them* be our leaders!
Almost at once, we should be lost!
Even the cat-lovers, those special pleaders,
would admit the terrible cost

of letting cats, on our journeys, be in charge.
Animals that, with no warning, can go to sleep
on their way somewhere! Cats, small or large,
that all of a sudden run wild and leap,

chasing the leaves, or even chasing the flies—
it would be silly to give *them* any responsibility.
They can't be trained like dogs (that's no surprise).
Train a cat if you can! It's a rare ability!

# EVE MERRIAM
## 1916–1992

### *Weather*

Dot a dot dot dot a dot dot
Spotting the windowpane.

Spack a spack speck flick a flack fleck
Freckling the windowpane.

A spatter a scatter a wet cat a clatter
A splatter a rumble outside.

Umbrella umbrella umbrella umbrella
Bumbershoot barrel of rain.

Slosh a galosh slosh a galosh
Slither and slather a glide

A puddle a jump a puddle a jump
A puddle a jump puddle splosh

A juddle a pump a luddle a dump
A pudmuddle jump in and slide!

### *Lullaby*

Purple,
Purple,
Twilight
Sky light.

Purple as a king's cape
Purple as a grape.

Purple for the evening
When daylight is leaving.

Soft and purry,
Gentle and furry,
Velvet evening-time.

Purple,
Purple,
Sky light
Goodbye light.

Dusky
Musky
Into night.

# GWENDOLYN BROOKS

## 1917–

### *a song in the front yard*

I've stayed in the front yard all my life.
I want a peek at the back
Where it's rough and untended and hungry weed grows.
A girl gets sick of a rose.

I want to go in the back yard now
And maybe down the alley,
To where the charity children play.
I want a good time today.

They do some wonderful things.
They have some wonderful fun.
My mother sneers, but I say it's fine
How they don't have to go in at quarter to nine.

My mother, she tells me that Johnnie Mae
Will grow up to be a bad woman.
That George'll be taken to Jail soon or late
(On account of last winter he sold our back gate).

But I say it's fine. Honest, I do.
And I'd like to be a bad woman, too,
And wear the brave stockings of night-black lace
And strut down the streets with paint on my face.


## Michael Is Afraid of the Storm

Lightning is angry in the night.
Thunder spanks our house.
Rain is hating our old elm—
It punishes the boughs.

Now, I am next to nine years old,
And crying's not for me.
But if I touch my mother's hand,
Perhaps no one will see.

And if I keep herself in sight—
Follow her busy dress—
No one will notice my wild eye.
No one will laugh, I guess.


# CHARLES CAUSLEY

## 1917–

### Nursery Rhyme of Innocence and Experience

I had a silver penny
    And an apricot tree
And I said to the sailor
    On the white quay

'Sailor O sailor
  Will you bring me
If I give you my penny
  And my apricot tree

'A fez from Algeria
  An Arab drum to beat
A little gilt sword
  And a parakeet?'

And he smiled and he kissed me
  As strong as death
And I saw his red tongue
  And I felt his sweet breath

*'You may keep your penny*
  *And your apricot tree*
*And I'll bring your presents*
  *Back from sea.'*

O the ship dipped down
  On the rim of the sky
And I waited while three
  Long summers went by

Then one steel morning
  On the white quay
I saw a grey ship
  Come in from sea

Slowly she came
  Across the bay
For her flashing rigging
  Was shot away

All round her wake
  The seabirds cried
And flew in and out
  Of the hole in her side

Slowly she came
  In the path of the sun
And I heard the sound
  Of a distant gun

And a stranger came running
  Up to me
From the deck of the ship
  And he said, said he

*'O are you the boy*
  *Who would wait on the quay*
*With the silver penny*
  *And the apricot tree?*

*'I've a plum-coloured fez*
  *And a drum for thee*
*And a sword and a parakeet*
  *From over the sea.'*

'O where is the sailor
  With bold red hair?
And what is that volley
  On the bright air?

'O where are the other
  Girls and boys?
And why have you brought me
  Children's toys?'

## I Saw a Jolly Hunter

I saw a jolly hunter
  With a jolly gun
Walking in the country
  In the jolly sun.

In the jolly meadow
Sat a jolly hare.
Saw the jolly hunter.
Took jolly care.

Hunter jolly eager—
Sight of jolly prey.
Forgot gun pointing
Wrong jolly way.

Jolly hunter jolly head
Over heels gone.
Jolly old safety catch
Not jolly on.

Bang went the jolly gun.
Hunter jolly dead.
Jolly hare got clean away.
Jolly good, I said.


## Figgie Hobbin

Nightingales' tongues, your majesty?
    Quails in aspic, cost a purse of money?
Oysters from the deep, raving sea?
    Grapes and Greek honey?
Beads of black caviare from the Caspian?
    Rock melon with corn on the cob in?
*Take it all away!* grumbled the old King of Cornwall.
    *Bring me some figgie hobbin!*

Devilled lobster, your majesty?
    Scots kail brose or broth?
Grilled mackerel with gooseberry sauce?
    Cider ice that melts in your mouth?
Pears filled with nut and date salad?
    Christmas pudding with a tanner or a bob in?
*Take it all away!* groused the old King of Cornwall.
    *Bring me some figgie hobbin!*

Amber jelly, your majesty?
    Passion fruit flummery?
Pineapple sherbet, milk punch or Pavlova cake,
    Sugary, summery?
Carpet-bag steak, blueberry grunt, cinnamon crescents?
    Spaghetti as fine as the thread on a bobbin?
*Take it all away!* grizzled the old King of Cornwall.
    *Bring me some figgie hobbin!*

So in from the kitchen came figgie hobbin,
    Shining and speckled with raisins sweet,
And though on the King of Cornwall's land
    The rain it fell and the wind it beat,
As soon as a forkful of figgue hobbin
    Up to his lips he drew,
Over the palace a pure sun shone
    And the sky was blue.
*THAT'S what I wanted!* he smiled, his face
    Now as bright as the breast of the robin.
*To cure the sickness of the heart, ah—*
    *Bring me some figgie hobbin!*

    *figgie hobbin*  a Cornish pudding made with raisins

## Colonel Fazackerley

Colonel Fazackerley Butterworth-Toast
Bought an old castle complete with a ghost,
But someone or other forgot to declare
To Colonel Fazack that the spectre was there.

On the very first evening, while waiting to dine,
The Colonel was taking a fine sherry wine,
When the ghost, with a furious flash and a flare,
Shot out of the chimney and shivered, 'Beware!'

Colonel Fazackerley put down his glass
And said, 'My dear fellow, that's really first class!
I just can't conceive how you do it at all.
I imagine you're going to a Fancy Dress Ball?'

At this, the dread ghost gave a withering cry.
Said the Colonel (his monocle firm in his eye),
'Now just how you do it I wish I could think.
Do sit down and tell me, and please have a drink.'

The ghost in his phosphorous cloak gave a roar
And floated about between ceiling and floor.
He walked through a wall and returned through a pane
And backed up the chimney and came down again.

Said the Colonel, 'With laughter I'm feeling quite weak!'
(As trickles of merriment ran down his cheek).
'My house-warming party I hope you won't spurn.
You *must* say you'll come and you'll give us a turn!'

At this, the poor spectre—quite out of his wits—
Proceeded to shake himself almost to bits.
He rattled his chains and he clattered his bones
And he filled the whole castle with mumbles and moans.

But Colonel Fazackerley, just as before,
Was simply delighted and called out, 'Encore!'
At which the ghost vanished, his efforts in vain,
And never was seen at the castle again.

'Oh dear, what a pity!' said Colonel Fazack.
'I don't know his name, so I can't call him back.'
And then with a smile that was hard to define,
Colonel Fazackerley went in to dine.

## Infant Song

Don't you love my baby, mam,
Lying in his little pram,

Polished all with water clean,
The finest baby ever seen?

*Daughter, daughter, if I could
I'd love your baby as I should,*

*But why the suit of signal red,
The horns that grow out of his head,*

*Why does he burn with brimstone heat,
Have cloven hooves instead of feet,*

*Fishing hooks upon each hand,
The keenest tail that's in the land,*

*Pointed ears and teeth so stark
And eyes that flicker in the dark?*

Don't you love my baby, mam?

*Dearest, I do not think I can.
I do not, do not think I can.*

## I am the Song

I am the song that sings the bird.
I am the leaf that grows the land.
I am the tide that moves the moon.
I am the stream that halts the sand.
I am the cloud that drives the storm.
I am the earth that lights the sun.
I am the fire that strikes the stone.
I am the clay that shapes the hand.
I am the word that speaks the man.

# JOHN HEATH-STUBBS
## 1918–

### *The History of the Flood*

Bang Bang Bang
Said the nails in the Ark.

It's getting rather dark
Said the nails in the Ark.

For the rain is coming down
Said the nails in the Ark.

And you're all like to drown
Said the nails in the Ark.

Dark and black as sin
Said the nails in the Ark.

So won't you all come in
Said the nails in the Ark.

But only two by two
Said the nails in the Ark.

So they came in two by two,
The elephant, the kangaroo,
And the gnu,
And the little tiny shrew.

Then the birds
Flocked in like wingèd words:
Two racket-tailed motmots, two macaws,
Two nuthatches and two
Little bright robins.

And the reptiles: the gila monster, the slow-worm,
The green mamba, the cottonmouth and the alligator—
All squirmed in;
And after a very lengthy walk,
Two giant Galapagos tortoises.

And the insects in their hierarchies:
A queen ant, a king ant, a queen wasp, a king wasp,
A queen bee, a king bee,
And all the beetles, bugs, and mosquitoes,
Cascaded in like glittering, murmurous jewels.

But the fish had their wish;
For the rain came down.
People began to drown:
The wicked, the rich—
They gasped out bubbles of pure gold,
Which exhalations
Rose to the constellations.

So for forty days and forty nights
They were on the waste of waters
In those cramped quarters.
It was very dark, damp and lonely.
There was nothing to see, but only
The rain which continued to drop.
It did not stop.

So Noah sent forth a Raven. The raven said 'Kark!
I will not go back to the Ark.'
The raven was footloose,
He fed on the bodies of the rich—
Rich with vitamins and goo.
They had become bloated,
And everywhere they floated.
The raven's heart was black,
He did not come back.
It was not a nice thing to do:

Which is why the raven is a token of wrath,
And creaks like a rusty gate
When he crosses your path; and Fate
Will grant you no luck that day:
The raven is fey:
You were meant to have a scare.
Fortunately in England
The raven is rather rare.

Then Noah sent forth a dove
She did not want to rove.
She longed for her love—
The other turtle dove—
(For her no other dove!)
She brought back a twig from an olive-tree.
There is no more beautiful tree
Anywhere on the earth,
Even when it comes to birth
From six weeks under the sea.

She did not want to rove.
She wanted to take her rest,
And to build herself a nest
All in the olive grove.
She wanted to make love.
She thought that was the best.

The dove was not a rover;
So they knew that the rain was over.
Noah and his wife got out
(They had become rather stout)
And Japhet, Ham, and Shem.
(The same could be said of them.)
They looked up at the sky.
The earth was becoming dry.

Then the animals came ashore—
There were more of them than before:
There were two dogs and a litter of puppies;
There were a tom-cat and two tib-cats

And two litters of kittens—cats
Do not obey regulations;
And, as you might expect,
A quantity of rabbits.

God put a rainbow in the sky.
They wondered what it was for.
There had never been a rainbow before.
The rainbow was a sign;
It looked like a neon sign—
Seven colours arched in the skies:
What should it publicize?
They looked up with wondering eyes.

It advertises Mercy
Said the nails in the Ark.
Mercy Mercy Mercy
Said the nails in the Ark.

Our God is merciful
Said the nails in the Ark.

Merciful and gracious
Bang Bang Bang Bang.

## The Kingfisher

When Noah left the Ark, the animals
Capered and gambolled on the squadgy soil,
Enjoying their new-found freedom; and the birds
Soared upwards, twittering, to the open skies.
But one soared higher than the rest, in utter ecstasy,
Till all his back and wings were drenched
With the vivid blue of heaven itself, and his breast scorched
With the upward-slanting rays of the setting sun.
When he came back to earth, he had lost the Ark;
His friends were all dispersed. So now he soars no more;
A lonely bird, he darts and dives for fish,
By streams and pools—places where water is—
Still searching, but in vain, for the vanished Ark
And rain-washed terraces of Ararat.

### The Jays

Two jays came down my street.
I heard them screeching, mate to his mate.
They kept well under cover, in hedges and shrubbery,—

The bright, conspicuous, winged with azure,
Cinnamon-coloured birds.
I guess they were casing the joint.

# SPIKE MILLIGAN
## 1918–

### Bad Report—Good Manners

My daddy said, 'My son, my son,
This school report is bad.'
I said, 'I did my best I did,
My dad my dad my dad.'

'Explain, my son, my son,' he said,
'Why *bottom* of the class?'
'I stood aside, my dad my dad,
To let the others pass.'

# WILLIAM JAY SMITH
## 1918–

### The Toaster

A silver-scaled Dragon with jaws flaming red
Sits at my elbow and toasts my bread.
I hand him fat slices, and then, one by one,
He hands them back when he sees they are done.

# YVONNE GREGORY
## 1919–

### *Christmas Lullaby for a New-Born Child*

'Where did I come from, Mother, and why?'
'You slipped from the hand of Morn.
A child's clear eyes have wondered why
Since the very first child was born.'

'What shall I do here, Mother, and when?'
'You'll dream in a waking sleep,
Then sow your dreams in the minds of men
Till the time shall come to reap.'

'What do men long for, Mother, and why?'
'They long for a star's bright rays,
And when they have glimpsed a tiny light
They follow with songs of praise.'

'Where does that star shine, Mother, and when?'
'It glows in the hearts of a few.
So close your eyes, while I pray, dear child,
That the star may shine in you.'


# MAY SWENSON
## 1919–1989

### *The Centaur*

The summer that I was ten—
Can it be there was only one
summer that I was ten? It must

have been a long one then—
each day I'd go out to choose
a fresh horse from my stable

which was a willow grove
down by the old canal.
I'd go on my two bare feet.

But when, with my brother's jack-knife,
I had cut me a long limber horse
with a good thick knob for a head,

and peeled him slick and clean
except a few leaves for the tail,
and cinched my brother's belt

around his head for a rein,
I'd straddle and canter him fast
up the grass bank to the path.

trot aong in the lovely dust
that talcumed over his hoofs,
hiding my toes, and turning

his feet to swift half-moons.
The willow knob with the strap
jouncing between my thighs

was the pommel and yet the poll
of my nickering pony's head.
My head and my neck were mine,

yet they were shaped like a horse.
My hair flopped to the side
like the mane of a horse in the wind.

My forelock swung in my eyes,
my neck arched and I snorted.
I shied and skittered and reared,

stopped and raised my knees,
pawed at the ground and quivered.
My teeth bared as we wheeled

and swished through the dust again.
I was the horse and the rider,
and the leather I slapped to his rump

spanked my own behind.
Doubled, my two hoofs beat
a gallop along the bank,

the wind twanged in my mane,
my mouth squared to the bit.
And yet I sat on my steed

quiet, negligent riding,
my toes standing the stirrups,
my thighs hugging his ribs.

At a walk we drew up to the porch.
I tethered him to a paling,
Dismounting, I smoothed my skirt

and entered the dusky hall.
My feet on the clean linoleum
left ghostly toes in the hall.

*Where have you been?* said my mother.
*Been riding.* I said from the sink,
and filled me a glass of water.

*What's that in your pocket?* she said.
*Just my knife.* It weighted my pocket
and stretched my dress awry.

*Go tie back your hair*, said my mother,
and *Why is your mouth all green?*
*Rob Roy, he pulled some clover
as we crossed the field*, I told her.

# MAX FATCHEN
1920–

## *Hullo, Inside*

Physical-education slides
Show us shots of our insides.
Every day I pat my skin,
'Thanks for keeping it all in.'

# EDWIN MORGAN
1920–

## *The Computer's First Christmas Card*

jollymerry
hollyberry
jollyberry
merryholly
happyjolly
jollyjelly
jellybelly
bellymerry
hollyheppy
jollyMolly
merryJerry
merryHarry
hoppyBarry
heppyJarry
boppyheppy
berryjorry
jorryjolly
moppyjelly
Mollymerry
Jerryjolly
bellyboppy
jorryhoppy

h o l l y m o p p y
B a r r y m e r r y
J a r r y h e p p y
h a p p y b o p p y
b o p p y j o l l y
j o l l y m e r r y
m e r r y m e r r y
m e r r y m e r r y
m e r r y C h r i s
a m m e r r y a s a
C h r i s m e r r y
asMERRY CHR
YSANTHEMUM

# GREGORY HARRISON

## *c*.1920

### *The Playground*

Fred Pickering never asked why
It was wrong
To watch the cotton-wool clouds
That floated like neatly-strung
Parcels of smoke
Against the back-cloth of the sky;
And no one spoke,
Only the teacher's
'Pickering'
Flung,
Like the tip of a long whip,
Jerked his head back
To the long,
Over-long,
Long multiplication sum,
Which came out better if you dug your teeth
Into the bony hardness of your thumb.
Fred knew some things well—
You set the sum down wide

To get all the columns of figures inside,
And left lots of room
When you had to divide,
After you'd added;

But he couldn't be sure—
It was all such a jumble in his head—
Whether he should be subtracting instead.
He'd get three out of ten,
But he'd set them down neat
And with luck in ten minutes
The curve of his feet
Would be trapping a ball
Before smashing it hard at the foot of the wall.

It was lovely to feel
The thing flow like a story
Into your feet,
Which lay toe-curled, ball-knowing
Under your seat.

If someone at playtime
Skied the ball
And you lost it in the grimy grass,
You could stand by the railings
And watch the froth fall,
Froth scooped from the river
By the black wind,
Froth which ballooned, skipped,
Sagged drunkenly,
Dipped
And tore itself to little stars
On the spikes of the railings,
Or slimed down the wind-screens of the cars,
Detergent fluff,
Off the greasy water whipped
To flurry and feather
And candy-floss
The old man's creased, coal-veined neck,
The off-pink baby gurgling in the pram.

You could stand by the railings,
Flake the rust with your nail
From the cankered lances,
And sniff smoke from the chemical-works,
Smoke like a yellow feather;
Or bound
Across the yelling asphalt struggle
Of dusty playground
To more bars,
And grit,
A humpbacked pit,
A stilted winding-wheel,
And the steel chuckle,
Of acid tankers buffering
In the sidings
Of a different chemical-works,
Where you can feel
With eyes and nose
The cream stroke
On the edge of the stack
Of the soft, ferret body of smoke.

Fred Pickering,
Back on his own railings,
Back from the country with his wheezy chest,
From the great empty moors,
The green, grey rain;
The stink of the steaming muck-heap,
And the yellow gutters of urine;
The dark nights under the farm rafters,
And the frightening cavern of quiet.
What would the doctor know
Of shunting trucks,
The smell of the smoke,
Telly and a bag of chips,
The river and the froth,
Mates in the playground,
And the curve of the ball
On your foot,
And the bell,

And even sums—
You know about sums,
And getting them wrong,
You cough a bit,
But you know.

# LESLIE NORRIS

1921–

## *Mice in the Hay*

out of the lamplight
  *whispering worshipping*
the mice in the hay

timid eyes pearl-bright
  *whispering worshipping*
whisking quick and away

they were there that night
  *whispering worshipping*
smaller than snowflakes are

quietly made their way
  *whispering worshipping*
close to the manger

yes, they were afraid
  *whispering worshipping*
as the journey was made

from a dark corner
  *whispering worshipping*
scuttling together

But He smiled to see them
  *whispering worshipping*
there in the lamplight

stretched out His hand to them
   they saw the baby king
hurried back out of sight
   *whispering worshipping*


# RICHARD WILBUR

## 1921–

### *'What is the opposite of* nuts?'

What is the opposite of *nuts*?
It's *soup*! Let's have no ifs or buts.
In any suitable repast
The soup comes first, the nuts come last.
Or that is what *sane* folk advise;
You're nuts if you think otherwise.


# VERNON SCANNELL

## 1922–

### *The Apple-raid*

Darkness came early, though not yet cold:
Stars were strung on the telegraph wires;
Street lamps spilled pools of liquid gold;
The breeze was spiced with garden fires.

That smell of burnt leaves, the early dark.
Can still excite me but not as it did
So long ago when we met in the park—
Myself, John Peters and David Kidd.

We moved out of town to the district where
The lucky and wealthy had their homes
With garages, gardens, and apples to spare
Clustered in the trees' green domes.

We chose the place we meant to plunder
And climbed the wall and tip-toed through
The secret dark. Apples crunched under
Our feet as we moved through the grass and dew.

We found the lower boughs of a tree
That were easy to reach. We stored the fruit
In pockets and jerseys until all three
Boys were heavy with their tasty loot.

Safe on the other side of the wall
We moved back to town and munched as we went.
I wonder if David remembers at all
That little adventure, the apples' fresh scent.

Strange to think that he's fifty years old.
That tough little boy with scabs on his knees;
Stranger to think that John Peters lies cold
In an orchard in France beneath apple trees.

## Hide and Seek

Call out. Call loud: 'I'm ready! Come and find me!'
The sacks in the toolshed smell like the seaside.
They'll never find you in this salty dark,
But be careful that your feet aren't sticking out.
Wiser not to risk another shout.
The floor is cold. They'll probably be searching
The bushes near the swing. Whatever happens
You mustn't sneeze when they come prowling in.
And here they are, whispering at the door;
You've never heard them sound so hushed before.
Don't breathe. Don't move. Stay dumb. Hide in your blindness.
They're moving closer, someone stumbles, mutters;
Their words and laughter scuffle, and they're gone.
But don't come out just yet; they'll try the lane
And then the greenhouse and back here again.
They must be thinking that you're very clever,
Getting more puzzled as they search all over.

It seems a long time since they went away.
Your legs are stiff, the cold bites through your coat;
The dark damp smell of sand moves in your throat.
It's time to let them know that you're the winner.
Push off the sacks. Uncurl and stretch. That's better!
Out of the shed and call to them. 'I've won!
Here I am! Come and own up I've caught you!'
The darkening garden watches. Nothing stirs.
The bushes hold their breath; the sun is gone.
Yes, here you are. But where are they who sought you?

## Poem on Bread

The poet is about to write a poem;
He does not use a pencil or a pen.
He dips his long thin finger into jam
Or something savoury preferred by men.
This poet does not choose to write on paper;
He takes a single slice of well-baked bread
And with his jam or marmite-nibbed forefinger
He writes his verses down on that instead.
His poem is fairly short as all the best are.
When he has finished it he hopes that you
Or someone else—your brother, friend or sister—
Will read and find it marvellous and true.
If you can't read, then eat: it tastes quite good.
If you do neither, all that I can say
Is he who needs no poetry or bread
Is really in a devilish bad way.

# JAMES KIRKUP
## 1923–

### *Scarecrows*

Where I live, there are more
scarecrows than human beings.
They would not lift their hats
even if the Queen passed by.

A scarecrow is born old
and stupid. The birds
steal the seeds at his foot.
They know he can't kick back.

The autumn sparrows flit
from one scarecrow to the next.
Their rags and bones are
covered with falling leaves.

And once the harvest's in,
the scarecrow's no more use.
Winter comes, and the crows
perch on his battered straw hat.

Never ask a scarecrow
if he's feeling cold.
The pitiless wind and rain
have numbed him to the bone.

He seems to sleep standing.
The farmer goes to check
if he's still awake, and
kicks him just to make sure.

In the icy moonlight he looks
like some poor lost child.
And when it's raining
he almost seems human.

He turns his back on
the rays of the setting sun.
But his twisted shadow stretches
right across the lane.

Even a silly scarecrow
still has a nose and a mouth
and his big round eyes—more
frightening than any human's.

The old country folk here
are all bent and thin:
ashamed to be seen standing
next to their scarecrow ghosts.


# JOAN AIKEN

## 1924–

### *Palace Cook's Tale*

The two little princesses
live in this palace
large as the whole of Birmingham
they aren't allowed to meet
except for five minutes every day
they are not allowed to play.

I take up their midmorning snack
a glass of buttermilk and a piece of hardtack.

Stick primroses through all the holes in a colander
you will have some notion
of their pretty ways;
yellowhaired they are, pale as the sky;
poor little dears, they hardly seem human
their smiles are like
thin thin slices of lemon.

I take up their teatime tray
black bread and a glass of whey.

They write each other letters
Dear Queenie, Dearest Regina
I was so happy to see you today
we smiled at each other
you borrowed my copy of *The Borrowers*
I think I heard you practising the piano
from far away.

Poor little things
when they grow up they will marry foreign kings.


## Do It Yourself

Buy our little magazine
Quite the smallest ever seen
Printed on a square of tissue
Just
One
Letter
In
Each
Issue.
With each issue, given free
A seed pearl and a pinch of tea.

Thread the seed pearl, save the pinch,
Make a necklace, inch by inch,
Fill a warehouse, ton by ton,
Save the letters, one by one,

Lay
The
Letters
In
A
Row
Make the rhyme you're reading now

# JAMES BERRY
## 1924–

### *Girls Can We Educate We Dads?*

Listn the male chauvinist in mi dad—
a girl walkin night street mus be bad.
He dohn sey, the world's a free place
for a girl to keep her unmolested space.
Instead he sey—a girl is a girl.

He sey a girl walkin swingin hips about
call boys to look and shout.
He dohn sey, if a girl have style
she wahn to sey, look
I okay from top to foot.
Instead he sey—a girl is a girl.

Listn the male chauvinist in mi dad—
a girl too laughy-laughy look too glad-glad
jus like a girl too looky-looky roun
will get a pretty satan at her side.
He dohn sey—a girl full of go
dohn wahn stifle talent comin on show.
Instead he sey—a girl is a girl.

## One

Only one of me
and nobody can get a second one
from a photocopy machine.

Nobody has the fingerprints I have.
Nobody can cry my tears, or laugh my laugh
or have my expectancy when I wait.

But anybody can mimic my dance with my dog.
Anybody can howl how I sing out of tune.
And mirrors can show me multiplied
many times, say, dressed up in red
or dressed up in grey.

Nobody can get into my clothes for me
or feel my fall for me, or do my running.
Nobody hears my music for me, either.

I am just this one.
Nobody else makes the words
I shape with sound, when I talk.

But anybody can act how I stutter in a rage.
Anbody can copy echoes I make.
And mirrors can show me multiplied
many times, say, dressed up in green
or dressed up in blue.

# RUSSELL HOBAN
## 1925–

## *The Pedalling Man*

We put him on the roof and we painted him blue,
And the pedalling man knew what to do—
He just pedalled, yes he pedalled:
He rode through the night with the wind just right
And he rode clear into the morning,
Riding easy, riding breezy, riding
Slow in the sunrise and the wind out of the east.

A weathervane was what he was—
Cast-iron man with a sheet-iron propeller, riding a
Worm gear, holding a little steering wheel,
Iron legs pumping up and down—show him a
Wind and he'd go. Work all day and
All his pay was the weather. Nights, too,
We'd lie in bed and hear him
Creak up there in the dark as he
Swung into the wind and worked up speed,
Humming and thrumming so you could
Feel it all through the house—
The more wind, the faster he went, right through
Spring, summer, and fall.

He rode warm winds out of the south,
Wet winds out of the east, and the
Dry west winds, rode them all with a
Serious iron face. Hard-nosed, tight-mouthed
Yankee-looking kind of an iron man.
'Show me a wind and I'll go,' he said.
'I'm a pedalling fool and I'm heading for weather.'
The weather came and he kept on going, right into
Winter, and the wind out of the north and no let-up—
We lived on a hill, and wind was what we got a lot of.

Then a night came along, and a blizzard was making,
Windows rattling and the whole house shaking,
But the iron man just hummed with the blast,
Said, 'Come on, wind, and come on fast,
Show me your winter, make it nice and cool,
Show me your weather—I'm a pedalling fool!'
Gears all spinning, joints all shivering,
Sheet-iron clattering, cast-iron quivering till WHOMP!
The humming stopped, and we all sat up in bed with
Nothing to listen to but the wind right through into morning.

And there he was when we dug him out, propeller all bent.
One eye in the snow and one eye
Staring up at the sky, still looking for weather.
He never let on he was beat, not him.

Well, my father put him up on the roof again, this time
Without the propeller.
'Let him ride easy,' he said. 'A man can only take
Just so much north wind, even if he's iron.'

## Small, Smaller

I though that I knew all there was to know
Of being small, until I saw once, black against the snow,
A shrew, trapped in my footprint, jump and fall
And jump again and fall, the hole too deep, the walls too tall.

# JAMES K. BAXTER
## 1926–1972

## The Firemen

*Clang! Clang! Clang!*
Says the red fire bell—
'There's a big fire blazing
At the Grand Hotel!'

The firemen shout
As they tumble out of bed
And slide down the pole
To the fire engine shed.

The fire engine starts
With a cough and a roar
And they all climb aboard
As it shoots from the door.

The firemen's helmets,
The ladders and hoses,
Are brassy and bright
As a jug full of roses.

*Whee! Whee! Whee!*—
You can hear the cry
Of the siren shrieking
As they hurtle by.

At the Grand Hotel
There is smoke and steam,
Flames at the windows
And people who scream.

The biggest fireman
Carries down
A fat old lady
In her dressing gown.

When the fire is finished
The firemen go
Back through the same streets
Driving slow.

Home at the station
The firemen stay
And polish up the nozzles
For the next fire day.

## *Twenty Little Engines*

Twenty little engines
Whistling in the yard—
One lost his whistle
And he cried SO hard

That every little engine
STOPPED in the yard
And the stationmaster ran
And BELLOWED to the guard,

'Tommy's lost his whistle,
His long, loud whistle,
And no one can shunt
When he's crying SO hard.'

The guard said 'WHAT?'
And the guard said, 'WHO?'
I've a brand new whistle
That I think will do;

'It's made of copper
And it's made of tin;
There's a hole at the bottom
Where the steam goes in;

'There's a hole at the top
Where the steam goes out,
Just like the whistle
On a tea kettle spout.

'It goes—*Peep! Peep!*
And it goes—*Hoo! Hoo!*
It's just the kind of whistle
That will do for you.'

Twenty little engines
Shunting in the sun—
Tommy got his whistle
and the work WAS DONE.

# ELIZABETH JENNINGS
## 1926–

### *The Ugly Child*

I heard them say I'm ugly.
I hoped it wasn't true.
I looked into the mirror
To get a better view,
And certainly my face seemed
Uninteresting and sad.
I *wish* that either it was good
Or else just very bad.

My eyes are green, my hair is straight,
My ears stick out, my nose
Has freckles on it all the year,
I'm skinny as a hose.
If only I could look as I
Imagine I might be.
Oh, all the crowds would turn and bow.
They don't—because I'm me.

### *Afterthought*

For weeks before it comes I feel excited, yet when it
At last arrives, things all go wrong:
My thoughts don't seem to fit.
I've planned what I'll give everyone and what they'll give to me,
And then on Christmas morning all
The presents seem to be

Useless and tarnished. I have dreamt that everything would come
To life—presents and people too.
Instead of that, I'm dumb,

And people say, 'How horrid! What a sulky little boy!'
And they are right. I *can't* seem pleased.
The lovely shining toy

I wanted so much when I saw it in a magazine
Seems pointless now. And Christmas too
No longer seems to mean

The hush, the star, the baby, people being kind again.
The bells are rung, sledges are drawn,
And peace on earth for men.


# NAOMI LEWIS
## fl. 1983

### *A Footprint on the Air*

'Stay!' said the child. The bird said, 'No,
My wing has mended, I must go.
I shall come back to see you though,
One night, one day—'
                          'How shall I know?'
'Look for my footprint in the snow.'

'The snow soon goes—oh, that's not fair!'
'Don't grieve, Don't grieve. I shall be there
In the bright season of the year,
One night, one day—'
                          'But tell me, where?'
'Look for my footprint on the air.'

# ALASTAIR REID
## 1926–

## *A Spell for Sleeping*

Sweet william, silverweed, sally-my-handsome.
Dimity darkens the pittering water.
On gloomed lawns wanders a king's daughter.
Curtains are clouding the casement windows.
A moon-glade smurrs the lake with light.
Doves cover the tower with quiet.

Three owls whit-whit in the withies.
Seven fish in a deep pool shimmer.
The princess moves to the spiral stair.

Slowly the sickle moon mounts up.
Frogs hump under moss and mushroom.
The princess climbs to her high hushed room,

Step by step to her shadowed tower.
Water laps the white lake shore.
A ghost opens the princess' door.

    Seven fish in the sway of the water.
    Six candles for a king's daughter.
    Five sighs for a drooping head.
    Four ghosts to gentle her bed.
    Three owls in the dusk falling.
    Two tales to be telling.
    One spell for sleeping.

Tamarisk, trefoil, tormentil.
Sleep rolls down from the clouded hill.
A princess dreams of a silver pool.

The moonlight spreads, the soft ferns flitter.
Stilled in a shimmering drift of water,
Seven fish dream of a lost king's daughter.

# MYRA COHN LIVINGSTON
## 1926–

### *Lazy Witch*

Lazy witch,
What's wrong with you?
  Get up and stir your magic brew.
  Here's candlelight to chase the gloom.
  Jump up and mount your flying broom
  And muster up your charms and spells
  And wicked grins and piercing yells.
  It's Halloween! There's work to do!
Lazy witch,
What's wrong with you?

### *Swimming Pool*

Floating, floating weightless
In the nothingness of pool,
I am all wet thoughts.

Water-soaked, whirling hair
Melts into my skin.
I am bathed in blue.

Nothing beneath to feel.
Nothing but sky overhead.
I live outside myself.

## Coming from Kansas

Whenever they come from Kansas
they stay for nearly a week
and they live with Grandma in Council Bluffs
because her house has room enough,
and we go over the day they arrive.
Everyone shouts when they pull in the drive.
We kiss and hug and I get to play
with my cousin Joan most every day
   *and the grown-ups cry when they leave.*

Whenever they say they're coming,
we make a lot of plans.
Joan and I like to put on a play
and we start to write it the very first day.
There're costumes and sets and curtains to do;
we write a part for the neighbor boy, too,
Denny, who comes in the very first scene
to introduce Joan, who's always the queen
   *and I have to be the king.*

And when it's hot in the afternoons
we get a big glass of Kool-Aid
and play cribbage or jacks on the vestibule floor
and Denny, the boy who lives next door,
comes over and dares us to go up the hill
where the cemetery, dark and still,
lies spooky with ghosts. We go before night,
but Denny and Joan always get in a fight
   *and I have to take Joan's side.*

Whenever they come in summer,
Joan tells me about her friends.
She says that Kansas is better, too,
there's always more fun and things to do.

But when we visited there last year
I saw her friends, and they all were queer,
And I told her so, and her face got tight
And then we had a terrible fight
   *and we pulled each other's hair.*

When we go to Grandma's in autumn,
Joan isn't there any more,
And Denny comes over. There's so much to do
like racing down North Second Avenue
or daring each other to slide down the eaves
or sloshing the puddles and jumping in leaves
and if we decide to write out a scene
Denny will always let me be queen
   *and I don't have to bother with Joan!*


# PETER DICKINSON

## 1927–

### *Moses and the Princess*

Ah, ah, ah,
The soldiers came
   Hunting for the baby boy
      And his name was Moses.
His sister took him
   Hid him in the river reeds
      And his name was Moses.

Sleep, my darling,
No such soldiers here.

Ah, ah, ah,
The Princess came
   Found him in the river reeds
      And his name was Moses.
The Princess took him
   Stole away the baby boy
      And his name was Moses.

Sleep, my darling
No such Princess here.

Ah, ah, ah,
His sister saw—
   Do you want a nurse, Princess?
     And his name was Moses.
His mother nursed him
   Never let the Princess know
     And his name was Moses.

Sleep, my darling,
Just your mother here.


# IAIN CRICHTON SMITH
## 1928–

### *The Ghost*

Who is this coming towards you
with his blank face?

Who is this coming towards you
legless yet walking?

Who is this in the evening
without eyes or forehead?

I tell you it's a ghost
on his way nowhere.

The evening empty as drawers
opens in his mind.

Goodbye, then, poor ghost!
Raise your hand to wave to him.

Raise your hand to wave to him,
if you have a hand.

And then walk away from him
if you have any legs.

But the ghost is looking back again
with his astonished eyes.

# THOM GUNN

### 1929—

## *Cannibal*

Shark, with your mouth tucked under
That severs like a knife,
You leave no time for wonder
In your swift thrusting life.

You taste blood. It's your brother's,
And at your side he flits.
But blood, like any other's.
You bite him into bits.

## *The Aquarium*

The dolphins play
Inside their pool all day
And through its bright blue water swing and wheel.
Though on display
They send out on their way
A song that we hear as a long light squeal.

But what they say
Is 'Oh the world is play!
Look at these men we have no cause to thank:
If only they
Would free themselves in play,
As we do even in this confining tank.'

# X. J. KENNEDY

1929–

## Hummingbird

Cried a scientist watching this creature dart by,
'Why its wings are too small for it! How dare it fly?'

So he figured and figured and finally found
That it just couldn't possibly get off the ground,

And they made him Professor. But still, hummingbird
Kept on flying to flowerbeds. It hadn't heard.

## Lighting a Fire

One quick scratch
Of a kitchen match
And giant flames unzip!

How do they store
So huge a roar
In such a tiny tip?

# TED HUGHES

1930–

## I See a Bear

I see a bear
Growing out of a bulb in wet soil licks its black tip
With a pink tongue its little eyes
Open and see a present an enormous bulging mystery package
Over which it walks sniffing at seams

Digging at the wrapping overjoyed holding the joy off
    sniffing and scratching
Teasing itself with scrapings and lickings and the thought of it
And little sips of the ecstasy of it

O bear do not open your package
Sit on your backside and sunburn your belly
It is all there it has actually arrived
No matter how long you dawdle it cannot get away
Shamble about lazily laze there in the admiration of it
With all the insects it's attracted all going crazy
And those others the squirrel with its pop-eyed amazement
The deer with its pop-eyed incredulity
The weasel pop-eyed with envy and trickery
All going mad for a share wave them off laze
Yawn and grin let your heart thump happily
Warm your shining cheek fur in the morning sun

You have got it everything for nothing


## Roe-Deer

In the dawn-dirty light, in the biggest snow of the year
Two blue-dark deer stood in the road, alerted.

They had happened into my dimension
The moment I was arriving just there.

They planted their two or three years of secret deerhood
Clear on my snow-screen vision of the abnormal

And hesitated in the all-way distintegration
And stared at me. And so for some lasting seconds

I could think the deer were waiting for me
To remember the password and sign

That the curtain had blown aside for a moment
And there where the trees were no longer trees, nor the road a road

The deer had come for me.

Then they ducked through the hedge, and upright they rode their legs
Away downhill over a snow-lonely field

Towards tree-dark—finally
Seeming to eddy and glide and fly away up

Into the boil of big flakes.
The snow took them and soon their nearby hoofprints as well

Revising its dawn inspiration
Back to the ordinary.


## Amulet

Inside the wolf's fang, the mountain of heather.
Inside the mountain of heather, the wolf's fur.
Inside the wolf's fur, the ragged forest.
Inside the ragged forest, the wolf's foot.
Inside the wolf's foot, the stony horizon.
Inside the stony horizon, the wolf's tongue.
Inside the wolf's tongue, the doe's tears.
Inside the doe's tears, the frozen swamp.
Inside the frozen swamp, the wolf's blood.
Inside the wolf's blood, the snow wind.
Inside the snow wind, the wolf's eye.
Inside the wolf's eye, the North star.
Inside the North star, the wolf's fang.


## *'Yesterday he was nowhere to be found'*

Yesterday he was nowhere to be found
In the skies or under the skies.

Suddenly he's here—a warm heap
Of ashes and embers, fondled by small draughts.

A star dived from outer space—flared
And burned out in the straw.
Now something is stirring in the smoulder.
We call it a foal.

Still stunned
He has no idea where he is.
His eyes, dew-dusky, explore gloom walls and a glare doorspace.
Is this the world?
It puzzles him. It is a great numbness.

He pulls himself together, getting used to the weight of things
And to that tall horse nudging him, and to this straw.

He rests
From the first blank shock of light, the empty daze
Of the questions—
What has happened? What am I?

His ears keep on asking, gingerly.

But his legs are impatient,
Recovering from so long being nothing
They are restless with ideas, they start to try a few out,
Angling this way and that,
Feeling for leverage, learning fast—

And suddenly he's up

And stretching—a giant hand
Strokes him from nose to heel
Perfecting his outline, as he tightens
The knot of himself.
                              Now he comes teetering
Over the weird earth. His nose
Downy and magnetic, draws him, incredulous,
Towards his mother. And the world is warm
And careful and gentle. Touch by touch
Everything fits him together.

Soon he'll be almost a horse.
He wants only to be Horse,
Pretending each day more and more Horse

Till he's perfect Horse. Then unearthly Horse
Will surge through him, weightless, a spinning of flame
Under sudden gusts,

It will coil his eyeball and his heel
In a single terror—like the awe
Between lightning and thunderclap.

And curve his neck, like a sea-monster emerging
Among foam,

And fling the new moons through his stormy banner,
And the full moons and the dark moons.


## 'Rooks love excitement'

Rooks love excitement. When I walked in under the rookery
A gale churned the silvery, muscular boughs of the beeches, and the
    wet leaves streamed—
It was like a big sea heaving through wreckage—

And the whole crew of rooks lifted off with a shout and floated clear.
I could see the oiled lights in their waterproofs
As the blue spilled them this way and that, and their cries stormed.

Were they shouting at me? What did they fear?
It sounded
More like a packed football stadium, at the shock of a longed-for
    goal—

A sudden upfling of everything, a surfing cheer.

## 'An October robin'

An October robin kept
Stringing its song
On gossamer that snapped.
The weir-pool hung
Lit with honey leaves.
Ploughed hills crisp as loaves

In the high morning.
I waded the river's way
Body and ear leaning
For whatever the world might say
Of the word in her womb
Curled unborn and dumb.

Still as the heron
I let the world grow near
With a ghostly salmon
Hanging in thin air
So real it was holy
And watching seemed to kneel.

And there I saw the vixen
Coiled on her bank porch.
Her paws were bloody sticks.
Ears on guard for her searchers
She had risked a sleep
And misjudged how deep.

# GERARD BENSON
## 1931–

### *The Cat and the Pig*

Once, when I wasn't very big
I made a song about a pig
    Who ate a fig
    And wore a wig
And nimbly danced the Irish jig.

And when I was as small as THAT
I made a verse about a cat
    Who ate a rat
    And wore a hat
And sat (you've guessed) upon the mat.

    And that, I thought, was that.

But yesterday upon my door
I heard a knock; I looked and saw
    A hatted cat
    A wiggèd pig
    Who chewed a rat
    Who danced a jig
    On my door mat!

They looked at me with faces wise
Out of their bright enquiring eyes,
'May we come in? For we are yours,
Pray do not leave us out of doors.
We are the children of your mind
Let us come in. Be kind. Be kind.'

So now upon my fireside mat
There lies a tireless pussy cat
Who all day long chews on a rat
    And wears a hat.
And round him like a whirligig
Dancing a frantic Irish jig
Munching a fig, cavorts a big
    Wig-headed pig.

They eat my cakes and drink my tea.
There's hardly anything for me!
And yet I cannot throw them out
For they are mine without a doubt.

But when I'm at my desk tonight
I'll be more careful what I write.

I'll be more careful what I write.


## Play No Ball

What a wall!
Play No ball,
It tells us all.
Play No Ball,
    By Order!

Lick no lolly.
Skip no rope.
Nurse no dolly.
Wish no hope.
Hop no scotch.
Ring no bell.
Telly no watch.
Joke no tell.
Fight no friend.
Up no make.
Penny no lend.
Hand no shake.

Tyre no pump.
Down no fall.
Up no jump.
Name no call.
  And . . .
Play No Ball.
No Ball. No Ball.
  BY ORDER!


# ALAN BROWNJOHN
## 1931–

### *Common Sense*

An agricultural labourer, who has
A wife and four children, receives 20s a week.
¾ buys food, and the members of the family
Have three meals a day.
How much is that per person per meal?
—*From Pitman's Common Sense Arithmetic, 1917*


A gardener, paid 24s a weeks, is
Fined ⅓ if he comes to work late.
At the end of 26 weeks, he receives
£30.5.3. How
Often was he late?
—*From Pitman's Common Sense Arithmetic, 1917*


A milk dealer buys milk at 3d a quart. He
Dilutes it with 3% water and sells
124 gallons of the mixture at
4d per quarter. How much of his profit is made by
Adulterating the milk?
—*From Pitman's Common Sense Arithmetic, 1917*

The table printed below gives the number
Of paupers in the United Kingdom, and
The total cost of poor relief.
Find the average number
Of paupers per ten thousand people.
—*From Pitman's Common Sense Arithmetic, 1917*

An army had to march to the relief of
A besieged town, 500 miles away, which
Had telegraphed that it could hold out for 18 days.
The army made forced marches at the rate of 18
Miles a day. Would it be there in time?
—*From Pitman's Common Sense Arithmetic, 1917*

Out of an army of 28,000 men,
15% were
Killed, 25% were
Wounded. Calculate
How many men there were left to fight.
—*From Pitman's Common Sense Arithmetic, 1917*

These sums are offered to
That host of young people in our Elementary Schools, who
Are so ardently desirous of setting
Foot upon the first rung of the
Educational ladder . . .
—*From Pitman's Common Sense Arithmetic, 1917*

### 'We are going to see the rabbit'

We are going to see the rabbit,
We are going to see the rabbit,
Which rabbit, people say?
Which rabbit, ask the children?
Which rabbit?
The only rabbit,
The only rabbit in England,
Sitting behind a barbed-wire fence
Under the floodlights, neon lights,

Sodium lights,
Nibbling grass
On the only patch of grass
In England, in England
(Except the grass by the hoardings
Which doesn't count.)
We are going to see the rabbit,
And we must be there on time.

First we shall go by escalator,
Then we shall go by underground,
And then we shall go by motorway
And then by helicopterway,
And the last ten yards we shall have to go
On foot.

And now we are going
All the way to see the rabbit.
We are nearly there,
We are longing to see it,
And so is the crowd
Which is here in thousands
With mounted policemen
And big loudspeakers
And bands and banners,
And everyone has come a long way.
But soon we shall see it
Sitting and nibbling
The blades of grass
On the only patch of grass
In—but something has gone wrong!
Why is everyone so angry,
Why is everyone jostling
And slanging and complaining?

The rabbit has gone,
Yes, the rabbit has gone.
He has actually burrowed down into the earth

And made himself a warren, under the earth.
Despite all these people,
And what shall we do?
What *can* we do?

It is all a pity, you must be disappointed.
Go home and do something else for today,
Go home again, go home for today.
For you cannot hear the rabbit, under the earth.
Remarking rather sadly to himself, by himself,
As he rests in his warren, under the earth:
'It won't be long, they are bound to come,
They are bound to come and find me, even here.'


# GEOFFREY SUMMERFIELD
## 1931–1991

### *Washday Battles*

On washday in the good old bad old days
Before the launderette, machine and drier,
My mother used to use her own bare hands,
A posher, mangle, line, a wooden horse and fire.

At dawn she blew small coals into a blaze
Under well-water in a brim-full copper.
Soon as the water seethed and steamed into a haze
The clothes were seized. They plunged, and came a cropper.

Submerged, they scalded, lunged and tossed,
Squelched by fire-water through and through,
Until she gripped her soggy wooden stick
And levered them, steaming, out, all black and blue,

Carried them soggy and limply dripping,
Chucked them onto the washboard-tub,
Where she set to, and thumped and slapped
And poshed and punched them, rub-a-dub.

Then she grabbed each punch-drunk one in turn
Wrung its neck, squeezed all its juice outright.
Corkscrewed and throttled, flat out it lay, quite dead,
And then she set to again, and beat it white.

Straightaway she fed it to the lion-roaring mangle,
Into tight-rolling rubber lips, which sucked it in
Then slurped it out again, pancaked
To a wafer, breathless, depressed, and thin.

And then she flung them over her arm,
Hauled them out to the windy backyard plot,
Shook them out, cracked them like a whip,
Then strung them up and hanged the lot.

Soon as the wind possessed those wretched shapes,
Their arms would wildly wave, their legs kick free,
The skirts would billow out, voluminous,
And all the washing blew out, flew out, on the spree.

Mimicking Nelson's flags (England expects . . .)
They semaphored 'A Terrible To-do!'
'Clothes Saved From Drowning.' 'All Hands Saved!'
'Housewife Fails Again To Drown This Gallant Crew!'

# KARLA KUSKIN

## 1932–

### *The Witches' Ride*

Over the hills
Where the edge of the light
Deepens and darkens
To ebony night,
Narrow hats high
Above yellow bead eyes,
The tatter-haired witches
Ride through the skies.

Over the seas
Where the flat fishes sleep
Wrapped in the slap of the slippery deep,
Over the peaks
Where the black trees are bare,
Where boney birds quiver
They glide through the air.
Silently humming
A horrible tune,
They sweep through the stillness
To sit on the moon.


# ADRIAN MITCHELL

## 1932–

### *Dumb Insolence*

I'm big for ten years old
Maybe that's why they get at me

Teachers, parents, cops
Always getting at me

When they get at me

I don't hit em
They can do you for that

I don't swear at em
They can do you for that

I stick my hands in my pockets
And stare at them

And while I stare at them
I think about sick

They call it dumb insolence

They don't like it
But they can't do you for it

## Nothingmas Day

No it wasn't.

It was Nothingmas Eve and all the children in Notown were not
tingling with excitement as they lay unawake in their heaps.
D
  o
    w
      n
        s
          t
            a
              i
                r
                  s their parents were busily not placing the last
crackermugs, glimmerslips and sweetlumps on the Nothingmas
Tree.

Hey! But what was that invisible trail of chummy sparks or
vaulting stars across the sky
        Father Nothingmas—drawn by 18 or 21 rainmaidens!
        Father Nothingmas—his sackbut bulging with air!
        Father Nothingmas—was not on his way!
(From the streets of the snowless town came the quiet of
unsung carols and the merry silence of the steeple bell.)

Next morning the children did not fountain out of bed with cries
of WHOOPERATION! They picked up their Nothingmas
Stockings and with traditional quiperamas such as: 'Look what
I haven't got! It's just what I didn't want!' pulled their stockings
on their ordinary legs.

For breakfast they ate—breakfast.

After woods they all avoided the Nothingmas Tree, where
Daddy, his face failing to beam like a leaky torch, was not
distributing gemgames, sodaguns, golly-trolleys, jars of
humdrums and packets of slubberated croakers.

Off, off, off went the children to school, soaking each other with no howls of 'Merry Nothingmas and a Happy No Year!', and not pulping each other with no-balls.

At school Miss Whatnot taught them how to write No Thank You Letters.

Home they burrowed for Nothingmas Dinner.
The table was not groaning under all manner of
    NOT TURKEY
    NO SPICED HAM
    NO SPROUTS
    NO CRANBERRY JELLYSAUCE
    NO NOT NOWT
There was not one (1) shout of glee as the Nothingmas Pudding, unlit, was not brought in. Mince pies were not available, nor was there any demand for them.

Then, as another Nothingmas clobbered to a close, they all haggled off to bed where they slept happily never after.

    and that is not the end of the story . . . . . .

# JOHN UPDIKE

### 1932–

## *January*

The days are short,
    The sun a spark
Hung thin between
    The dark and dark.

Fat snowy footsteps
    Track the floor.
Milk bottles burst
    Outside the door.

The river is
  A frozen space
Held still beneath
  The trees of lace.

They sky is low.
  The wind is gray.
The radiator
  Purrs all day.

## May

Now children may
  Go out of doors,
Without their coats,
  To candy stores.

The apple branches
  And the pear
May float their blossoms
  Through the air,

And Daddy may
  Get out his hoe
To plant tomatoes
  In a row,

And, afterwards,
  May lazily
Look at some baseball
  On TV.

# ALDEN NOWLAN
## 1933–

### *I, Icarus*

There was a time when I could fly. I swear it.
Perhaps, if I think hard for a moment, I can even tell you the year.
My room was on the ground floor at the rear of the house.
My bed faced a window.
Night after night I lay on my bed and willed myself to fly.
It was hard work, I can tell you.
Sometimes I lay perfectly still for an hour before I felt my body rising
      from the bed.
I rose slowly, slowly until I floated three or four feet above the floor.
Then, with a kind of swimming motion, I propelled myself toward the
      window.
Outside, I rose higher and higher, above the pasture, fence, above the
      clothesline, above the dark, haunted trees beyond the pasture.
And, all the time, I heard the music of flutes.
It seemed the wind made this music.
And sometimes there were voices singing.

# ALAN GARNER
## 1934–

### *Summer Solstice*

The mountain's green and shining
And white rocks at the top.
It's the longest day of the year.
It'll never be lighter than this.

I climb in good boots,
Sure on the slopes,
Proof against the wind
And bright against loss,
(These anoraks can be seen at a mile).

Behind me the sun slips.
I climb fast.
It's the longest day of the year.
The mountain's purple, and I reach
The black rocks at the top.
I mean well,
But I can't climb faster
Than the world turns.
It'll never be lighter than this.

# SONIA SANCHEZ

### 1934–

## *To P. J. (2 yrs old who sed write a poem for me in Portland, Oregon)*

if i cud ever write a
poem as beautiful as u
little 2/yr/old/brotha,
i wud laugh, jump, leap
up and touch the stars
cuz u be the poem i try for
each time i pick up a pen and paper.
u. and Morani and Mungu
be our blue/blk/stars that
will shine on our lives and
makes us finally B E.
if i cud ever write a poem as beautiful
as u, little 2/yr/old/brotha,
poetry wud go out of bizness.

## Song No. 3

(FOR 2ND & 3RD GRADE SISTERS)

cain't nobody tell me any different
i'm ugly and you know it too
you just smiling to make me feel better
but i see how you stare when nobody's watching you.

i know i'm short black and skinny
and my nose stopped growin fo it wuz 'posed to
i know my hair's short, legs and face ashy
and my clothes have holes that run right through to you.

so i sit all day long just by myself
so i jump the sidewalk cracks knowing i cain't fall
cuz who would want to catch someone who looks like me
who ain't even cute or even just a little tall.

cain't nobody tell me any different
i'm ugly anybody with sense can see.
but, one day i hope somebody will stop me and say
looka here, a pretty little black girl lookin' just like me.

# TED WALKER

### 1934–

## Owl

'In here,' our teacher said,
    'I have a bird.'
He held a block of wood.
    'Don't be absurd,'
We said, 'that's not a box.'
'If we had several blocks
The same,' he said, 'we could
Have not one bird, but flocks.'

He gave us lumps of oak.
  'All right,' we said.
'We know you like a joke;
  Is your bird dead?'
Miracles happen in schools.
We watched, ignorant fools,
As he began to stroke
His owl alive with tools.

The chips and shavings fell.
  Every feather
He found, and wings, and bill.
  He said, 'Whether
Your owls will live or die,
Whether fall or whether fly,
Depends upon the skill
You learn.' We said we'd try.

### Goldfish in the Garden Pond

Basking close to the sun as they are able,
They turn the afternoon into a fable:
Spillings of rich coins on a miser's table.

# VALERIE WORTH

## 1935−

### Sun

The sun
Is a leaping fire
Too hot
To go near,

But it will still
Lie down
In warm yellow squares
On the floor

Like a flat
Quilt, where
The cat can curl
And purr.

# LUCILLE CLIFTON
## 1936–

### *Listen Children*

listen children
keep this in the place
you have for keeping
always
keep it all ways

we have never hated black

listen
we have been ashamed
hopeless      tired      mad
but always
all ways
we loved us

we have always loved each other
children      all ways

pass it on

### *December*

'The end of a thing
is never the end,
something is always
being born like
a year or a baby.'

'I don't understand,'
Everett Anderson says.
'I don't understand where
the whole thing's at.'

'It's just about Love,'
his Mama smiles.
'It's all about Love and
you know about that.'

# MARGARET MAHY
## 1936–

### The Dictionary Bird

Through my house in sunny weather
Flies the Dictionary Bird
Clear to see on every feather
Is some outlandish word.

'Hugger Mugger' 'gimcrack' 'guava'
'Waggish' 'mizzle' 'swashing rain'
Bird—fly back into my kitchen,
Let me read those words again.

# GARETH OWEN
## 1936–

### Gathering in the Days

I saw my grandad late last evening
On a hillside scything hay
Wiped his brow and gazed about him
Gathering in the day.

My grandmother beside the fireplace
Sleeps the afternoons away
Wakes and stirs the dying embers
Gathering in the day.

Heard screams and laughter from the orchard
Saw a boy and girl at play
Watched them turn their heads towards me
Gathering in the day.

And my mother at a window
On some long-forgotten May
Lifts her eyes and smiles upon us
Gathering in the day.

And all the people I remember
Stopped their lives and glanced my way
Shared the selfsame sun an instant
Gathering in the day.


# JOHN FULLER

## 1937–

### *A Whole New Scene*

God leaned out of himself one day,
Said Hey out there, now what do you say?
I want to do something, I don't know what,
But whatever it is, I want it a lot.
He looked around, said Well, I declare!
There's absolutely nothing there!
He scratched his head and rubbed his chin:
What a predicament I'm in!

I've got to
Make a
Six-day war on chaos,
Six-day war on the Primitive Soup. I've got
Just six days in which to do it,
Six of the best for the empty vacuum,
A week of wonder for a whole new scene.

So God created the firmament
But God only knows what he thought he meant:
He put angels here and angels there
With nothing to do and no one to care.
He looked around, said Bless my soul!
That Satan thinks he's top of the poll.
Can't have him prying into my affairs.
I'll clip his wings and kick him downstairs.
    I've got to
    Make a
Six-day war on pride.
Six-day war on disobedience. I've got
Just six days in which to do it,
Six of the best for the Prince of Darkness.
A week of wonder for a whole new scene.

Then God got back to work and soon
He'd earth and trees and sun and moon.
What an invention! What an invention!
Come along to the World Convention!
Flowers burst open, fishes swim
And little birds fly up to him.
He's put those atoms through their paces
And now they're wearing their birthday faces
    Because he's
    Made a
Six-day war on chaos,
Six-day war on the Great Big Nothing. He had
Just six days in which to do it,
Six of the best (and by God he did it),
A week of wonder for a whole new scene.

# ROGER McGOUGH
### 1937–

## *First Day at School*

A millionbillionwillion miles from home
Waiting for the bell to go. (To go where?)
Why are they all so big, other children?
So noisy? So much at home they
must have been born in uniform.
Lived all their lives in playgrounds.
Spent the years inventing games
that don't let me in. Games
that are rough, that swallow you up.

And the railings.
All around, the railings.
Are they to keep out wolves and monsters?
Things that carry off and eat children?
Things you don't take sweets from?
Perhaps they're to stop us getting out
Running away from the lessins. Lessin.
What does a lessin look like?
Sounds small and slimy.
They keep them in glassrooms.
Whole rooms made out of glass. Imagine.

I wish I could remember my name
Mummy said it would come in useful.
Like wellies. When there's puddles.
Yellowwellies. I wish she was here.
I think my name is sewn on somewhere
Perhaps the teacher will read it for me.
Tea'cher. The one who makes the tea.

## Prayer to Saint Grobianus

(THE PATRON SAINT OF COARSE PEOPLE)

Intercede for us dear saint we beseech thee
   we fuzzdutties and cullions
   dunderwhelps and trollybags
   lobcocks and loobies.

On our behalf seek divine forgiveness for
   we puzzlepates and pigsconces
   ninnyhammers and humgruffins
   gossoons and clapperdudgeons.

Have pity on we poor wretched sinners
   we blatherskites and lopdoodles
   lickspiggots and clinchpoops
   quibberdicks and quakebuttocks.

Free us from the sorrows of this world
and grant eternal happiness in the next
   we snollygosters and gundyguts
   gongoozlers and groutheads
   ploots, quoobs, lurds and swillbellies.

As it was in the beginning, is now, and ever shall be,
world without end. OK?


## The Kleptomaniac

Beware the Kleptomaniac
Who knows not wrong from right
He'll wait until you turn your back
Then steal everything in sight:

The nose from a snowman
(Be it carrot or coal)

The stick from a blindman
From the beggar his bowl

The smoke from a chimney
The leaves from a tree

A kitten's miaow
(Pretty mean you'll agree)

He'll pinch a used teabag
From out of the pot

A field of potatoes
And scoff the whole lot

(Is baby still there,
Asleep in its cot?)

He'll rob the baton
From a conductor on stage

All the books from the library
Page by page

He'll snaffle your shadow
As you bask in the sun

Pilfer the currants
From out of your bun

He'll lift the wind
Right out of your sails

Hold your hand
And make off with your nails

When he's around
Things just disappear

F nnily eno gh I th nk
Th re's one ar und h re!

# ALLAN AHLBERG

1938–

## *Only Snow*

Outside, the sky was almost brown.
The clouds were hanging low.
Then all of a sudden it happened:
The air was full of snow.

The children rushed to the windows.
The teacher let them go,
Though she teased them for their foolishness.
After all, it was only snow.

It was only snow that was falling,
Only out of the sky,
Only onto the turning earth
Before the blink of an eye.

What else could it do from up there,
But fall in the usual way?
It was only *weather*, really.
What else could you say?

The teacher sat at her desk
Putting ticks in a little row,
While the children stared through steamy glass
At the only snow.

## *The Boy without a Name*

I remember him clearly
And it was thirty years ago or more:
A boy without a name.

A friendless, silent boy,
His face blotched red and flaking raw,
His expression, infinitely sad.

Some kind of eczema
It was, I now suppose,
The rusty iron mask he wore.

But in those days we confidently swore
It was from playing near dustbins
And handling broken eggshells.

His hands, of course, and knees
Were similarly scabbed and cracked and dry.
The rest of him we never saw.

They said it wasn't catching: still, we knew
And strained away from him along the corridor,
Sharing a ruler only under protest.

I remember the others: Brian Evans,
Trevor Darby, Dorothy Cutler.
And the teachers: Mrs Palmer, Mr Waugh.

I remember Albert, who collected buttons.
And Amos, frothing his milk up with a straw.
But *his* name, no, for it was never used.

I need a time-machine.
I must get back to nineteen fifty-four
And play with him, or talk, at least.

For now I often wake to see
His ordinary, haunting face, his flaw.
I hope his mother loved him.

Oh, children, don't be crueller than you need.
The faces that you spit on or ignore
Will get you in the end.

## The Trial of Derek Drew

*The charges*

Derek Drew:
For leaving his reading book at home.
For scribbling his handwriting practice.
For swinging on the pegs in the cloakroom.
For sabotaging the girls' skipping.
For doing disgusting things with his dinner.

*Also charged*

Mrs Alice Drew (née Alice Jukes):
For giving birth to Derek Drew.
Mr Dennis Drew:
For aiding and abetting Mrs Drew.
Mrs Muriel Drew and Mr Donald Drew:
For giving birth to Dennis Drew, etc.
Mrs Jane Jukes and Mr Paul Jukes:
For giving birth to Alice Jukes, etc.
Previous generations of the Drew and Jukes families:
for being born, etc., etc.

*Witnesses*

'He's *always* forgetting his book.' Mrs Pine.
'He *can* write neatly, if he wants to.' Ditto.
'I seen him on the pegs, Miss!'
'And me!' 'And me!' Friends of the accused.
'He just kept jumpin' in the rope!' Eight third-year girls
In Miss Hodge's class.
'It was disgusting!' Mrs Foot (dinner-lady).

*For the defence*

'I was never *in* the cloakroom!' Derek Drew.

*Mitigating circumstances*

This boy is ten years old.
He asks for 386 other charges to be taken into consideration.
'He's not like this at home,' his mother says.

*The verdict*
Guilty.

*The sentence*
Life!
*And* do his handwriting again.

# WES MAGEE
## 1939–

### Giant Rocket

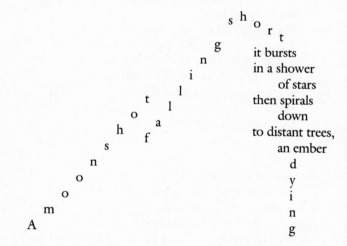

### *How to Reach the Sun . . .*
### *on a Piece of Paper*

Take a sheet of paper
and fold it,
and fold it again,
and again, and again.
By the 6th fold
it is 1 centimetre thick.

By the 11th fold
it will be 32 centimetres thick,
and by the 15th fold
—5 metres.

At the 20th fold
it measures 160 metres.
At the 24th fold,
—2.5 kilometres
and by fold 30
is 160 kilometres high.

At the 35th fold
—5000 kilometres.
At the 43rd fold
it will reach to the moon.

And by fold 52
will stretch from here
        to the sun!
Take a sheet of paper.
Go on.
        Try it!


# JANE YOLEN
## 1939–

### First Robin

As puffed up
as a tag-team wrestler,
he hops around the arena
of our lawn.
Finding a worm,
he slips a half-nelson
on its slim wriggle.
One pull, two, three,
and the worm is up,

then down for the count,
down his winning throat.
He bobs his head
for my applause,
then looks for another worm,
another arena,
before the game is over,
before the crowds
have moved on.

# JACK PRELUTSKY
## 1940–

### Mother Goblin's Lullaby

Go to sleep, my baby goblin,
hushaby, my dear of dears,
if you disobey your mother,
she will twist your pointed ears.

Little goblin, stop complaining,
time for all your eyes to close,
if you make your mother angry,
she will bite your tiny nose.

Slumber sweetly till tomorrow,
do not worry, Mother's near,
dream of demons weirdly screaming,
hushaby, my goblin dear.

# JOHN MOLE

1941–

## *Taking the Plunge*

One day a boy said to a girl in a swimming pool
'I'm going to dive in, are you?' She replied
'No thanks. I bet you can't anyway.' So the boy
got on the diving board and dived and said
'See.' The girl replied 'Flipping eck!'
   (Simon Wilkinson, Margaret Wix Junior School, St Albans)

Flipping eck, cor blimey, strewth,
You're my hero, that's the honest truth.

Lummy, crikey, lordy lord,
It's a long way down from that diving board.

Itchy beard and stone the crows,
Don't you get chlorine up your nose?

Luv a duck and strike me pink,
You're slicker than the soap in the kitchen sink.

Knock me down with a sparrow's feather,
How about us going out together?

Groovy, t'riffic, brill and smashing,
Me 'n' you, we could start things splashing.

Watcha cocky, tara, see ya,
Meet me for a coke in the cafeteria.

Halleluja and Amen,
If you like this poem you can read it again.

## Jack-in-the-Box

Jack-in-the-Box is faithful,
Jack-in-the-Box is true,
But Jack-in-the-Box
Is alone in his box
And Jack-in-the-Box wants you.

Jack-in-the-Box is cunning,
Jack-in-the-Box is sly,
Can Jack-in-the-Box
Get out of his box?
Oh Jack-in-the-Box will try.

## The Trick

One night, when I couldn't sleep,
My dad said
*Think of the tomatoes in the greenhouse*

And I did.
It wasn't the same as counting sheep
Or anything like that.

It was just not being in my room forever
On a hot bed
Restless, turning and turning,

But out there, with the patient gaze of moonlight
Blessing each ripe skin
And our old zinc watering-can with its sprinkler,

Shining through a clear glass pane
Which slowly clouded over into
Drowsy, comfortable darkness

Till I woke and came downstairs to breakfast
Saying *Thank you, Dad,*
*I thought of them. It did the trick.*

# JUDITH NICHOLLS
## 1941–

### *Polar Cub*

This way, that way?
Step out,
little five-toe flat-foot,
squint-eye,
cave-dazed,
into the sun!

*Eyes left,*
*ears right,*
*nose to the wind!*

*The coast is clear!*
Run, roll, lollop;
winter's done!
Enjoy the pause;
make your mark
on this blank page—
the world is yours!

# J. PATRICK LEWIS
## 1942–

### *Stories*

Circling by the fire,
My dog, my rough champion
Coaxes winter out of her fur.
She hears old stories
Leaping in the flames:
The hissing names of cats,
Neighbors' dogs snapping

Like these gone logs,
The cracking of ice . . .
Once, romping through the park,
We dared the creaking pond.
It took the dare and half
Of me into the dark below.
She never let go.

We watch orange tongues
Wagging in the fire
Hush to blue whispers.
Her tail buffs my shoe.
She has one winter left.

Maybe two.

# NIKKI GIOVANNI

## 1943–

### Knoxville, Tennessee

I always like summer
best
you can eat fresh corn
from daddy's garden
and okra
and greens
and cabbage
and lots of
barbecue
and buttermilk
and homemade ice-cream
at the church picnic
and listen to
gospel music
outside
at the church
homecoming

and go to the mountains with
your grandmother
and go barefooted
and be warm
all the time
not only when you go to bed
and sleep


## poem for my nephew

(BROTHER C. B. SOUL)

i wish i were
a shadow
oh wow! when they put
the light on
me i'd grow
longer and taller and
BLACKER


## basketball

when spanky goes
to the playground all the big boys say
    hey big time—what's happenin'
'cause his big brother plays basketball for their high school
and he gives them the power sign and says
    you got it
but when i go and say
    what's the word
they just say
    your nose is running junior

one day i'll be seven feet tall
even if i never get a big brother
and i'll stuff that sweaty ball down
their laughing throats

# BRIAN PATTEN

## 1946–

### *How the New Teacher Got Her Nickname*

When the new teacher said,
'I'm going to be frank with you,'
I burst out laughing
'What are you laughing about?' she asked.
'It's hard to explain, Frank,' I said.
From that moment on Miss Jones became Frank.
For that, she has me to thank.

# MICHAEL ROSEN

## 1946–

### *This Morning*

This morning my father looks out of the window, rubs his nose
and says: Let's go and saw up logs
me and you.
So I put on my thick blue socks
and he puts on his army vest
and he keeps saying: Are you ready are you ready
It's a snorter of a day just look at the trees
and I run downstairs to get my old bent boots
that everybody says go round corners on their own they're so bent
and he comes in saying that his tobacco is like old straw
which means that he is going to smoke his pipe today
So he says to Mum: We'll be back in an hour or two
which means not for ages
but Mum doesn't hear, because we lumberjacks are out of the door
     in a flash

## Eddie and the Birthday

When Eddie had his second birthday
he got lots of cards,
and he had a cake and all kinds of presents
and we sang Happy Birthday.
'Happy Birthday to you
Happy Birthday to you
Happy Birthday, dear Eddie . . .'
and all that.
He liked that very much
So he goes:
'More. Sing it again.'
So we sang it again.
'Happy Birthday to you
Happy birthday to you
Happy birthday, dear Eddie . . .'
and all that.
And he goes,
'More. Sing it again.'
So we sang it again.
'Happy birthday to you
da de da de da, dear Eddie
da de da to you . . .'
And he goes.
'More. Sing it again.'
It felt like we sang Happy Birthday about
Two hundred and twenty-three times.

And the candles. On the cake.
He loved them.
'Eddie, blow.'
He blew.
And the moment he blew it out
he wanted more.
'More candle.'
So we light it.
'More Eddie blow.'
Eddie blew.

'More candle.'
We light.
'More Eddie blow.'
'More candle.'
That felt like two hundred and twenty-three times as well.

And he loved the cards.
Everyone who sent him a card
seemed to think he'd like one
with pictures of big fat animals.

Elephants and hippos.
He got about ten of them.
Imagine.
Your second birthday
and everyone sends you pictures of
hippopotamuses.
Maybe they think he *is* a hippo.

Anyway he had a nice birthday.
Next day he gets up
comes downstairs
and he looks round
and he goes,
'More happy birfdy.'
So I go,
'That was yesterday, Eddie.'
'More happy birfdy.'
'But it isn't your birfdy – I mean birthday . . .'
'More happy birfdy.'

Now, you don't cross Eddie.
He has rages.
We call them wobblies.
'Look out, he's going to throw a wobbly!'
And the face starts going red,
the arms start going up and down,
the screaming starts winding up
he starts jumping up and down
and there he is—
throwing a wobbly.

So I thought,
'We don't want to have a wobbly over this one.'
So we started singing happy birthday all over again.
Two hundred and twenty-three times.
Then he says
'More candles.'

'We haven't got any,' we say
(Lies, of course, we had).
'More candles . . .'
So out came the candles
and yes—
'Eddie blow.'
He blew.
'More candle.'
And off we go again—
Two hundred and twenty-three times.

And then he says,
'Letters, More.'
Well, of course no one sent him any more,
so while I'm singing more happy birfdy's,
my wife was stuffing all the cards
into envelopes and sticking them down.
So we hand over all his cards again
and out came all the hippopotamuses again.

So he's very pleased.
And that's how Eddie had two birthdays.
Lucky for us
he'd forgotten by the third day.

Maybe he thinks when you're two you have two birthdays
and when you're three you have three birthdays
and when you're seventy-eight you . . .

# MICHAEL ROSEN AND SUSANNA STEELE
## 1948–

### *Humpty Dumpty*

(WRITTEN USING ONLY NAMES FROM THE
TELEPHONE DIRECTORY)

Humm Tee Dim Tay
Sato Nawol
Huntly Dumke
Hudd Agate Fall
Alder King Soss
Isan Dorley Kinsman
Coode Dant Pot
Humphrey Duhig Adda Arr Gaine

# MARLENE NOURBESE PHILIP
## 1947–

### *Oliver Twist*

Oliver Twist can't do this
if so do so
touch your toe under we go
touch the ground and a merry go round,
and mother oh lady says to jump
mother oh grady says to cry
mother oh lady says be white
mother oh grady says be black,
  brown black
  yellow black
  black black
  black pickney stamped English
singing brown skin girl
stay home and mind baby,
growing up la di dah polite

pleasing and thank you ma'am, yet so savage
        union jacked in red
        in white
        in blue
and dyed in black to welcome Her
tiny hand moving slowly backward
slowly forward
painted smile on regal face
from the stately 'buh look how shiny'
black limousine with air conditioned crawl,
and little children faint and drop
black flies in the heat singing
Britons never never never
shall be slaves and
all that land of hope and glory
that was not,
black flies in the heat singing
of Hector and Lysander
and such great names as these,
but of all the world's great heroes
there's none that can compare
with a tow row row row row row
of the British Grenadiers and
little black children
marching past stiffly white bloused
skirted blue
overalled and goin' to one big school
feelin' we self look so proper—
a cut above our parents you know,
man we was black
an' we was proud
we had we independence
an' massa day done,
we goin' to wear dat uniform
perch dat hat
'pon we hot comb head
jus' like all dem school girls
roun' de empire
learning about odes to nightingales
forget hummingbirds,

a king that forgot
Harriet Tubman, Sojourner Truth
and burnt his cakes,
about princes shut in towers
not smelly holds of stinking ships
and pied piper to our blackest dreams
a bastard mother, from her weaned
on silent names of stranger lands.

# CLYDE WATSON

## 1947–

### 'Knickerbocker Knockabout'

Knickerbocker Knockabout
Sausages & Sauerkraut
Run! Run! Run! The hogs are out!
Knickerbocker Knockabout

# BRIAN MORSE

## 1948–

### A Day on the Planet

OR INVASION THWARTED
THE SCHOOL TRIP THAT WENT RIGHT
*For Alan Tucker*

To The Supreme Commander, Sirian Forces,
Solar System

Hail!
Greetings!

We landed, ten and a half hours local time,
at a large habitation, Weston Manor, our spy-ship
reconnoitred in the middle of last Terran winter.
However conditions had changed and
instead of being deserted the grounds were occupied
by a large number of Young Earthlings
being moved about in classes or 'showers'
as they are referred to by the smaller number
of Adult Earthlings who were leading them.

At first it was thought to have become
a correction centre with the young creatures
('school children' as they are called)
being exercised or punished in this random fashion
but we later realized that, on the contrary,
it was the Older Earthlings
(or 'school teachers' as they are called)
being tested or examined.
These school teachers seemed inoffensive
but were armed with weapons such as
'detentions' and 'lines' and 'tell your parents'
which, however, were concealed about their persons.

Taking upon ourselves our disguises
we infiltrated the house
which we found was also occupied by the school children.
They were everywhere and being shouted at
by a different species of school teacher called 'guides',
mainly ill-tempered older women in tweed skirts
with immaculately groomed grey hair,
who expostulated nauseatingly upon
the supposed glories of the Manor,
its pictures, carpets and furniture,
at the same time issuing constant commands
'Not To Touch!'

This made us realize there was danger in these objects
so we abandoned our intention of placing the M.U.S.P.MO.
(Mark IV Ultra Sonic Population Subjugation Module)
on the chair in the dining room

(this Chippendale must be a powerful magician
to command such respect—
if nothing else is learnt from Earth I humbly suggest
we at least investigate the source of his power).
We left it instead on the floor in the entrance hall,
a mistake for it was immediately spotted by an 'idiot'
(singular of 'school children')
who pocketed it.
The idiot no sooner had it in his possession
than he was grabbed by an inside teacher
who told him in a loud whisper
'if there was any more malarkey'
he would be 'out on his neck'
(another terrible Earth punishment).
(On our preliminary visit we, of course,
had no direct contact with the dominant species
especially this aggressive sub-group.)
We assumed appropriate disguises and followed,
though our next glimpse of the M.U.S.P.MO.
came only when the idiot engaged in
bartering it for a bag of something that appeared edible.

There followed a bewildering series of exchanges
in which the Subjugation Module changed pockets
at least ten times, finishing by being exchanged
for a small round coloured glass object,
the purpose of which was not ascertained.
Not only, however, did it pass from one idiot
to another but also from shower to shower.
Twice it was taken back into the house
(the inside teachers were by now even more aggressive—
on a scale from 1 to 7 they were 6.3 and rising).
Finally one of the school teachers (or 'berks')
spotted it being thrown from idiot to idiot
and 'confiscated' it.

Fearing the worst of this 'confiscated' we assumed
even more appropriate disguises.
The school teacher examined, then attempted to open it
with a screwdriver—happily it resisted

all his frenzied assaults,
but remained in his pocket
as he marched his shower here and there
from what he called one 'attraction' to another
until tiring of this game, or perhaps having passed—
or failed—his test (it was difficult to decide which)
he led the school children
to a large multi-windowed motor vehicle
in which another shower was already seated.
We made a last attempt at retrieval.

I ordered storm-trooper Markee
to assume an appropriate disguise
and follow the M.U.S.P.MO. onto the 'coach'
(name of the vehicle).
Unfortunately this began to move off
almost immediately.
The last we saw of Markee
(his emergency beacon continued to broadcast distress calls
for a quarter of an Earth hour)
he was being passed from idiot to idiot
in the backseat of the coach
while being waved with considerable loss of dignity
to the accompaniment of raucous cheers
at the occupants of other coaches.
Random aggression readings on the charge-persons
of these coaches deterred any attempts at following—
any attempt to recover the M.U.S.P.MO. or Markee
would have led to considerable loss of life.
We therefore left Earth
and forward this preliminary report
as we return with all haste to the Mother Vehicle.

# JOHN AGARD
## 1949–

### *Don't Call Alligator Long-Mouth Till You Cross River*

Call alligator long-mouth
call alligator saw-mouth
call alligator pushy-mouth
call alligator scissors-mouth
call alligator raggedy-mouth
call alligator bumpy-bum
call alligator all dem rude word
but better wait
                till you cross river.

### *Poetry Jump-Up*

Tell me if ah seeing right
Take a look down de street

Words dancin
words dancin
till dey sweat
words like fishes
jumpin out a net
words wild and free
joinin de poetry revelry
words back to back
words belly to belly

Come on everybody
come and join de poetry band
dis is poetry carnival
dis is poetry bacchanal
when inspiration call
take yu pen in yu hand
if yu dont have a pen
take yu pencil in yu hand

if you dont have a pencil
what the hell
so long de feeling start to swell
just shout de poem out

Words jumpin off de page
tell me if Ah seeing right
words like birds
jumping out a cage
take a look down de street
words shakin dey waist
words shakin dey bum
words wit black skin
words wit white skin
words wit brown skin
words wit no skin at all
words huggin up words
an saying I want to be a poem today
rhyme or no rhyme
I is a poem today
I mean to have a good time

Words feelin hot hot hot
big words feelin hot hot hot
lil words feelin hot hot hot
even sad words cant help
tappin dey toe
to de riddum of de poetry band
Dis is poetry carnival
dis is poetry bacchanal
so come on everybody
join de celebration
all yu need is plenty perspiration
an a little inspiration
plenty perspiration
an a little inspiration

# RICHARD EDWARDS
## 1949–

### *Recollections of an Old Spook*

Quite a posh old house was this,
Years and years ago,
Red fires crackled in the hearths
Where now tongues of snow
Poke down broken chimney pots
When the rude winds blow.

Quite a posh old house was this,
Solid, waterproof,
Keeping all its gentlefolk
Sheltered and aloof,
Now the common sparrows squat
Cheeping in the roof.

Quite a posh old house was this,
Full of chinless earls
Dressed in frilly shirts of silk
Chasing silly girls
While the powdered chaperones
Twiddled with their pearls.

Quite a posh old house was this,
Now nobody cares,
Perhaps it's just as well to lose
All those snobby airs,
Still, I did enjoy myself:
Haunting down the stairs,

Chasing Lady Otterbourne,
Making Lord Snoot shriek,
Kissing, quite invisibly,
Rosie's rosy cheek—
Now it's just a wandering rat
If the floorboards creak.

Time for me to make a move,
Find a newer place,
Somewhere more appreciative
Of my ghostly grace,
Somewhere snug and double-glazed
With less draughty space.

Where though? Perhaps a penthouse flat
With a city view,
Perhaps a bed-sit, perhaps a pub,
Even digs would do,
Anywhere that's . . . unpossessed . . .
Perhaps I'll call on
You!

# GRACE NICHOLS

## 1950–

### *Wha Me Mudder Do*

Mek me tell you wha me Mudder do
wha me mudder do
wha me mudder do

Me mudder pound plantain mek fufu
Me mudder catch crab mek calaloo stew

Mek me tell you wha me mudder do
wha me mudder do
wha me mudder do

Me mudder beat hammer
Me mudder turn screw
she paint chair red
then she paint it blue

Mek me tell you wha me mudder do
wha me mudder do
wha me mudder do

Me mudder chase bad-cow
with one 'Shoo'
she paddle down river
in she own canoe
Ain't have nothing
dat me mudder can't do
Ain't have nothing
dat me mudder can't do

Mek me tell you


# DOUGLAS FLORIAN
### 1950–

### *First*

First things first,
Last things last.
Hours
          pass
                    slowly.
Years pass fast.


### *Send My Spinach*

Send my spinach
Off to Spain.
Parcel post it
On a train.
Mail it,
Sail it,
On a ship.
Just don't let it
Touch my lip.

# JOY HARJO
## 1951–

### *Remember*

Remember the sky you were born under,
know each of the star's stories.
Remember the moon, know who she is.
Remember the sun's birth at dawn is the
strongest point of time. Remember sundown
and the giving away to night.
Remember your birth, how your mother struggled
to give you form and breath. You are evidence of
her life, and her mother's, and hers.
Remember your father. He is your life, also.
Remember the earth whose skin you are:
red earth, black earth, yellow earth, white earth
brown earth, we are earth.
Remember the plants, trees, animal life who all have their
tribes, their families, their histories, too. Talk to them,
listen to them. They are alive poems.
Remember the wind. Remember her voice. She knows the
origin of this universe.
Remember you are all people and that all people are you.
Remember you are the universe and this universe is you.
Remember all is in motion, is growing, is you.
Remember language comes from this.
Remember the dance language is, that life is.
Remember.

# JON WHYTE
## fl. 1985

### *Coyotes*

The coyotes are howling;
   it's forty below.
The moon is silvering
   shivering snow.

```
                         .ipipip.                                              o
        .pipipipi      ipi   ipi                                          o oo
Kee   i                        pip                                      o
                                  oo                                  o
          kaiueoo   oooo              yup                          o
              eeee                                              oooo
                                                          o  oo
                                                      ooooo
        eeeeyayayayaya                  ooooo    o oooooo
                            ooooooo  ooooo    o
ooooooooooooo        ooooooo                                   ap
              puka                                          ap  ap
                  aa                                           ap
                    aa                                           ap ap
                      a                                            ap
          kee                              kyip
             oo haha                                  haa
                   ha  hahahaahaa
```

How many coyotes
do you think there are?
One for the moon
and one for each star.

```
                  oooouiiiiui   w w w w wa
aueeeeoooo                     wa a a a a  wa      i
                                            i i ii ii ii  a
                                            a a a a a
          yute yiee                         a
      eae       yeet yite
         ee
           ee eee
              ee   eeee            eee c
                       eeee  ee
                           ee
```

The coyotes are crying;
   the night is awake
with their crying at midnight
   on the frozen lake.

# MICK GOWAR
## 1951–

## *Rat Trap*

Do you know the story of Hamelin Town?
How the Pied Piper came in his coloured gown
And piped the plague of rats away;
And then, double-crossed, lured the children from play
Through a mountain door to a land far away?
'A pretty good story,' you'd probably say.
'But believe it? You're joking!
What, *me*? Get away!'

But every story that's ever been told
Has a kernel of truth—like a nugget of gold
Encased in base rock—this tale's no exception.
So sit up straight and pay attention,
And I'll tell you a version of what I think may
Have happened in Hamelin that fateful day
When the piper strode out and started to play.

To begin at the beginning . . .

Hamelin Town was a shambles,
Hamelin Town was a dump;
The prices were soaring in all of the shops
And no one had any idea where they'd stop.
The place was deep in a slump.

And why? Because of the taxes!
There was a tax on windows, a tax on doors;
A tax on roofs, a tax on floors;
A tax on heads, a tax on hats;
A tax on trousers, a tax on spats;
There was even a tax on dogs and cats!
To get to the real nitty-gritty:
Hamelin Town was *Bad Time City*.

But not everyone was depressed and blue;
Not everyone was malcontent.
One group of people were quite content.
Can you guess who?
Where do you think the taxes went?

Yes, the mayor and the aldermen strolled around town
In silken stockings and ermine gowns.
The mayor and his mates had their hands in the till,
But behind their backs the curses rang shrill!
The citizens held a big demonstration;
They yelled: 'Down with the mayor and the corporation!
Let's boot them all out!
They're the absolute pits!
They're as bent as a purse full of nine-guilder bits!'

The mayor called a special council meeting.
He said, 'Listen to that: we're in for a beating!
We'd better face facts, lads, we're in disgrace.
We've made a pig's ear out of running this place!'

All his cronies looked glum, as well they should.
'Unless . . .' said the mayor, 'unless we could . . .'
Somewhere deep in his sneaky mind
An idea was forming. 'Unless we can find
A scapegoat, a whipping-boy of some kind?'
He was interrupted by scratching and squealing
From over their heads; there were *rats* in the ceiling!

'That's it!' cried the mayor. 'We'll blame the rats!'
'The *what*?' asked the burghers. 'The rats! The rats!'
Yelled the mayor. 'Why, only the other day
I overheard a physician say
That rats caused the plague we had last May!'
The councillors all guffawed and teeheed.
'Stupid, I know,' the mayor agreed.
'But if people will swallow nonsense like that
They'll believe in our *new plague*—
A great plague of rats!'

So, on to the balcony strode the mayor,
And started to speak to the crowd in the square:
'Dear friends, hear me out. I have something to say.
Don't boo, please don't hiss—
I have come here today
To tell you of something so utterly vile
It makes the blood boil, it curdles the bile!
Our beautiful town is caught in the grip
Of a great plague of rats. They came on a ship
From a far foreign land. And *that* is the cause
Of your mouldering houses—the plague rats have gnawed
All the wealth of our city! It's the God's truth, I swear!
Only one man can save you: yours truly, the mayor!'

Some words have the power to make the skin creep,
Like 'snake', 'worm' and 'vampire bat'.
Somewhere down deep, just the word chills the blood,
Sets the nerve-endings twitching.
For example: say 'flea' and who *doesn't* start itching.
Thus it happened that day, when the mayor blamed the rats,
A thousand spines chilled, and beneath all their hats
The townsfolk's hair rose.
But then up spoke one voice:
'Don't trust him again! Don't squander your choice!
A rat plague! What phooey!
It's a lie, don't you see?
Who's seen all these thousands of rats? Not me!'

'*Aha!*' yelled the mayor.
'That just shows, don't you see,
How cunning your average rat can be!
They're hiding in corners and lurking in lofts,
Making their plans and hatching their plots,
And breeding lots and lots and *lots*
Of baby rats. While we wait in dread
For the rats to murder us all in our beds!'

So off went the crowd, started spreading the word . . .

And the mayor's plan worked *too* well,
It was quite absurd:
Reports flooded in of
Rats in flats and rats in houses,
Rats found nesting in frocks and trousers,
Rats in sheds and rats in tents,
Rats in the Ladies, rats in the Gents.
The town went rat-mad that very same day:
Rat Paranoia ruled, O K!

A new demonstration formed in the square,
Demanding that something be done then and there
To save Hamelin Town from doom and despair.
The councillors met once again. Said the mayor:
'We need a solution to this plague we've been faking.
We're stuck in a rat trap of our own making!
We need the best rat-catcher money can buy.
Has anyone any ideas? Come on, *try*!'

The burghers all frowned. Then a low voice said, 'I
Can solve all your problems, don't worry. So why
Not give me a chance?' The burghers turned round
And saw a strange man in a long coloured gown.
'Who are *you*?' asked the mayor.
'The Pied Piper,' said he,
'Street theatre, kid's parties—and for a small fee
I'll find your rats. I've a workable plan
To mobilize all of the boys in your land.
You've brought them all up to be tough, hard and fit.
*They'll* kill all the rats, if encouraged a bit.
For boys will be boys, as has often been said,
So we'll form a Town Rat Corps, with me at the head.
Give each lad a badge, a stick and a trap—
Leave the training to me, don't panic and flap.
Just trust me: we'll have a great Rat-killing Day,
And the mayor can give prizes . . . well, what do you say?'
'You're hired!' said the mayor. 'Let's get started, today!'

So posters were printed, and handbills were sent
To all of the schools:
      'The Great Ratting Event!
Catch a rat for the good of your school and your town!
And on Saturday week, get a stick—come on down
To the banks of the Weser, for the great jamboree
And Rat-killing Bash-up, and barbecue—free!'

With the Piper in front, the procession set out:
Each boy had a rat, and a stick broad and stout.
On the banks of the Weser, the rats were let out.
Each boy grasped his stick.

It would make me quite sick
To describe how the rats—yes, vermin, I know—
Were slaughtered that day. And how, with each blow,
A taste for blood-letting started to grow.

And then, at the very end of the show
The Piper said: 'Pay me!'
The mayor said: 'No!'

'Stop!' yelled the Piper. 'Boys, listen to me!
The rats are all dead—but the rat-*men* are free!
Yes, the rats were mere agents, their masters you see
Here, standing before you!
So, boys, follow me!
Let's finish the job we started today:
Cleanse Hamelin Town properly!
What do you say?'

A forest of sticks was raised in salute.
In reply, the Piper lifted his flute . . .
'I give in,' said the mayor. 'I'll pay you your fee.
But first, our dear children. You must set them free
From this terrible spell.
Just look at them—there!
How their lips seem to snarl,
How their eyes seem to stare.'
The Piper just grinned: 'Some things can't be undone:
We've taught them the pleasure of killing for *fun*.

Yes, you and I, mayor, must both share the blame,
For your dearly loved children will not be the same.
You have lost both your rats and your sons here today!
So, goodbye, Mr Mayor. I must be on my way.
All these souls! Many thanks!
I must bid you farewell . . .'

And so saying, the Devil
                                went
                                     back
                                          down
                                               to
                                                    Hell.


# PAUL FLEISCHMAN

## 1952–

### *Fireflies*

#### [FOR TWO VOICES]

| | |
|---|---|
| Light | Light |
| | is the ink we use |
| Night | Night |
| is our parchment | |
| | We're |
| | fireflies |
| fireflies | flickering |
| flitting | |
| | flashing |
| fireflies | |
| glimmering | fireflies |
| | gleaming |
| glowing | |
| Insect calligraphers | Insect calligraphers |
| practicing penmanship | |
| | copying sentences |
| Six-legged scribblers | Six-legged scribblers |
| of vanishing messages, | |

fleeting graffiti
Fine artists in flight

bright brush strokes
Signing the June nights
as if they were paintings
We're
fireflies
flickering
fireflies.

Fine artists in flight
adding dabs of light

Signing the June nights
as if they were paintings

flickering
fireflies
fireflies.

# GARY SOTO

1952–

## *Teaching Numbers*

The moon is one,
The early stars a few more . . .
The sycamore is lean
With sparrows, four perhaps,
Three hunched like hoods
And one by itself,
Wiping a beak
In the rag of its shoulder.

From where we sit
We could count to a thousand
By pointing at oranges
On trees, bright lanterns
Against the dusk, globes
Of water that won't come down.

Follow me with this, then:
A stray on two legs
At a trash can, one kite in a tree,
And a couple with four hands,
Three in pockets and one scratching
An ear busy with sound:
Door, cat, scrambling leaf.

(The world understands numbers—
At birth, you're not much
And when lowered into the earth
You're even less, a broken
Toy of 108 bones and 23 teeth
That won't stop laughing.)

But no talk of this
For the dog is happy with an eggshell
And oranges are doing wonders
At this hour in the trees
And there is popcorn to pick
From my smal bowl of hands.

Let's start again,
With numbers that will help.

The moon is one,
The early stars a few more . . .

### Brown Girl, Blonde Okie

Jackie and I cross-legged
In the yard, plucking at
Grass, cupping flies
And shattering them against
Each other's faces—
Smiling that it's summer,
No school, and we can
Sleep out under stars
And the blink of jets
Crossing up our lives.
The flies leave, or die,
And we are in the dark,
Still cross-legged,
Talking not dogs or baseball,
But whom will we love,
What brown girl or blonde

Okie to open up to
And say we are sorry
For our faces, the filth
We shake from our hair,
The teeth without direction.
'We're ugly,' says Jackie
On one elbow, and stares
Lost between jets
At what this might mean.
In the dark I touch my
Nose, trace my lips, and pinch
My mouth into a dull flower.
Oh God, we're in trouble.

# DIONNE BRAND

## 1953–

### *Wind*

I pulled a hummingbird out of the sky one day but let it go,
I heard a song and carried it with me on my cotton streamers,
I dropped it on an ocean and lifted up a wave with my bare hands,
I made a whole canefield tremble and bend as I ran by,
I pushed a soft cloud from here to there,
I hurried a stream along a pebbled path,
I scooped up a yard of dirt and hurled it in the air,
I lifted a straw hat and sent it flying,
I broke a limb from a guava tree,
I became a breeze, bored and tired,
and hovered and hung and rustled and lay where I could.

# JULIE O'CALLAGHAN
## 1954–

### *Taking my Pen for a Walk*

Tonight I took the leash off my pen.
At first it was frightened,
looked up at me with confused eyes, tongue panting.
Then I said, 'Go on, run away,'
and pushed its head.
Still it wasn't sure what I wanted;
it whimpered with its tail between its legs.
So I yelled, 'You're free, why don't you run—
you stupid pen, you should be glad,
now get out of my sight.'
It took a few steps.
I stamped my foot and threw a stone.
Suddenly, it realised what I was saying
and began to run furiously away from me.

# SANDRA CISNEROS
## 1954–

### *Good Hot Dogs*

#### FOR KIKI

Fifty cents apiece
To eat our lunch
We'd run
Straight from school
Instead of home
Two blocks
Then the store
That smelled like steam
You ordered
Because you had the money
Two hot dogs and two pops for here

Everything on the hot dogs
Except pickle lily
Dash those hot dogs
Into buns and splash on
All that good stuff
Yellow mustard and onions
And french fries piled on top all
Rolled up in a piece of wax
Paper for us to hold hot
In our hands
Quarters on the counter
Sit down
Good hot dogs
We'd eat
Fast till there was nothing left
But salt and poppy seeds even
The little burnt tips
Of french fries
We'd eat
You humming
And me swinging my legs

# BILL NEIDJIE

## fl. 1987

### 'This earth'

This earth . . .
I never damage,
I look after.
Fire is nothing,
just clean up.
When you burn,
new grass coming up.
That mean good animal soon . . .
might be goose, long-neck turtle, goanna, possum.
Burn him off . . .
new grass coming up,
new life all over.

# SHONTO BEGAY
## 1954–

### *Mother's Lace*

In the morning when I leave my hogan,
the mesa echoes with cries of birds.
The air is crisp and clean.
It flows through me, washing away
all ills in my spirit.

Down past the dry wash and slickrock,
across an old wagontrail to my holy ground.
This is the season when the mother
wears lace of ice.

As the sun blazes up from the mesa top,
I sprinkle my corn pollen,
tracing the path of the sun,
as prayer silently leaves my lips.
Prayer of humility, prayer of another day.
Prayer for family, for animals, for travelers.
Prayer especially for *hózhó*, for harmony.
My prayer is strong today.

Far above, a young black hawk spirals,
rising with the fog.
My head is clear, my vision bright;
happiness and love dwell in my heart—
this day starts as all days must,
blessed with prayer.

*Beauty before me I walk*
*Beauty behind me I walk*
*Beauty above me I walk*
*Beauty below me I walk*
*Beauty all about me I walk*
*In beauty all is made whole*
*In beauty all is restored.*

*hogan* traditional Navajo dwelling      *mesa* plateau

## MICHAEL SMITH
### 1954–1983

### *Black and White*

Went to an all black school
with an all black name
all black principal
black teacher

graduated
with an all black concept

with our blackety blackety frustration
we did an all black march
with high black hopes
and an all black song

got a few solutions
not all black

went to a show
and saw our struggles
in black and white

Lawwwwwd have mercy

# VALERIE BLOOM
### 1956–

### *Sun-a-shine, Rain-a-fall*

Sun a-shine an' rain a-fall,
The Devil an' him wife cyan 'gree at all,
The two o' them want one fish-head,
The Devil call him wife bonehead,
She hiss her teeth, call him cock-eye,
Greedy, worthless an' workshy,
While them busy callin' name,
The puss walk in, sey is a shame
To see a nice fish go to was'e,
Lef' with a big grin pon him face.

# BENJAMIN ZEPHANIAH
### 1958–

## ACCORDING TO MY MOOD

 I have *poetic* licence, i WriTe thE way i waNt.
i *drop* my **full stops** where *i* like**...**
**MY CAPITAL L**eteRs go where i li**KE**,
i **order** from **MY** PeN, i verse **the way** i like
( **i do** *my spelling write* )
Acording to My *MO*od.
i **HA**ve Poetic **licence**,
i put my **commers** where **I** like,,**((0).**
**(((my** brackets *are* **write((**
**I REPEAT WH**en i lik**E**.
**i** can't **go rong.**
i *look* and **i.c.**
It's **rite.**
i**I REPEAT WH**en i lik**E**. i **have**
*poetic* licence!
**don't** question me?**?**?**?**

# JACKIE KAY
## 1961–

### *English Cousin Comes to Scotland*

See when my English cousin comes,
it's so embarrassing so it is, so it is.
I have to explain everything
I mean Every Thing, so I do, so I do.
I told her, 'know what happened to me?
I got skelped, because I screamed when a skelf
went into my pinky finger: OUCH, loud.
And ma ma dropped her best bit of china.
It wis sore, so it wis, so it wis.
I was scunnert being skelped
when I wis already sore.
So I ran and ran, holding
my pinky, through the park,
over the burn, up the hill.
I was knackered and I fell
into the mud and went home
mocket and got skelped again.
So I locked myself in the cludgie
and cried, so I did, so I did,
pulling the long roll of paper
onto the floor. Like that dug Andrex.'
Whilst I'm saying this, my English cousin
has her mouth open. Glaikit.
Stupit. So she is, so she is.
I says, 'I'm going to have to learn you
what's what.' And at that the wee git
cheers up; the wee toffee nose says,
'not learn you, teach you,' like she's scored.

| | | | |
|---|---|---|---|
| *skelped* spanked | *skelf* splinter | *scunnert* fed up | *pinky* finger |
| *mocket* filthy | *cludgie* toilet | *dug* dog | *glaikit* silly |

### What Jenny Knows

'I didn't come out my mummy's tummy.
No I didn't,' I says to my pal Jenny.
But Jenny says, 'you must have.
How come?' And I replies,

'I just didn't. Get it. I didn't.'
'Everybody does' says Jenny,
who is fastly becoming an enemy.
'Rubbish,' I say. 'My mummy got me.

She picked me. She collected me.
I was in a supermarket,
on the shelf and she took me off it.'
'Nonsense,' says Jenny. 'Lies.'

'Are you calling me a liar?'
I'm getting angry. It's not funny.
'No, but you have a tendency'
(a word from her aunty, probably)

'To make things up.'
'Look. I'm speaking the Truth.'
I say, 'Cross my heart.'
'Don't hope to die,' shouts Jenny.

Awful superstitious, so she is.
'I'm adopted,' I says, 'adopted.'
'I know That!' says Jenny,
'But you still came out

Somebody's tummy. Somebody
had to have you. Didn't they?'
'Not my mummy. Not my mummy,' I says.
'Shut your face. Shut your face.'

## The Stincher

When I was three, I told a lie.
To this day that lie is a worry.

Some lies are too big to swallow;
some lies so gigantic they grow

in the dark, ballooning and blossoming;
some lies tell lies and flower,

hyacinths; some develop extra tongues,
purple and thick. This lie went wrong.

I told my parents my brother drowned.
I watched my mother chase my brother's name,

saw her comb the banks with her fingers
down by the river Stincher.

I chucked a stone into the deep brown water,
drowned it in laughter; my father, puffing,

found my brother's fishing reel and stool
down by the river Stincher.

I believed in the word disaster.
Lies make things happen, swell, seed, swarm.

Years from that away-from-home lie,
I don't know why I made my brother die.

I shrug my shoulders, when asked, raise my
eyebrows: *I don't know, right, I was three.*

Now I'm thirty-three. That day they rushed me
to the family friends' where my brother sat

undrowned, not frothing at the mouth, sat
innocent, quiet, watching the colourful TV.

Outside, the big mouth of the river Stincher
pursed its lips, sulked and ran away.


# PAULINE STEWART
## 1962–

### *Singing down the Breadfruit*

Her father blended truth and myth
so finely that each became the other.
'Well' he would start,
'fac is fac . . . is fac dat we is
good singers—right?'
—'Ee-hee.' She would reply.
'Well is for a purpose.'
—'What purpose, poopa?'
'See how coconut tree tallaway,
swipple an' hard fe scale?'
—'Ee-hee.'
'Well, when we cyan go no more,
we jus' sing dung de coconut,
sing dung de mangoes an' de breadfruit dem.'
'Sing dem dung?'
'Yes, all de way
dung
to
de
grung.'
—'like de wind?'
'Just like de wind.'

# JANET S. WONG
## 1962–

### *Good Luck Gold*

When I was a baby
one month old,
my grandparents gave me
good luck gold:
a golden ring
so soft it bends,
a golden necklace
hooked at the ends,
a golden bracelet
with coins that say
I will be rich
and happy someday.

I wish that gold
would work
real soon.
I need my luck
this afternoon.

# BIBLIOGRAPHY

BADHAM-THORNHILL, DESMOND, *Three Poets Two Children*. Gloucester: Thornhill Press, 1975.

BENNETT, JILL, and CHAMBERS, AIDAN, *Poetry for Children: A Signal Bookguide*. South Woodchester: The Thimble Press, 1984, rev. 1986.

CARPENTER, HUMPHREY, and PRICHARD, MARI, *The Oxford Companion to Children's Literature*. Oxford: Oxford University Press, 1984.

CHEVALIER, TRACEY, *Twentieth-Century Children's Writers*. 3rd edn., Chicago: St James Press, 1989.

DARTON, F. J. HARVEY, *Children's Books in England*. 3rd edn., rev. Brian Alderson, Cambridge: Cambridge University Press, 1982.

HALL, DONALD, *The Oxford Book of Children's Verse in America*. New York: Oxford University Press, 1985.

HAVILAND, VIRGINIA, and SMITH, WILLIAM JAY, *Children and Poetry: A Selective Annotated Bibliography*. 2nd edn., Washington, DC: Library of Congress, 1979.

HUGHES, TED, *Poetry in the Making*. London: Faber & Faber, 1967.

MCCORD, DAVID, 'Poetry for Children', in Sara Innis Fenwick (ed.), *A Critical Approach to Children's Literature*. Chicago: The University of Chicago Press, 1967.

MEARNS, HUGHES, *Creative Youth: How a School Environment Set Free the Creative Spirit*. Garden City, NY: Doubleday, Doran & Company, 1928.

MEEK, MARGARET, 'The Signal Poetry Award', *Signal: Approaches to Children's Books*, 44 (May 1984).

—— 'The Signal Poetry Award', *Signal: Approaches to Children's Literature*, 50 (May, 1986).

MORSE, BRIAN, *Poetry Books for Children: A Signal Bookguide*. South Woodchester: The Thimble Press, 1992.

OPIE, IONA, and OPIE, PETER, *The Oxford Book of Children's Verse*. Oxford: Oxford University Press, 1973.

PIRRIE, JILL, *Apple Fire: The Halesworth Middle School Anthology*. Newcastle upon Tyne: Bloodaxe Books, 1993.

REEVES, JAMES, *How to Write Poetry for Children*. London: Heinemann, 1971.

ROGERS, TIMOTHY, *Those First Affections: An Anthology of Poems Composed between the Ages of Two and Eight*. London: Routledge & Kegan Paul, 1979.

ROSEN, MICHAEL, 'Memorable Speech?', *The Times Educational Supplement* (9 Mar. 1984).

SHAW, JOHN MACKAY, *Childhood in Poetry*. Detroit: Gale Research Company, 1968. First Suppl. 1972; Second Suppl. 1976; Third Suppl. 1980.

STYLES, MORAG, 'Lost from the Nursery: Women Writing Poetry for Children 1800 to 1850', *Signal: Approaches to Children's Books*, 63 (Sept. 1990).

—— and TRIGGS, PAT, *Poetry 0–16: A BFK Guide*. London: Books for Keeps, 1988.

SUTTON-SMITH, BRIAN, 'Early Stories as Poetry', in *Children's Literature*, vol. ix. New Haven: Yale University Press, 1981.

TOWNSEND, JOHN ROWE, *Written for Children*. 6th edn., London: The Bodley Head, 1990.

TUCKER, ALAN, *Poetry Books for Children: A Signal Booklist*. South Woodchester: The Thimble Press, 1976, rev. 1979.

# PUBLISHER'S ACKNOWLEDGEMENTS

The editor and publisher are grateful for permission to include the following copyright poems:

The poem which appears in the Introduction, 'Once upon a Time' from Brian Sutton-Smith, 'Early Stories as Poetry' in *Children's Literature*, vol. 9 (Yale, 1981), copyright © 1981 by The Children's Literature Foundation, Inc., reprinted by permission of Yale University Press.

John Agard, 'Don't Call Alligator Long-Mouth Till You Cross River' from *Say It Again Granny* (Bodley Head, 1989), and 'Poetry Jump-Up' from *Get Back Pimple* (Viking, 1996), reprinted by permission of John Agard, c/o Caroline Sheldon Literary Agency.

Allan Ahlberg, 'Only Snow' from *Please Mrs Butler* (Kestrel, 1983), copyright © Allan Ahlberg, 1983, 'The Boy Without a Name' and 'The Trial of Derek Drew' from *Heard It In the Playground* (Kestrel, 1989), copyright © Allan Ahlberg, 1989, all reprinted by permission of Penguin Books Ltd.

Joan Aiken, 'Palace Cook's Tale' and 'Do It Yourself' from *The Skin Spinners* (Viking, 1976), copyright © 1960, 1973, 1974, 1975, 1976 by Joan Aiken Enterprises Ltd, reprinted by permission of A. M. Heath & Co. Ltd, and Brandt & Brandt Literary Agents, Inc.

J. K. Annand, 'Mavis' and 'Heron' from *Sing It Aince for Pleisure* (Macdonald, 1965), and 'I Winna Let On' from *Thrice to Show Ye* (Macdonald, 1979), reprinted by permission of The Saltire Society.

George Barker, 'How Many Apples Grow on the Tree?' from *Runes and Rhymes and Tunes and Chimes* (1969), reprinted by permission of the publishers, Faber & Faber Ltd.

James K. Baxter, 'The Fireman' and 'Twenty Little Engines' from *Collected Poems of James K. Baxter* edited by John Weir (Oxford University Press Australia and New Zealand), reproduced by permission of the publishers.

Shonto Begay, 'Mother's Lace' from *Navajo Visions and Voices*, copyright © 1995 by Shonto Begay, reprinted by permission of Scholastic Inc.

Hilaire Belloc, 'The Frog' and 'Jim' from *Cautionary Verses* (Cape), reprinted by permission of the Peters Fraser & Dunlop Group Ltd.

Stephen V. Benét, 'A Nonsense Song' and 'A Sad Song' from *Ballads and Poems 1915–1930* (Doubleday, 1931).

Gerard Benson, 'The Cat and the Pig' and 'Play No Ball' from *The Magnificent Callisto* (Blackie, 1992), copyright © Gerard Benson, reprinted by permission of Penguin Books Ltd.

James Berry, 'Girls Can We Educate We Dads' and 'One' from *When I Dance* (Hamish Hamilton Children's Books, 1988), copyright © 1988 by James Berry, reprinted by permission of Penguin Books Ltd.

Elizabeth Bishop, 'Manners' from *The Complete Poems 1927–1979*, copyright © 1979, 1983, by Alice Helen Methfessel, reprinted by permission of Farrar, Straus & Giroux, Inc.

Valerie Bloom, 'Sun a-shine, Rain a-fall' from *Duppy Jamboree* (CUP, 1992), reprinted by permission of the author and Cambridge University Press.

Gwendolyn Brooks, 'A Song in the Front Yard' from *Blacks* (The David Co., 1987), and 'Michael is Afraid of the Storm' from *Bronzeville Boys and Girls* (Harper & Brokes, 1956).

Alan Brownjohn, 'Common Sense' and 'We are Going to See the Rabbit' from *Collected Poems* (Secker & Warburg), copyright © Alan Brownjohn 1983, reprinted by permission of Rosica Colin Ltd.

Charles Causley, 'I Saw a Jolly Hunter', 'I am the Song', 'Nursery Rhyme of Innocence & Experience', 'Figgie Hobbin', 'Infant Song', and 'Colonel Fazackerly', all from *Collected Poems* (Macmillan), reprinted by permission of David Higham Associates.

John Ciardi, ' All About Boys and Girls' from *You Read to Me, I'll Read to You* (HarperCollins, 1982) and 'Sometimes Even Parents Win' from *The Hopeful Trout* (Houghton Mifflin, 1989), reprinted by permission of the Ciardi Family Publishing Trust.

Sandra Cisneros, 'Good Hot Dogs' from *My Wicked Wicked Ways* (published by Alfred A. Knopf, 1989, originally published in paperback by Third Woman Press), copyright © by Sandra Cisneros 1987, reprinted by permission of Third Woman Press and the author via Susan Bergholz Literary Services.

John Clare, 'Clock a Clay' and 'Little Trotty Wagtail' from *John Clare* (The Oxford Authors Series) edited by Eric Robinson and David Powell (OUP, 1984), copyright Eric Robinson, reproduced by permission of Curtis Brown Group Ltd, London.

Leonard Clark, 'Singing in the Streets' from *Singing in the Streets* (Dobson, 1972), reprinted by permission of the Literary Executor of Leonard Clark.

Lucille Clifton, 'Listen Children', copyright © 1987 by Lucille Clifton, from *Good Woman: Poems and a Memoir 1969–1980* by Lucille Clifton, reprinted with the permission of BOA Editions Ltd, 92 Park Ave., Brockport, NY 14420; 'December' from *Everett Anderson's Year*, copyright © 1974 by Lucille Clifton, reprinted by permission of Henry Holt and Co., Inc.

Frank Collymore, 'Ballad of an Old Woman' from *Collected Poems* (Advocate Co., 1959), reprinted by permission of Mrs E. Collymore.

Frances Cornford, 'A Child's Dream' from *Collected Poems* (Cresset Press, 1954), reprinted by permission of Random House UK Ltd, on behalf of the Estate of Frances Cornford.

Countee Cullen, 'Incident' from *Color* by Countee Cullen, copyright © 1925 by Harper & Brothers; copyright renewed 1953 by Ida M. Cullen, reprinted by permission of GRM Associates, Inc., agents for the Estate of Ida M. Cullen.

E. E. Cummings, 'in Just-', 'hist whist', and 'maggie and milly and molly and may', from *Complete Poems 1904–1962*, edited by George J. Firmage, by permission of W. W. Norton & Company Ltd, copyright © 1920, 1976, 1991 by the Trustees for the E. E. Cummings Trust and George James Firmage.

Beatrice Curtis Brown, 'Jonathan Bing' from *Jonathan Bing and Other Verses*, copyright 1936 by Oxford University Press, renewed © 1964 by Beatrice Curtis Brown, reproduced by permission of Curtis Brown, London.

Walter de la Mare, 'The Silver Penny', 'Hi', 'The Storm', and 'The Listeners', all from *Collected Rhymes and Verse* (Faber, 1970), reprinted by permission of The

Literary Trustees of Walter de la Mare, and The Society of Authors as their representative.

Emily Dickinson, Poem no. 1185 and poem no. 1521 from *The Poems of Emily Dickinson*, edited by Thomas H. Johnson (The Belknap Press of Harvard University Press, Cambridge, Mass.), copyright © 1951, 1955, 1979, 1983 by the President and Fellows of Harvard College, reprinted by permission of the publishers and the Trustees of Amherst College; poem no. 1590 from *Life and Letters of Emily Dickinson*, edited by Martha Dickinson Bianchi, copyright 1924 by Martha Dickinson Bianchi, © renewed 1952 by Alfred Leete Hampson, reprinted by permission of Houghton Mifflin Company. All rights reserved.

Peter Dickinson, 'Moses and the Princess' from *City of Gold* (Victor Gollancz, 1980), reproduced by permission of Victor Gollancz Ltd.

Richard Edwards, 'Recollections of an Old Spook' from *A Mouse in My Roof* (Orchard Books, 1988), reprinted by permission of the author.

T. S. Eliot, 'Mr Mistoffelees' from *Old Possum's Book of Practical Cats*, copyright 1939 by T. S. Eliot and renewed 1967 by Esme Valerie Eliot, reprinted by permission of the publishers, Faber & Faber Ltd and Harcourt Brace & Company.

Gavin Ewart, 'Who Likes the Idea of Guide Cats? ' from *Like It or Not* (Bodley Head, 1992).

Eleanor Farjeon, 'The Tide in the River' from *Invitation to a Mouse* (Hodder & Stoughton), and 'Good Night' from *Silver Sand and Snow* (Michael Joseph), reproduced by permission of David Higham Associates.

Max Fatchen, 'Hullo Inside' from *Wry Rhymes for Troublesome Times* (Kestrel, 1983), copyright © 1983 by Max Fatchen, reprinted by permission of Penguin Books Ltd.

Rachel Field, 'Skyscrapers', copyright 1924 by Yale University Press, from *Taxis and Toadstools*, reprinted by permission of Bantam Doubleday Dell Books for Young Readers.

Aileen Fisher, 'Fair Exchange' from *Up the Windy Hill* (Abelard Press, 1958), reprinted by permission of the author.

Paul Fleischman, 'Fireflies' from *Joyful Noise*, text copyright © 1988 by Paul Fleischman, reprinted by permission of HarperCollins Publishers, New York.

Douglas Florian, 'First' and 'Send My Spinach' from *Bing Bang Boing: Poems and Drawings*, copyright © 1994 by Douglas Florian, reprinted by permission of Harcourt Brace & Company.

Robert Frost, 'The Last Word of a Bluebird' from *The Poetry of Robert Frost*, edited by Edward Connery Lathem (Cape/Holt), copyright 1944 by Robert Frost, copyright 1916 © 1969 by Henry Holt & Co., Inc., reprinted by permission of Henry Holt & Co., Inc., and Random House UK Ltd on behalf of the Estate of the author.

John Fuller, 'A Whole New Scene', lines from 'Adam's Apple' from *Come Aboard and Sail Away* (Salamander Press, 1983), reprinted by permission of the author.

Rose Fyleman, 'Solo with Chorus' from *Runabout Rhymes* (Methuen, 1941), reprinted by permission of the Society of Authors as the literary representative of the Estate of Rose Fyleman. 'Punch and Judy' and 'The Cat' from *Fifty One New Nursery Rhymes* (Methuen/Doubleday, 1931), copyright 1931, 1932 by Doubleday, a division of Bantam Doubleday Dell Publishing Group, Inc., reprinted by permission of the Society of Authors as the literary representative of the Estate of Rose Fyleman, and of Bantam Doubleday Dell Books for Young Readers.

Alan Garner, 'Summer Solstice', copyright © Alan Garner 1971, from *The Burning Thorn*, edited by G. Greaves (Hamish Hamilton, 1971), reprinted by permission of Richard Scott Simon Ltd.

Nikki Giovanni, 'Poem for My Nephew' from *Ego Tripping and Other Poems* (Lawrence Hill Books), reprinted by permission of Chicago Review Press; 'Basketball' from *Spin a Soft Black Song* (Farrar, Straus & Giroux, 1985), copyright © 1971, 1985 by Nikki Giovanni, reprinted by permission of Farrar, Straus & Giroux, Inc.; and 'Knoxville, Tennessee' from *Black Feeling, Black Talk, Black Judgment*, copyright © 1968, 1970 by Nikki Giovanni, reprinted by permission of William Morrow and Company, Inc.

Elizabeth Godley, 'Ninety-Nine' from *Green Outside* (Chatto, 1931), reprinted by permission of Random House UK Ltd.

Mick Gowar, 'Rat Trap' from *Carnival for the Animals and Other Poems* (Viking, 1992), text copyright © Mick Gowar, 1992, reprinted by permission of Penguin Books Ltd.

Robert Graves, extract from 'The Mirror' from *Poems Abridged for Dolls and Princes* and extracts from 'Henry and Mary', 'Love Without Hope', 'Vain and Careless', and 'Warning to Children' all from *Collected Poems*, reprinted by permission of Carcanet Press Ltd and of A..P. Watt Ltd on behalf of The Trustees of the Robert Graves Copyright Trust.

Thom Gunn, 'Cannibal' and 'The Aquarium' from 'Three for Children' in *Collected Poems*, copyright © 1994 by Thom Gunn, reprinted by permission of the publishers, Faber & Faber Ltd. and Farrar, Straus & Giroux, Inc.

Joy Harjo, 'Remember' from *She Had Some Horses* by Joy Harjo, copyright © 1996 by Joy Harjo, reprinted by permission of the publisher, Thunder's Mouth Press.

Gregory Harrison, 'The Playground' from *Posting Letters* (OUP, 1968), copyright © Gregory Harrison 1968, reprinted by permission of the author.

John Heath-Stubbs, 'The History of the Flood', 'The Jays', and 'The Kingfisher', from *Collected Poems* (Carcanet), reproduced by permission of David Higham Associates.

Russell Hoban, 'The Pedalling Man' and 'Small, Smaller' from *The Pedalling Man* (Heinemann, 1969), reprinted by permission of David Higham Associates.

Langston Hughes, 'April Rain Song', 'Tambourines', 'I, Too', 'Ultimatum: Kid to Kid', 'My People', and 'Children's Rhymes', all from *Collected Poems* (Knopf, 1994), copyright © 1994 by the Estate of Langston Hughes, reprinted by permission of David Higham Associates and Alfred A. Knopf Inc.

Ted Hughes, 'I See a Bear', 'Roe-Deer', and 'Amulet' from *Moon Bells and Other Poems* (Chatto, 1978), reprinted by permission of Faber & Faber Ltd; 'Yesterday He Was Nowhere to be Found', 'Rooks Love Excitement' and 'An October Robin Kept' from *What is the Truth?: A Farmyard Fable for the Young*, text copyright © 1984 by Ted Hughes, reprinted by permission of the publishers, Faber & Faber Ltd and HarperCollins Publishers, Inc.

Christopher Isherwood, 'The Common Cormorant', copyright The Estate of Christopher Isherwood, reproduced by permission of Curtis Brown Ltd, London on behalf of the Executors of the Estate of Christopher Isherwood.

Elizabeth Jennings, 'The Ugly Child' and 'Afterthought' from *The Secret Brother* (Macmillan, 1966), reprinted by permission of David Higham Associates.

Jackie Kay, 'English Cousin Comes to Scotland' and 'What Jenny Knows' from *Two's Company* (Blackie, 1992), copyright Jackie Kay, 1992, and 'The Stincher' from *Three Has Gone* (Blackie, 1994), text copyright © Jackie Kay, 1994, all reprinted by permission of Penguin Books Ltd.

X. J. Kennedy, 'Hummingbird' and 'Lighting a Fire' from *The Forgetful Wishing Well* (Atheneum, 1985), text copyright © 1985 X. J. Kennedy, reprinted by permission of Margaret K. McElderry Books, an imprint of Simon & Schuster, and Curtis Brown Ltd, New York.

James Kirkup, 'Scarecrows' from *Look at it This Way!* (Rockingham Press, 1994), reprinted by permission of the publishers.

Karla Kuskin, 'The Witches Ride' from *Dogs & Dragons, Trees & Dreams*, copyright © 1980 by Karla Kuskin, reprinted by permission of HarperCollins Publishers, New York.

Lois Lenski, 'Sing a Song of People' from *The Life I Live*, copyright © 1965 by Lois Lensky, reprinted by permission of Arthur F. Abelman, Moses & Singer, New York, on behalf of the Lois Lensky Covey Foundation.

J. Patrick Lewis, 'Stories' from *Two-Legged, Four-Legged, No-Legged Rhymes* by J. Patrick Lewis (Knopf, 1991), text copyright © 1991 by J. Patrick Lewis, reprinted by permission of Alfred A. Knopf, Inc., and the author.

Naomi Lewis, 'A Footprint in the Air' from *A Footprint in the Air* (Hutchinson, 1983), reprinted by permission of Random House UK Ltd.

Vachel Lindsay, 'The Moon's the North Wind's Cooky' and 'The Little Turtle' from *Collected Poems* (Macmillan, New York, 1934).

Myra Cohn Livingston, 'Lazy Witch' from *A Song I Sang to You* (Harcourt Brace, 1958), copyright © 1984, 1969, 1967, 1965, 1959, 1958 Myra Cohn Livingston, and 'Swimming Pool' from *The Way Things Are and Other Poems* (Atheneum, 1974), copyright © 1974 Myra Cohn Livingston, both reprinted by permission of Marian Reiner; 'Coming from Kansas' from *Worlds I Know and Other Poems*, text copyright © 1985 Myra Cohn Livingston, reprinted by permission of Marian Reiner and Margaret K. McElderry Books, an imprint of Simon & Schuster.

Hugh Lofting, 'Picnic' from *Porridge Poetry*, copyright Christopher Lofting, reprinted by permission of Christopher Lofting.

David McCord, 'Five Chants' and 'Father and I in the Woods' from *One at a Time* by David McCord, copyright © 1952 by David McCord, reprinted by permission of Little, Brown and Company.

Roger McGough, 'Prayer to St Grobianus' from *Nailing the Shadow* (Penguin, 1987), 'The Kleptomaniac' from *Pillow Talk* (Penguin, 1990), and 'First Day at School' from *In the Glassroom* (Cape, 1976), all reprinted by permission of the Peters Fraser & Dunlop Group Ltd.

Irene McLeod, 'Lone Dog' from *Songs to Save a Soul* by Irene Rutherford McLeod (Chatto & Windus), reprinted by permission of Random House UK Ltd.

Wes Magee, 'Giant Rocket' from *Morning Break and Other Poems* (CUP, 1989), reprinted by permission of Cambridge University Press; 'How to Reach the Sun . . . on a Sheet of Paper', copyright © Wes Magee 1995 from *Sandwich Poets: Matt, Wes and Pete* by M. Simpson, W. Magee, and P. Dixon (Macmillan, 1995), reprinted by permission of the author.

Margaret Mahy, 'The Dictionary Bird' from *Nonstop Nonsense* (J. M. Dent, 1977), reprinted by permission of The Orion Publishing Group.

Eve Merriam, 'Lullaby' from *There is No Rhyme for Silver*, copyright © 1962 Eve Merriam, © renewed 1990 Eve Merriam, and 'Weather' from *Catch a Little Rhyme*, copyright © 1966 Eve Merriam, © renewed 1994 Dee Michel and Guy Michel, both reprinted by permission of Marian Reiner.

Edna St Vincent Millay, 'The Bean Stalk', 'Counting-out Rhyme', and 'From a Very Little Sphinx (I–VI)' from *Collected Poems* (HarperCollins), copyright © 1921, 1928, 1929, 1948, 1955, 1956 by Edna St Vincent Millay and Norma Millay Ellis, reprinted by permission of Elizabeth Barnett, literary executor.

Spike Milligan, 'Bad Report, Good Manners' from *Unspun Socks From A Chicken's Laundry* (Michael Joseph, 1981), reprinted by permission of Spike Milligan Productions Ltd.

A. A. Milne, 'Bad Sir Brian Botany', 'Happiness', and 'Disobedience' from *When We Were Very Young* (Methuen Children's Books, 1924), copyright 1924 by E. P. Dutton, renewed 1952 by A. A. Milne, reprinted by permission of Reed Books and Dutton Children's Books, a division of Penguin Books USA, Inc.

Adrian Mitchell, 'Nothingmas Day' and 'Dumb Insolence' from *Nothingmas Day* (Allison & Busby Ltd, 1984), reprinted by permission of the Peters Frazer & Dunlop Group Ltd.

John Mole, 'Jack in the Box' and 'Taking the Plunge' from *Boo to a Goose* (Peterloo, 1987), and 'The Trick' from *The Mad Parrot's Countdown* (Peterloo, 1990), all reproduced by permission of the author.

Edwin Morgan, 'The Computer's First Christmas Card' from *Collected Poems 1949–1989* (Carcanet, 1990), reprinted by permission of Carcanet Press Ltd.

Brian Morse, 'A Day on the Planet' from *Picnic on the Moon* by Brian Morse, (Turton & Chambers, 1990), copyright © 1990 by Brian Morse, reprinted by permission of Turton & Chambers.

Ogden Nash, 'Nature Gets More Wonderful Everyday: The Eel', copyright © 1941 by Ogden Nash, renewed, and 'Adventures of Isobel: The Modern Girl', copyright © 1936 by Ogden Nash, renewed, both from *Parents Keep Out* (J. M. Dent, 1962), reprinted by permission of Curtis Brown Ltd, New York and Little, Brown and Company.

Judith Nicholls, 'Polar Cub', copyright © Judith Nicholls 1994 from *Storm's Eye* (OUP, 1994), reprinted by permission of Oxford University Press.

Grace Nichols, 'Wha Me Mudder Do' from *Come On Into My Tropical Garden* (A. & C. Black, 1988), copyright © Grace Nichols, 1988, reproduced by permission of Curtis Brown on behalf of Grace Nichols.

Norman Nicholson, 'Carol for the Last Christmas Eve' from *The Candy Floss Tree* (OUP, 1984), reproduced by permission of David Higham Associates.

Leslie Norris, 'Mice in the Hay' from *Norris's Ark*, (The Tidal Press, Portsmouth, N.H., 1988), reprinted by permission of the author.

Alden Nowlan, 'I, Icarus' from *Bread, Wine and Salt* (Clark Irwin Inc., 1967), reprinted by permission of Stoddart Publishing Co. Ltd, Don Mills, Ont. Canada.

Alfred Noyes, 'Daddy Fell Into the Pond' and 'The Highwayman' from *Collected Poems*, reprinted by permission of John Murray (Publishers) Ltd.

Julie O'Callaghan, 'Taking My Pen for a Walk' from *Bright Lights Blaze Out* (OUP, Three Poets Series, 1986), reprinted by permission of the author.

Gareth Owen, 'Gathering in the Days' from *The Fox on the Roundabout* (Collins Children's Books, 1995), copyright © Gareth Owen, 1995, reprinted by permission of the author, c/o Rogers, Coleridge & White Ltd, 20 Powis Mews, London W11 1JN.

Brian Patten, 'How the New Teacher Got Her Nickname' from *Thawing Frozen Frogs* (Viking Children's Books, 1990), text copyright © Brian Patten 1990, reprinted by permission of Penguin Books Ltd.

Mervyn Peake, 'O Here It Is! And There It Is' and 'I Cannot Give the Reasons' from *A Book of Nonsense* (Peter Owen, 1972), reprinted by permission of David Higham Associates.

Lydia Pender, 'The Lizard' from *Morning Magpie* (Angus & Robertson, 1984), reprinted by permission of the author.

H. D. C. Pepler, 'Concerning Dragons', from privately published pamphlet *Concerning Dragons* (St Dominic's Press, Ditchling), reprinted by permission of Mr L. D. M. Pepler.

Marlene Philip, 'Oliver Twist' from *Thorns* (Williams-Wallace, 1983).

Ezra Pound, 'A Girl' from *Collected Shorter Poems*, reprinted by permission of the publishers, Faber & Faber Ltd.

Jack Prelutsky, 'Mother Goblin's Lullaby' from *Something BIG Has Been Here* (Wm. Morrow, 1990), copyright © 1990 by Jack Prelutsky, reprinted by permission of Greenwillow Books, a division of William Morrow & Co., Inc.

James Reeves, 'Slowly', 'W', 'Cows', and 'Giant Thunder', © James Reeves from *Complete Poems for Children* (Heinemann), and 'The Sea', © James Reeves from *The Wandering Moon and Other Poems* by James Reeves (Puffin Books), all reprinted by permission of the James Reeves Estate.

Alastair Reid, 'A Spell for Sleeping', copyright © Alastair Reid, reprinted by permission of the author.

Laura Riding, 'Toward the Corner' from *The Poems of Laura Riding* by Laura (Riding) Jackson, copyright © 1938, 1980 by Laura (Riding) Jackson, reprinted by permission of Carcanet Press and the author's Board of Literary Management. In conformity with the late author's wish, her Board of Literary Management asks us to record that, in 1941, Laura (Riding) Jackson renounced, on grounds of linguistic principle, the writing of poetry: she had come to hold that 'poetry obstructs general attainment to something better in our linguistic way-of-life than we have'.

Elizabeth Madox Roberts, 'Christmas Morning' and 'The People' from *Under the Tree*, copyright 1922 by B. W. Huebsch, Inc., renewed 1950 by Ivor S. Roberts. Copyright 1930 by Viking Penguin, Inc., renewed © 1958 by Ivor S. Roberts, reproduced by permission of Viking Penguin, a division of Penguin Books USA Inc.

Roland Robinson, 'Jarranguli' from *The Nearest the White Man Gets: Aboriginal narratives and poems of New South Wales*, collected by Roland Robinson (Hale & Iremonger, Sydney, Australia, 1989), reprinted by permission of Jane Diplock and the publishers.

Theodore Roethke, 'Child on Top of a Greenhouse', copyright 1946 by Editorial Publications, Inc., 'The Lizard', copyright © 1961 by Theodore Roethke, 'My Papa's Waltz', copyright 1942 by Hearst Magazines, Inc., and 'The Serpent', copyright 1950 by Theodore Roethke, all from *The Collected Poems of*

*Theodore Roethke* reproduced by permission of the publishers, Faber & Faber Ltd and Doubleday, a division of Bantam Doubleday Dell Publishing Group, Inc.

Michael Rosen, 'Humpty Dumpty' (with S. Steele) from *The Kingfisher Book of Children's Poetry*, edited by Michael Rosen (Kingfisher/Larousse), reprinted by permission of the Peters Fraser & Dunlop Group Ltd; 'This Morning' from *Mind Your Own Business* (Deutsch, 1974), and 'Eddie and the Birthday' from *Quick, Let's Get Out of Here* (Deutsch, 1983), reprinted by permission of Scholastic Publications Ltd.

Sonia Sanchez, 'Definition for Blk/children' (used in Introduction) from *Home Coming* (Broadside Press, 1979), 'To P. J. (2 yrs old who sed write a poem for me in Portland, Oregon)' from *It's a New Day* (Broadside Press, 1971), reprinted by permission of Broadside Press, and 'Song No 3' from *Under a Soprano Sky* (Africa World Press, 1987), all three poems reprinted by permission of the author.

Carl Sandburg, 'Auctioneer' and 'Be Ready', copyright © 1958 by Carl Sandburg and renewed 1986 by Margaret Sandburg, Janet Sandburg, and Helga Sandburg Crile; 'Stars', copyright © 1960 by Carl Sandburg and renewed 1988 by Margaret Sandburg, Janet Sandburg, and Helga Sandburg Crile, from *Wind Song*; 'Little Girl Be Careful What You Say' and 'We Must Be Polite' from *The Complete Poems of Carl Sandburg*, copyright 1950 by Carl Sandburg and renewed 1978 by Margaret Sandburg, Janet Sandburg, and Helga Sandburg Crile, all reprinted by permission of Harcourt Brace & Company.

May Sarton, 'Nursery Rhyme' from *Selected Poems of May Sarton*, edited by Serena Sue Hilsinger and Lois Byrnes, copyright © 1978 The Estate of the late May Sarton, reprinted by permission of A. M. Heath & Co. Ltd, and W. W. Norton & Co. Inc.

Vernon Scannell, 'The Apple Raid', 'Hide and Seek', and 'Poem on Bread' from *Apple Raid and Other Poems* (Chatto, 1974), reprinted by permission of the author.

Delmore Schwartz, 'I am Cherry Alive' and 'O Child, Do Not Fear the Dark and Sleep's Dark Possession' from *Selected Poems—Summer Knowledge*, copyright © 1959 by Delmore Schwartz, reprinted by permission of New Directions Publishing Corp., and Laurence Pollinger Ltd.

Ian Serraillier, 'Anne and the Field-Mouse' from *Happily Ever After* (OUP, 1963), reprinted by permission of Anne Serraillier.

Edith Sitwell, ' The King of China's Daughter' and 'Trams' from *The Wooden Pegasus* (Blackwell, 1920), reprinted by permission of David Higham Associates.

Ian Crichton Smith, 'The Ghost' from *River, River* (Macdonald Publ., 1978), reprinted by permission of the author.

Michael Smith, 'Black and White' from *It a Come*, copyright © Nerissa Smith, (Race Today Publications, 1986).

Stevie Smith, 'Fairy Story' from *Collected Poems of Stevie Smith*, copyright © 1972 by Stevie Smith (Penguin 20th-Century Classics), reprinted by permission of James MacGibbon and New Directions Publishing Corp.

William Jay Smith, 'The Toaster' from *Laughing Time: Collected Nonsense* (Faber, 1956), copyright © 1990 by William Jay Smith, reprinted by permission of Farrar, Straus & Giroux, Inc.

Gary Soto, 'Teaching Numbers', copyright © 1985 by Gary Soto from *Black Hair*

(Univ. of Pittsburgh Press, 1985), reprinted by permission of the author; and 'Brown Girl, Blonde Okie', from *New and Selected Poems* by Gary Soto © 1995 (Chronicle Books, San Francisco, 1995), reprinted by permission of Chronicle Books.

Gertrude Stein, 'The Teachers Taught Her that the World Was Round' from *The World Is Round* (Batsford, 1939), reprinted by permission of David Higham Associates.

Pauline Stewart, 'Singing Down the Breadfruit' from *Sing on Down the Breadfruit and Other Poems* (Hutchinson, 1993), reprinted by permission of Random House UK Ltd.

Geoffrey Summerfield, 'Washday Battles' from *Welcome and Other Poems* (1983), reprinted by permission of Scholastic Publications Ltd.

May Swenson, 'The Centaur' from *The Complete Poems to Solve*, copyright © 1956 May Swenson, copyright renewed 1984 May Swenson, reprinted by permission of Simon & Schuster Books For Young Readers.

Genevieve Taggard, 'Millions of Strawberries' from *The New Yorker* (8 June 1929), copyright © 1929, 1957 by The New Yorker Magazine, Inc., reprinted by permission of *The New Yorker*.

J. R. R. Tolkien, 'Oliphaunt' from *The Adventures of Tom Bombadil*, reprinted by permission of HarperCollins Publishers Ltd.

John Updike, 'January' and 'May' from *A Child's Calendar* (Knopf, 1965), copyright 1965 by John Updike and Nancy Burkert, reprinted by permission of Alfred A. Knopf Inc.

Ted Walker, 'Owl' and 'Goldfish in the Garden Pond', copyright © Ted Walker 1994, from *Grandad's Seagull* (Blackie, 1994), reprinted by permission of Sheil Land Associates.

John Walsh, 'I've Got an Apple Ready' from *Poets in Hand*, edited by Anne Harvey (Puffin, 1985).

Clyde Watson, 'Knickerbocker, Knockabout' from *Father Fox's Pennyrhymes* (Thomas Y. Crouch, 1971/Macmillan, London, 1972), text copyright © 1971 by Clyde Watson, reprinted by permission of HarperCollins Publishers, New York.

Jon Whyte, 'Coyotes' from *Prairie Jungle*, edited by W. McArthur and G. Ursel (Coteau Books, 1985), reprinted by permission of Ted Hart, Literary Executor.

Anna Wickham, 'Letter to a Boy at School' and 'Nursery Song' from *The Writings of Anna Wickham*, edited by R. D. Smith (Virago, 1984), reprinted by permission of George Hepburn and Margaret Hepburn.

Richard Wilbur, 'What is Opposite of Nuts?' from *Opposites: Poems and Drawings*, copyright © 1973 by Richard Wilbur, reprinted by permission of Harcourt Brace & Company.

Janet S. Wong, 'Good Luck Gold' from *Good Luck Gold and Other Poems*, copyright © 1994 Janet S. Wong, reprinted by permission of Margaret K. McElderry Books, an imprint of Simon & Schuster.

Valerie Worth, 'Sun' from *All the Small Poems and Fourteen more* (Farrar, Straus & Giroux, 1987), copyright © 1994 by Valerie Worth, reprinted by permission of Farrar, Straus & Giroux, Inc.

Jane Yolen, 'First Robin' from *Bird Watch* by Jane Yolen, copyright © 1990 by Jane Yolen, reprinted by permission of Philomel Books, The Putnam and Grosset Group.

Benjamin Zephaniah, 'According to my Mood' from *Talking Turkeys* (Viking, 1994), text copyright © Benjamin Zephaniah, 1994, reprinted by permission of Penguin Books Ltd.

Despite every effort to contact copyright holders and obtain permission prior to publication in some cases this has not been possible. If notified, the publisher undertakes to rectify any errors or omissions at the earliest opportunity.

# INDEX OF AUTHORS

# INDEX OF TITLES
# AND FIRST LINES